Never Enough: The Carl Katz Story

by

ELISE GARIBALDI

Dedication

In Loving Memory of

Carl Katz,

The Cohen Family, The Frank Family, Rosa Gruenberg,

Marianne (Gruenberg) Katz,

& Sam (Schmuel) Berger

Table of Contents

Preface

Menachem Z. Rosensaft, Associate Executive Vice President and General Counsel, World Jewish Congress

As part of a naïve and mostly misguided attempt to enable Germans under Allied military occupation after World War II to feel that they were not being subjected to what was commonly referred to as "victor's justice," far too many participants in Nazi crimes were allowed and even encouraged to return to public roles in their communities. Among them was a quite loathsome individual named Siegfried Höffler who had been a prosecutor in the Nazi special courts in Berlin and German-occupied Poland and became a state prosecutor in the German city of Bremen.

Unsurprisingly, Höffler retained his Nazi-era antisemitic mindset and proceeded to persecute Carl Katz, the head of the Bremen's minuscule post-Holocaust Jewish community, attempting maliciously and, thankfully, unsuccessfully to cast him as a villain in the deportation of Bremen's Jews to the Nazi death and concentration camps. Höffler's goal, not surprisingly, was to shift the spotlight from Germans who had perpetrated the greatest crime against humanity in history by seeking to cast blame and responsibility on the crime's victims.

In recent years, a descendant of a Gestapo functionary has similarly tried to falsify history by making provably false accusations against Katz.

Carl Katz, whom I had the privilege to know and whom I admire greatly, was a committed, profoundly decent, proud Jew who distinguished himself by his service to his fellow Jews in pre-Holocaust Bremen, in Theresienstadt, and in post-war Germany. He was one of the group of leaders who rebuilt Jewish life in Germany following the inglorious end of the Third Reich. The attempts to defame him are reprehensible.

1

In this meticulously researched and superbly written book, Katz's great-granddaughter, Elise Garibaldi, sets the record straight. *Never Enough, the Carl Katz Story* is an enormously important contribution to the history of the Holocaust and its aftermath. It belongs in every Holocaust library and on the bookshelves of every Holocaust scholar and researcher, if only as a stark reminder of and potent antidote to the increasingly prevalent distortion of history that is being perpetrated by Holocaust deniers and their acolytes.

Introduction

Frank Mecklenburg, Director of Research and Chief Archivist, New York & Berlin

In May 1945, came the end of the Nazi Regime, but the persecution of Jews did not stop. The same people who had sent Jews to their death often continued to serve in official functions after the war. Despite the control and supervision by the Allied forces, the old networks of members of the Gestapo and other agencies remained intact and served them to get back into positions of influence and power. In the city of Bremen, the post-war legal system employed a number of people of the former system, and aside from whitewashing themselves, they engaged in making the lives of those who returned from the concentration camps as miserable as they could.

In *Never Enough. The Carl Katz Story*, Carl Katz's great-granddaughter reconstructs from the files of various court cases and personal documents the story of the continued persecution of the head of the Bremen Jewish community during the war and after the war. The story is wild, it reads like fiction and the story sounds like fiction, but it is all true. How come that post-war ex-Nazis managed to accuse "The Jew" Carl Katz, who barely survived the Sachsenhausen concentration camp in 1938 and then the Theresienstadt concentration camp with most of his family, of "crimes against humanity"? Carl Katz's great-granddaughter, Elise Garibaldi, has meticulously reconstructed this case. With her knowledge of the family trauma and personal documents as well as having read and researched the files of the court proceedings, she is digging into the thicket of still raw emotions to present a reality that might seem too strange and too crazy for us today. But sometimes reality is stranger than fiction, you can't make it up.

Katz's sense of community and upholding the tradition led him to return to Bremen and to rebuild what his tormentors had been eager to destroy. Unlike most survivors who did not return to what was deemed the "blood soaked soil"

3

of Germany, and much against the Jewish community at large who considered it almost treasonous to go back to Germany after the Holocaust, Carl Katz had something else in mind. His great-granddaughter's book can only tell part of a larger story that has to wait to be told later. Almost single handedly he supported the re-establishment of the Bremen Jewish community largely with his own means. He pushed hard to build a new, high-capacity synagogue that opened only sixteen years after Katz's return from Theresienstadt in August of 1961, much to the surprise and consternation of everybody around him. And he didn't stop there. His visionary sense went beyond Bremen and a new Jewish life when he started to establish early East-West connections in raw and scrap materials trade between the two Germanys, participating in the annual commercial fairs in Leipzig, not afraid of attacks from the drivers of the Cold War.

The story of the Nazi years and deportation of the family to the concentration camp is not unfamiliar to informed readers. The specific circumstances tell us about survival and resilience. But what is truly strange, because largely unknown, is what followed after liberation and after the return to his home town Bremen. Especially what emerged during the de-Nazification proceedings of his former and current tormentors shown in chapters 22 and 23 must sound to our ears as complete fictional. How could that exchange between former Nazi officials and the camp survivor Carl Katz take place only a few years after the end of the persecution of Jews in Germany? But the court files of the case and the testimonies are there, preserved and open to the public in the local archives. Reality truly turned out stranger than fiction and tells us something about Germany's return to a new post-Nazi normalcy, that is, what the guilty and not-so-guilty former perpetrators and bystanders did. The myth of the zero hour, the new beginning after the fall of the Third Reich, was the fiction that many people were more than willing to buy into. And where Garibaldi's book ends is not the end of the story.

Fifteen years later, in another court case, all the same accusations and smears were warmed up again and repeated by one of Katz's former fellow Jewish administrators. However, at the end of the trial the accuser was simply declared as mentally incompetent, case closed, at least as far as the courts were concerned. And more so, the story resumed many years later. There is a brief epilogue about a recent book written only a few years ago by the grandson of one of the Nazi perpetrators which found broad acclaim in Bremen. In that book, again and yet so many years later, Carl Katz is portrayed the same way he had been denounced after the war, as the one who was truly guilty of the deportations of the Jews of Bremen, attempting again to whitewash the Nazi perpetrators.

What Garibaldi's book tells us about is the continuation of anti-Jewish sentiments after the war. It has to be said, however, that Katz's determination to return to Bremen and to stay and to rebuild the Jewish community was not a singular occurrence; it happened in a few other places as well, but it was extremely uncommon. Katz's commitment to the Jewish community was outstanding in its determination and resilience.

What could not be covered in this book, and what needs to be brought to light in a story still to be told, is the reputation that Carl Katz came to be known for— that is, the other side of the story. The struggles of the post-war Jewish community in Bremen, and elsewhere, needs to be told from the Jewish end and by way also of those non-Jewish Germans who wanted to break with the Nazi past. Katz's friendship with Leo Baeck that was forged in Theresienstadt continued until the last days of Leo Baeck's life in 1956. The connection Katz made immediately with the Bremen exile community in the United States right away after his return to Bremen in late 1945, when he was reporting about who had not survived, but were murdered.

What needs to be recognized is that Katz received the highest medal of merit of the Federal Republic, the Bundesverdienstkreuz, awarded to Katz in 1960. In 1959, the year prior, in the Festschrift for his 60th birthday, we find the contributions by Norbert Wollheim and Josef Rosensaft, two of the major fighters for the survivors. And there is more that is still to be told, details that are important for the local history of Bremen.

On the other hand, and maybe even more important, Carl Katz's story will resonate with families who suffered in similar ways. It is to be hoped that this book will convince people to listen more carefully to the voices that remained after the catastrophe to tell the story.

Chapter One
August 1949:
The Case

Siegfried Hoeffler. Courtesy of Staatsarchiv Bremen.

Siegfried Hoeffler left through the front door of his small furnished apartment on *Moselstrasse* in the *Neustadt* section of Bremen, Germany.

The small flower gardens to either side of the front path were overrun with weeds. *Somebody really ought to fix that up*, he thought to himself with distaste. It was difficult enough getting used to these humble surroundings in a middle-class section of town. He felt he had worked far too hard for far too long to live in this modest situation. Passing through the small iron gate and onto the gray flagstone sidewalk, he made his way to the tramway stop.

He hurried his tall, slim frame towards his destination near *Norderlander* Street. He wore his best summer suit and held a custom-made hat in place—careful not to mess his neatly slicked back hair. Hoeffler was determined to always maintain a cosmopolitan and sophisticated bearing. While he may not have been considered classically handsome by German standards, he managed to sustain his lean build from all those years of working the family's farm as a boy.

Upon introduction, no one could have ever guessed his humble origins. Born and raised in the countryside of Eastern Germany, his keen intelligence and determination produced a law degree from the prestigious Berlin University. He was even awarded the distinction of cum laude for his doctorate studies. But the loss of the war four years ago had not served him well. Directly following the collapse of the Third Reich, this former Prosecutor of the *SA* was reduced to performing low-level, menial labor for quite some time.

After waiting only a minute or two at the stop, Hoeffler jumped onto the pale yellow and red-trimmed trolley car after it came to a complete halt. He found a vacant seat adjacent to the window to watch through on his way to work in the center of town. The air was getting a little crisper now that the summer was nearing its end. He raised his chin to the incoming brilliance of the sun's rays, as he knew their days were now numbered. He was a bit saddened that the seemingly endless gray and overcast skies of Northwest Germany's fall and winter months were closely around the corner.

Seated upon his comfortable bench, he turned his attention away from an obnoxious driver blaring his horn directly behind the tram. Instead of focusing on all that was wrong so far this morning, he decided to remind himself about those others who fared far worse fates than he. Hoeffler made it an essential practice these days to try to focus on the positive. For example, whereas many were—and in some cases, still are— incarcerated by the Allied forces, Hoeffler was released from his detainment at his POW camp as early as November of 1945. And unlike so many of his peers, he didn't have to serve years for charges of "crimes against humanity." He credited his quick ability to manipulate "the system" among his God-given blessings. *There, that was good of me,* he reflected. *I feel tremendous gratitude for that.*

But on this fine August morning, Hoeffler was pulled from his determined attempt at positivity when the man in the car blasted his horn again.

Center square of Bremen's downtown in post-war, 1946. Trolley car pictured in the upper-right corner. Courtesy of the Weser Kurier. Photographer Georg Schmidt.

Right beside his window! The blaring of its klaxon rattled his teeth and had him jump right out of his seat. Unable to disregard this latest offence, he propped himself up further to get a better look. The infraction originated from a recent model chocolate brown Wanderer. Polished to a mirror-like sheen, it mocked Hoeffler as it bore his reflection along its elegantly arched hood. His heart center then ached a bit. It was not unlike the one he used to drive around in during the better war years. He could recall the luxury of running his hands over the large polished steering wheel. When he'd pull up to his destination with the grated fender and winged hood ornament, everyone would immediately understand that he was a man of importance. He angled his chin to get a better glance at the man behind the wheel in the contrast stitching leather bucket seats. No! It couldn't be. Was it? Was it the Jew, Katz?

Hoeffler had seen Carl Katz around town in this most affluent of cars. It was almost as though Katz were rubbing the impoverished Germans' noses in his recent, post-war prosperity. Katz had also become quite portly—unlike the rest of the population, who had grown painfully thin from lack of food. In fact, the Jews all received greater food rations than the rest of them. And here was Katz now, barely able to squeeze his round belly behind the wheel. Yes, yes, the Jews suffered. *But haven't we all?*

9

The Prosecutor was a man who had always done everything right. From a career standpoint, that is. Soon after he was absolved of all major wrongdoing by the Allies, he was reinstated to his former profession, but this time as an assistant to the State Prosecutor. He correctly deduced that the Americans, war-weary and missing home, wanted to finish their jobs as swiftly as possible. They were therefore content to have one less Nazi to process in their courts. And today, at forty-one years of age, Hoeffler was still young enough to rise back up the ranks of this new world order. He had done it before, and he was determined to do it again.

The man behind the Wanderer sped away before Hoeffler could accurately determine whether it was actually Katz. He therefore settled back into his seat. After a short ride into Bremen's city center, he bounded off at his stop. He headed toward the Landgericht Bremen building. Arguably one of the most beautiful and stately constructions of all of Bremen. The sprawling complex extended over an entire block. Along with his office, the courthouse was also located in this structure on the bustling Domsheide Square. Built in the French Renaissance style, it was mercifully spared from the effects of war.

Landgericht Bremen Building in Domsheide Square.
Gerichtsgebaeude_10, B-Karterei-04984_001. Courtesy of Staatsarchiv Bremen.

He struggled to pass by all the others heading to work. Within this busy square, there were also many young veterans hobbling upon their crutches. The pant legs of their missing limbs flapped about, as if mocking the relic of what once was. The pre-war Germany, with its pristine society and proper codes of conduct, felt like a lifetime ago. The once-proud Germans barely held onto their decorum since stricken with famine and living amongst the rubble and skeletons of homes and buildings from Allied airstrikes. Hoeffler briefly paused his pace as a small group of young children—the youngest byproducts of war—circled his steps before running off. Dressed in their summer sweaters and shorts, he should have found joy and promise in their smiling faces. But the truth was, they were mostly orphaned, and single-parented children. Most ran throughout the streets aimlessly without schools to attend or adults to watch after them. Hoeffler sighed at the thought. Germany was just now starting to get back on its feet, but to him it seemed like an all too slow and arduous process. Some days it was easier than others to maintain positivity and gratitude.

Photo: Magnus Iken, photoarchive SKB-Bremen.

11

The courthouse's magnificent engravings of lions, heads of Medusa, and dragons spouting rainwater granted his permission through its entrance. Enormous stained-glass windows depicting the Ten Commandments shadowed him as he walked into the expansive first floor lobby. He had already made this journey countless times, but the awareness that this homage to German prominence was where he belonged, never failed to light a fire in his heart.

After a few brief greetings, Hoeffler passed his secretary's writing table to enter his office. He placed his briefcase down upon his heavy, wooden desk. Before he could even organize his contents from out of his portfolio, his young assistant hastily appeared to offer him his daily paper and a drink. He assured her that he was in no immediate need of anything.

Hoeffler was recently given the task to come up with a case that would stand in court against *der Jude* (The Jew), Carl Katz. He appropriated the first hour of the morning to review the evidence provided. While Hoeffler may have been one of the best prosecutors in Germany, he realized that this one would not be a simple victory. To convince the already sympathetic Allies that this Jew was guilty of crimes against humanity, would take all of his ingenuity and resources. But then again, the naïve Americans helped place people like *him* in charge of trying his comrades for their war crimes. *Like him*—a former Nazi! He couldn't help but chuckle a bit at the humor and irony of it all. After all, Hoeffler was the one who would be known for his efficiency at acquitting his fellow Nazi wrongdoers, from "Killing Without a Whimper or Consequence." It wouldn't be so hard to convince those gullible Americans of Katz's guilt after all.

He was then pulled from his thoughts at the gentle rapping upon his door. His svelte secretary, in a tight black skirt and matching black cardigan, leaned slightly into the room to notify him of his visitor.

"Gerber is here to see you," she said, ever so politely.

Hoeffler immediately rose from his chair. "Yes, please let him in. Thank you," he replied, while taking a moment to watch the pretty young girl exit the room. Yes, her figure was more pleasing than his new wife's, he determined. *Shame at that.*

Gerber swiftly entered the office with a determined stride. There was no mistaking this man as anything other than who he was. The Police Investigator, wearing the customary beige three-piece suit characteristic of his employ, removed his hat before entering the room.

"Inspector," Hoeffler stated, while extending a hand.

"Good day, Mr. Prosecutor," Gerber replied in kind, grasping Hoeffler's outstretched hand firmly before taking a seat.

"I heard you have some good news for me," Hoeffler continued. The weighty, rectangular chair screeched loudly against the wood flooring, before he sat upon its upholstery.

"Yes. It does look good, and he is willing to officially testify," Gerber asserted.

"Fantastic! And you are absolutely certain that he is a full-blooded Jew?"

"Yes, one hundred percent certain of that. He is a journalist as well. This makes Arnold Schustermann by far our most credible witness. He just flew in from London, and is staying at his sister-in-law's here in the city," Gerber verified. His excitement just barely contained below the surface. He really was determined to obtain Hoeffler's approval.

"Wonderful. Will he state it? Is he willing to put it into writing?" Hoeffler demanded, glaring into the Inspector's simple, yet stern, brown eyes.

"We just received confirmation that Schustermann is prepared to testify that Carl Katz was the one responsible for placing his brother, Benno's, name on the transport list. He is thereby holding Katz responsible for Benno's murder in Auschwitz," Gerber answered. A small smile creeped up the corners of his mouth, in anticipation of Hoeffler's appreciation.

Hoeffler leaned back into his chair, and took in a deep breath. He folded his hands over his waist, and felt a sense of relief wash over him. This may be just what they needed to get their conviction.

After the Police Inspector's departure, Siegfried Hoeffler spent the rest of the workday with a fire in his belly. He loved the thrill of the hunt, and even began visualizing his victory. Perhaps the Prosecutor would legitimately find something to be grateful for today, after all.

He made sure to pass by the entrance of the courthouse room before leaving for the day. Standing just inside its doorway, he ingratiated himself with the smell of the rich, aged cedar. Opulent wood paneling covered every wall. He visualized himself pleading his case before the elevated bench of the judges. They would look down upon the assailant with intimidation and austerity. The Prosecutor proudly reflected back upon his cases during the war years—namely, his work on the Terror Trials of Krakow Poland. That it was *his* group who was awarded the title of most death verdicts, second only to Warsaw, against those deemed "enemies of the state." Today, however, the enormous American and British flags of the occupiers glared offensively at Hoeffler from behind the judges' chairs. *The tricolor black, red, and gold bands of Germany will reign over this institution and land again soon enough. Yes,* he vowed, *that day will soon come again.*

13

He left work at his usual time, and jumped in on his usual trolley. He got off at his usual stop, with the usual neighbors, before walking the usual distance home. With all his assets confiscated by the Russian occupiers of Eastern Germany in '45, he knew it would take some time yet before he could ever rebuild his fortune. For now, he had to resign himself to living in his modest furnished apartment in *Neustadt*—amongst the weeds.

But he would not let himself get used to it—to the usual circumstances of his life. No, if he did that, he was afraid he'd lose his ubiquitous desire for better. His motivation was everything—it had always served him well. Now he had a new incentive. Carl Katz had just purchased a large, three-story home on *Donandtstrasse*—in a very nice part of town. A home where that fancy chocolate brown car looked good parked in front. Katz actually owned several other properties in and around town, too. Sometimes Hoeffler would pass by them to see how their rebuilding was coming along. Katz was just now starting to reconstruct the bombed-out homes of those family members killed in the camps. Hoeffler was perpetually exasperated at this Jew's audacity. He shook his head at the thought of Katz profiting off his dead relatives' misfortune. Suspiciously enough, Katz's was one of the only Jewish families in Bremen to survive their annihilation.

Someone had to take this man down, and he was determined that he would be the one to do it.

Chapter Two
Thursday, November 10th, 1938:
The Night That Changed Everything

Carl Katz, 18, in his military uniform.

"Take your mother and grandmother to the taxi stand and go to *Frau* Beiser's home. She is not Jewish, you will be safe there," Carl Katz whispered to Inge, his fourteen-year-old daughter, his cheek pressed against her dark hair.

While considered a handsome man by anyone's standards, Carl was known more for his commanding presence and quick wit. His fast smile and blue-eyed charm always got him out of more trouble than he cared to admit. But he wasn't quite sure how he'd get out of this one—the Nazis forcibly removing him from his home.

As he let go of Inge and was led down the path away from their home on #33 *Isarstrasse* in Bremen, Germany, he drew in a modicum of comfort knowing that at least his daughter, wife, and mother-in-law were safe... for now. But when, if ever, would he be able to return to protect them? As Carl was being led away by the three young *SA* men, he knew his beautiful daughter must also be praying that this would not be the last time she would ever set eyes upon her father. While she was a sweet, quiet girl, Carl recognized a rare strength and capable nature far beyond her years. She was truly her father's daughter.

A few neighbors now stood peering out from behind their curtains, witnessing his arrest. They must have been curious upon hearing the sounds of the Katz home being vandalized. Surely they heard Carl's wife's frantic cries? Yet they stood there, watching, doing nothing. Carl raised his chin a bit higher as the Nazis led him into their awaiting car.

"*Schnell, einsteigen* (Quick, get in)!" one of the arrogant, heavily armed young men in leather boots and gray overcoats commanded.

He obediently followed the order, even though to do so went against every instinct coursing through his body. With a young daughter, a wife with a delicate constitution, an elderly mother-in-law, an ailing father, and a mother with dementia under his care, Carl simply could not risk doing anything foolish. It took all of his determination to let those men continue to do whatever it was they were ordered to do. Before driving away, he glanced back toward his pretty, two-story house with white-painted window frames. Rose bushes, both red and yellow, stood in the front yard. How he looked forward to bounding through the front gate and up the black and white tiled steps every day after work. He would then be embraced with the aroma of the stew his wife had been cooking.

But when would he be permitted to return to his normal life? He shuddered at the realization that he did not know. Looking back at the frame of his doorway now, he saw the silhouette of Inge. He knew she would remain there until her father was out of sight. With the roar of the ignition, he left Inge, his pretty home, and the rest of his family behind.

They drove for several minutes down the tree-lined residential streets on the way to an undisclosed destination. *Neustadt* was a quaint, middle-class section of town where most homes had overflowing flower boxes hanging outside every window. Carl felt that it made the crimes committed in this sweet and quiet neighborhood all the more jarring. He unbuttoned the front of his heavy woolen overcoat. Despite the brisk chill to the early morning air, the stress of these events made him sweat. The *SA* remained silent in the front seats and still had not given Carl a reason for his arrest.

As a young man, Carl Katz had served Germany on the front lines in The Great War. He was even awarded an Iron Cross for his service. But apparently, this was not enough for the Katz family and their home to be spared. Everything was destroyed. Anything ceramic was shattered, their fine china thrown to the floor, their windows were all broken. Even the family photos on the wall had the faces cut out by the edge of a Nazi sword. The Katzes may have thought of themselves as Germans, but it appeared that Germany officially thought of them only as Jews.

SA Plundering Jewish-owned stores on the morning of November 10th, 1938.
Courtesy of Staatsarchiv Bremen.

All along the streets, he saw non-Jewish people leaving for work and going about their day. It was as if nothing had happened, but for Carl and his family, it seemed their nightmare had just begun. He was then driven past some vandalized Jewish businesses. The *SA* looted them, while other officers stood guard to make sure no civilians joined in on the opportunity. He felt his temple pulsate with dread as he wondered how the other members of his community fared.

"You know why this is happening, don't you, *Drecksau* (filthy swine)?" one of the officers suddenly said to Carl.

"No, sir," Carl responded tentatively.

"You heard about the murder of Ernst vom Rath in Paris by one of your people, haven't you?" he inquired.

"Yes, sir." Carl sighed.

When the Third Secretary in the German Embassy in Paris was assassinated a few days ago by a Polish Jewish boy, the whole Jewish community in Bremen shuddered. Carl knew that any excuse to justify the further mistreatment of Jews in Germany would be exploited. Ever since the Nuremberg Laws of 1935, which stripped German Jews of their rights of citizenship, things had only gotten harder. The actions of the *SA* this past night, although extreme, began to make a bit more sense to Carl.

"Your kind is dangerous to us and a threat to Germany. You must be dealt with accordingly... and severely," the officer continued.

Through clenched teeth, Carl responded in the only way he was permitted. "Yes, sir. You are right."

The car turned by the entrance of a local school, the Altes Gymnasium, and stopped. They ushered Carl out of the vehicle and ordered him to stand in the center of the school's courtyard, amongst nearly a hundred other Jewish men already gathered. Many of those also served Germany in The Great War. Huddled inside the walls of a three-story, yellow brick building, they frantically muttered to each other in search of information.

While the men quietly spoke, Carl's eyes darted all around in search of his father. *He must be somewhere in this crowd.* The two of them had not been on the best of terms for the last few years, but none of that was important today. As he scanned the huddled masses of men, his eyes rested upon a familiar form.

No, it cannot be him.

This man did not hold himself in the same noble way as did *Herr* (Mister) Rudolph Katz. His white hair was disheveled, eyes bewildered, and he had nothing on but an overcoat over a crumpled nightshirt. Yet this man called out to Carl upon making eye contact. Carl's brother-in-law, Moritz, was also there beside him.

"Carl!" he shouted, pushing his way closer.

"*Papa* (Father)! Are you okay? Is Mom safe at the house?"

"Yes... No... I don't know. I had to leave her there. I explained to them that she needed me as she has dementia, but those brutes couldn't care less! They didn't even give me time to get dressed before they took me away." Rudolph looked down at his appearance, ashamed.

"Do you have your heart medication?" Carl asked, trying to prioritize their situation.

"No! I had no time. But more importantly, who will care for your mother?"

Carl tried his best to comfort his father. He was not used to seeing him this way. He appeared frail and confused, not at all like the argumentative, authoritative disciplinarian he had always known him to be. After assuring his dad that he'd figure something out, Carl prayed that he reflected confidence and capability. In truth, he was profoundly stunned and heartbroken.

Carl was also completely overwhelmed by the situation. He had no idea how to manage any of this. It was then that he noticed that the courtyard was filled with trees, some of their golden leaves still clinging to the overhanging branches. They swayed a bit in the November winds, shining brightly as the early morning sun illuminated their features. When he looked up in appreciation of their beauty, it only served to magnify the ugly and sorry state in which they all found themselves this morning. More importantly, it reminded him in some strange way that natural order did and could still exist. Newly composed, he then turned his attention to Moritz.

"Your wife, the children, is everyone alright? Were they all home safe when you left?"

"I suppose so," Moritz replied before casting a haggard expression upon his brother-in law. He ran a hand over his wayward, brown, curly hair, before using it to cover his gaping mouth. "Why do you ask? Why wouldn't they be safe? W-what do you think happened to them?"

"Of course, they are fine!" Carl responded, thinking quickly. He needed to calm the man down—immediately. The guards surrounding the perimeter looked toward the two conversing men in response to Moritz's sudden shrill, raised voice. One of them even casually rested his hand upon the butt of the gun in its holster. As the *SA* took a step toward Carl, he grabbed at Moritz's elbow, and spoke forcefully into his ear.

"Lower your voice, God damnit."

"What? Why?" Moritz replied, confused, as he instinctively looked around him. As he inevitably made eye contact with the Stormtrooper now approaching, he began to panic. "Oh shit, Carl," he whispered.

Thinking fast, Carl forcefully patted the fellow Jew on the shoulder while letting out a boisterous laugh. "That's great to hear!" Carl exclaimed loudly. "Tell the wife and kids hello for me!"

Now directly upon them, the *SA,* with a confused expression, addressed the detainees. "Keep it down!" he ordered, brows pressed crossly together.

Carl looked towards him with a friendly countenance, and flashed a broad, toothy, smile. He noticed that the hand of the young lad, however, was still gripping the pistol. He felt his heartrate quicken.

"My apologies, sir. Just catching up with an old friend. It won't happen again."

This seemed to please the capturer, as he finally released his grasp of the weapon, and redirected his attention. As he stepped back to rejoin his comrades, Carl scolded Moritz harshly.

"You had better pull yourself together," he warned the trembling, skinny man. His visible frailty in this moment concerned Carl. "Everyone is fine. All the women are together at my business partner's Aryan household. They are safe," Carl declared harshly before briskly walking away a little. He did not want to give the capturers any excuse to pursue disciplinary action.

Over the course of the morning, more men joined them in the courtyard. Carl went around to check on the others. There was really nothing he could do for anyone, much less himself. He didn't have an exact count, but estimated there to be between one and two hundred men and boys over the age of seventeen. Carl spotted a young *SA* soldier who he felt held some doubts about the role he was given to play this morning. There was hesitation and concern in his eyes when he looked upon the older men. Carl took a chance to approach him in a friendly tone.

"*Moin moin*, (slang for good morning)," Carl chirped.

"*Moin moin*," the young man responded. His long, gray overcoat with polished rows of brass buttons was cinched at the waist with a brown leather belt. His black boots appeared to be new, polished to a reflective veneer.

Carl figured that this fresh-faced young boy must have just gotten his uniform... and position. He may have been dressed up and given the power of a man, but he was barely more than a child.

"My father..." he pointed to Rudolf, "is really weak and forgot to bring his heart pills with him. He also takes care of my mother at home. She is all alone there right now and suffers from dementia."

"That's too bad," the young man replied, only encouraging Carl further.

"Yes! It is too bad. You know, I think a lot of these older gentlemen probably forgot their medication, too, and they've been standing outside in the cold for hours. Maybe we could let them go back home for a bit? What do you think?"

Carl tried his best to muster a grin at this pompous boy with the ruddy cheeks of a child. He desperately clung to the hope that the Stormtrooper remembered that in Germany, youth were raised to show respect to their elders—even if he was a dreadful Nazi. But the fair-haired youngster just looked at Carl before walking away. Disappointed, and with his pride compromised, he figured it was worth a try.

Maybe an hour or more passed before they made an announcement that they would be releasing his father and several other elderly men.

"You see? I told you!" Carl exclaimed as he turned toward his father beside him. "All is fine. Say hi to Mom, and I'll be by soon to check up on you," he said before Rudolf was led away.

Thank God there was one less thing Carl needed to worry about. He had no idea if they had planned on releasing the elderly all along, but Carl suddenly became hopeful. *Maybe I do have some control over my fate.*

By the time the afternoon approached, the men could sense the *SA* were readying themselves. After they hung a sign over the neck of Rabbi Aber that read, *Wir Sind Die Zerstoerer Deutschen Kultur* (We are the destroyers of German culture), the Jews were ordered to stand in a line, and remove their hats, to be marched through the city streets of Bremen. Embarrassed and ashamed, they had no option but to be bare-headed and do precisely as they were told.

The Jewish men over the age of 17 being marched through the city streets of Bremen.
Courtesy of Staatsarchiv Bremen.

Shortly upon leaving, but surely by no accident, the parade of demoralized and newly anointed "enemies of the state" was led past the only synagogue in the city. It was a small, purposefully indistinguishable building attached to others just like it. The two-story, gray stucco walls were intact, but you could see through the shattered windows that the insides had all been set on fire, still smoldering. The wooden pews where Carl's family sat in observance of his *bar mitzvah* as a young lad, then for his wedding to the beautiful love of his life, Marianne, to the naming of his sweet and reliable daughter, Inge, were now splintered and shattered. His heart ached a bit as he was forced to walk past the building.

The local firemen stood nearby, but they were there only to make sure the fire did not spread to the adjacent non-Jewish buildings. Even the firemen's uniforms were military in appearance these days. Moss green with red piping on the seams, it appeared that no one and nothing was immune from Nazi indoctrination. It took all of Carl's strength to step over a prayer book lying open on the street. Later, he would learn that his daughter would find it and pick it up.

Burning down of the synagogue while the firefighters stand by to make sure the adjacent buildings don't also catch fire. Courtesy of Staatsarchiv Bremen.

They were marched through the cobblestone streets of Bremen, under the scarlet red Nazi flags, without a word spoken. The citizens all gathered along the street, watching silently. Confused, the members of the *SA* tried to encourage the crowd's applause. A few did clap in response to their urging, while others smirked at their humiliation. But mostly, all just stood there silently. They appeared to be in as complete a state of shock of the treatment of the Jews as were the Jews themselves.

The parade was then led through the narrow streets of the old part of the town. These slender, winding passageways had uneven footpaths from centuries of people passing. This medieval city had a unique lure of outdoor markets, chocolate shops, and coffee breweries. The smell alone of baking *butterkuchen* (butter cake) and roasted morning coffee was reason enough to rise from bed. But all that charm was concealed

23

these days underneath the copious number of Nazi flags hung along the storefronts. The stench of the charred building housing the synagogue, and with it the hundreds of years of Germany's Jewish history now filled the air with a thick black smoke.

The Jews were then led down *Ostertorstrasse* towards the *Walle* section. Shortly thereafter, they continued on to *Groepelinger-Heerstrasse* on the way to *Oslebshausen* Prison. It was an excruciatingly long and burdensome walk.

The weight the elderly placed upon their wooden canes made them appear as though they would splinter and crack under the pressure. Carl couldn't help but take note of every uneven slope or raised pebble. God forbid one of the elderly would catch themselves and stumble over it. What then? He shuddered to think. No less than an hour passed. He wasn't sure if they could all make it much further. But just then a large looming structure appeared before them.

The men stopped their huffing and labored breaths just long enough to look upon the impending prison walls. A brick enclosure—maybe a foot thick and two stories high—was all lined with barbed wire. The men, all forcibly lined up in rows and pressed together, could never have imagined that this was where they were being led. Looking up toward the heavens for some sort of guidance, Carl's eyes paused upon the looming strips of barbed wire resting high above the fortifications. Many of the elderly and unwell continued to sway from the strain of the trudge. When they thought no one was looking, a few leaned against the wall to give their shaky, cane-holding hands a bit of a rest. Carl looked at them with concern, but there was nothing he could do. There were no chairs to offer, no glasses of water to provide. He let out a huge sigh of relief when many of those who couldn't endure the afternoon's walk were called out and released. Perhaps his small prayer had been answered after all.

Oslebshausen prison.

They passed through an enormous courtyard surrounded on all sides by five stories of celled men. These hardened criminals, now pressing themselves against the windows, jeered at the pitiful gang of men. Whistles and lewd comments taunted them as they tried their best to ignore the heckling. While most were teachers, shopkeepers, accountants, etc., the Jews had enough good sense to know not to allow any fear to cross their faces.

The frightening reality, however, was that they were to remain amongst these hooligans without any protection. Carl was awash with a feeling he hadn't experienced since his war years; that sense of vulnerability and hopelessness in the knowledge that within those trenches, you were just sitting prey to the enemy. Upon passing through the courtyard, they were led into a large open dormitory of the prison. Carl wearily staggered to a vacant area. Hungry and cold, he selected a cot, then gestured for his brother-in-law, Moritz, to grab the one beside him. He rolled his overcoat under his head as a pillow. Allocated a thin, woolen blanket, he pulled it up and over his shoulders. All the while, he kept an eye on the windows and doors. He had to be at the ready if any of the real inmates broke in and wanted to have a little fun assaulting unarmed Jews.

In the eerie darkness, he'd somehow accidentally drift off for a moment here and there, then suddenly jolt awake at the remembrance of his daughter, wife, and mother-in-law alone, without his protection. *Have they remained unharmed? Did the SA come*

25

back for them? Were they apprehended and imprisoned, too? These thoughts threaded together in his mind in an unending loop of anxiety and insanity. If that weren't enough to jar him from accidental bouts of slumber, then it was the random screams and howls just outside the walls of their dormitory. He pushed the cots closer so that he may keep his back pressed and close to Moritz . At least no one could attack them from behind. That was how he and his men slept in the foxholes during The Great War. He closed his hands in tight fists as he wondered if the guards would allow the inmates to pay the Jews a visit. He cursed that, unlike then, he did not have a rifle in his hands at the ready.

****

The following morning, weary, haggard, and thankfully unharmed, Carl and the rest of the men were led to the *Strassenbahn* (trolley car) to the tune of angry orders from *Gestapo* Agent Parchmann.

In their crumpled suits and with wayward hair prohibited from being concealed up under their hats, they obediently followed their captors' orders. They were walked through columns of enormous, blood red, swastika embossed banners arranged at the *Hauptbahnhof* (main train station). They were then instructed to walk the few steps up the concrete service staircase, and under the high, arched ceilings of the entrance. On the long departure platform with wood and metal benches scattered about, which they were prohibited to use, stood a "special train," which was indistinguishable from any other commuter car, waiting to transport them to another undisclosed location. The massive iron machinery stood idly still while awaiting its cargo. The train conductors blew on their shrill whistles, signaling the train to fire up its engines.

"Hurry up! The train needs to leave! *Schnell, einsteigen!* (Quick, enter!)," the high-ranking *Gestapo* kept shouting at them.

Forced onto the commuter train, it was only the second time Carl had ever been commanded with those angry words, yet they already served to trigger fearful shivers up his spine.

Once inside, Carl made his way to the first available space. He rested his head against its comfortable, high-backed gray seats, Moritz sitting beside him. Around him, the rest of the men nervously speculated about their fate. Carl just sat there silently for what was to be a several-hour train ride. He felt it far wiser to conserve his energy rather than waste it, like the others, on fear and theorizing. If he were going to make it through whatever was to happen to them, he was certain it would require all his strength and capability.

Chapter Three

August, 1949
The "Witness"

Heinrich Himmler, the second most powerful man of the Third Reich, visiting Bremen's police station, April 7th, 1934. Courtesy of Staatsarchiv Bremen.

Charles Gerber involuntarily shook his head a bit at the statement spoken by the Jewish witness before him. He realized he had done so when the man suddenly stopped his account to question him.

"What? What was wrong with what I just said?" Arnold Schustermann questioned.

"*Hmm*?" the Police Inspector asked, raising his gaze from his notetaking. He met the Jew's eager and pleading eyes with his own.

"Your head. You were just shaking your head at me. Why?" star witness for the prosecution, Arnold Schustermann, asked again.

27

Gerber reprimanded himself for his outward display of dissatisfaction. No witness would ever feel comfortable opening up if they felt disapproval from an investigator. That was a rookie mistake. But my God—*would anyone blame me?* He must have mentioned that he is an English journalist ten times already!

"My apologies. I was just reflecting on the evidence you are bringing against Katz," the Police Inspector politely responded. He himself had never had any trouble with Jews as a race. But it was common practice to be very, albeit overly, polite and friendly with these people in post-war Germany. The Allied occupiers had been punishing Germans who mistreated Jews for the past several years. He just wanted to do his job. He just wanted to take a salary back to his family. He had to somehow come up with the money for a suit for his son's upcoming confirmation. All Gerber needed right now was to be accused of impropriety to a Jew.

"Oh. Okay. Of course. I just thought that maybe I said something wrong." The witness shrugged apologetically.

Is this man for real? Gerber couldn't help but wonder to himself. He had never known a post-war Jew so desperate for the validation of a German working for former Nazi Party members. Had he seen Jews express anger? Most certainly. Fear? Absolutely. But seeking *approval?* This was a new experience for the Police Inspector.

Gerber, a simple man from humble beginnings, with an eighth grade education, a former political prisoner for communist ties during the Third Reich in the mid-1930s, and to top it all off, possessing the distinctive ruddy face of a country-dweller, had grown accustomed to being treated as though he were nothing. Therefore, he should have enjoyed this deferential interaction more. Instead, he found it rather unsettling.

Charles Gerber, SD Index File,
November 4th, 1936. Identified here as a communist. Courtesy of Staatsarchiv Bremen.

"Please, go on," he urged Schustermann, trying better to hide his repugnance.

"Yes, so as I was saying. As you know, I am a journalist—"

Oh for the love of God!

"—and so therefore, I don't frivolously make allegations. And as a journalist and citizen of England, I am used to seriously researching before making up my mind and bringing forth allegations," Arnold Schustermann said with a small smile. He was seated at the very front of his seat, and was clasping his hands upon the desk before him. He reminded Gerber of a school boy sitting in the front row of class after he had gifted his teacher a shiny red apple. Furthermore, he was almost certain that the "witness" was wearing his best summer suit for this occasion.

"Yes, of course, but could you please once again clarify how you believe Katz was the one responsible for the murder of your brother, Benno Schustermann, and for the incarceration of your nephew? I am just a little confused. My apologies. Until this moment, I was unaware that not only have you never met *Herr* Katz, but that you were never even in the city of Bremen, nor were you in the camps, Theresienstadt or Auschwitz, where these offences allegedly occurred."

This time, Gerber only shook his head within his own mind. Careful not to betray his encouraging veneer, Gerber was completely exasperated. Other than the fact that Arnold was a full-blooded Jew willing to speak against another Jew, no court of law would ever—*could* ever—consider this man's testimony, much less treat him as a "witness" to a murder.

"Yes, well, it is true that I have never met Katz, in either the camps or Bremen in the time in question, nor am I very familiar with the event firsthand." Arnold started shifting a bit nervously within his seat now. "But in the *Spruchkammer* (criminal trial for war crimes) against the former *Gestapo* Agent Nette, Nette accused Katz heavily of being guilty of the fate of many Jews—"

*Don't shake your head. Just keep writing all this down. Whatever you do, **do not** shake your head.*

"—and that Katz was an informer and collaborator of the *Gestapo*. Then a list of names was read out under which one was my nephew's name, Lothar. My nephew lived during the Nazi time in Bremen in *Vor dem Steintor* 45."

"Ah, pardon my interruption. You said that you heard this during Nette's criminal trial?"

"Oh no. I just arrived in Bremen. My sister-in-law, Johanna, Lothar's mother, told me that *she* heard this from her friend, *Frau* Haendler, during Nette's testimony."

"Right. Please continue," Gerber humored the man.

"Lothar was then just a young lad. Former *Gestapo*, Nette, claimed in his testimony that Lothar should not have been deported but was deported due to the actions of Katz."

"And why did Nette claim that? After all, wasn't it the very job of the *Gestapo* to have records on who qualified for deportation?" Gerber was now finding himself genuinely curious as to Arnold's reasoning. If for no other reason than the sheer entertainment value of interviewing a simpleton.

30

"Well, from what Johanna told me, is that *Frau* Haendler remembers that Nette said that he placed a call to Katz in his office whereby Nette said that he had Lothar there beside him. He asked Katz what he should do with him. Therefore, my nephew's deportation could only have occurred through the information that Katz had given to Nette," Arnold finished stating.

"Ah yes, I see. Thank you for bringing all this to my attention. Just a few quick questions. I want to make sure I have everything correct." Gerber started shuffling through his papers in order to reread them.

"So were you actually a witness to Katz telling the *Gestapo* agent, Nette, to deport Lothar?"

"Uh no. I heard that that is what the *Gestapo* agent said had happened."

"Of course. That's right. You heard from your sister-in-law's friend that the *Gestapo* agent, Nette, accused Katz of this when Nette was tried and later convicted of committing crimes against humanity against Jews?" Gerber tried his hardest to stifle a chuckle.

"Uh, yes."

"So, correct me if I am wrong, but according to the laws of that time, Lothar was due to go to the camps because he was biologically Jewish on his father's side, and attended a Jewish school. Correct?"

"Yes, I've heard that to be the case."

"So if it were law of that time, why, again, do you hold Katz responsible for his deportation?"

"That's easy, because my sister-in-law said that the only person that knew of him attending the Jewish school was Katz, and Katz betrayed his own people, by reporting it to the *Gestapo*," Arnold replied with a polite nod, as though confirming the script in his head he was given to recite.

"I'm sorry, did you say Katz was the only person that knew Lothar attended Jewish school?"

"Yes," Schustermann affirmed.

"The *only* person? In an *entire* school established for teaching Jewish culture to its citizens. For all those three years?" Gerber pressed.

"Oh, well, yes. That's what I was told." Arnold wasn't good at hiding his thoughts either, Gerber noted. Beads of sweat settled upon his brow as the realization of the illogical nature of his comment hit him. It didn't stop him one bit, however. Gerber

31

wondered what—or rather, *who*—it was that compelled this man to give his laughably flawed testimony.

"Um, may—" he cleared his throat with a dry cough, "may I have a glass of water, please?" Arnold requested apologetically.

"Absolutely, right away." Gerber gestured to the stenographer sitting beside the two men.

She quickly reached toward the tray and politely poured the men some water into two glasses from a pitcher. Schusterman gulped his drink hastily, seemingly disappointed that it was such a short process. He didn't appear quite as eager to continue with his testimony as he had when he initially entered the office at the *Polizeihaus (*Police station).

Now growing impatient, Gerber asked his next question before Schusterman had even a chance to place down his empty glass. "You also mentioned earlier that you know your brother was shipped to the death camp, Auschwitz, from the labor camp, Theresienstadt, because of Katz?"

"Yes, in hindsight, I hold this as suspicion," he answered.

"Suspicion?"

"Yes, I have no proof of this, but I assume this because of my nephew's experience. Last evening, I also just heard from Johanna and her friends that my brother was in fact murdered. He was gassed in Auschwitz."

"You just found this out *last night*? Did I hear that correctly? After all these years? No one, including your sister-in-law or nephew, ever gave you corroboration of your brother's death before *last night*?"

"Well, no." He shifted uncomfortably, suggesting that the oddness of that fact just occurred to him in this very moment. "It's been years since he went missing, so I *assumed*—" He stopped his thought mid-phrase.

Gerber wondered if it was from the emotion of learning of his brother's passing, or at the betrayal of the withheld information.

"Anyway," he continued, "I guess you can say that I now have confirmation of Katz's involvement of my brother's now definite murder. I would therefore like to acknowledge that I have given my testimony freely and I am willing to testify in front of a court of law."

"Well, thank you so much for coming in, *Herr* Schustermann." Gerber abruptly rose from his seat, eager to see this man off.

"Oh, I am not done yet," Arnold quickly stated.

Gerber inaudibly sighed as he repositioned himself back in his chair. "I didn't realize. Please, what other evidence would you like to share with me?"

"Not evidence so much, but a request," Schustermann corrected.

"A request? By all means."

"As brother of murdered Benno Schustermann, I politely request your assistance with the board of the Jewish community for Johanna's acceptance into the Jewish community to be granted as quickly as possible."

"She wants to be part of the Jewish community? Why? She is not a Jew," Gerber asked, genuinely curious.

"Well, actually she is now, as she just converted. Also, she is the widow to my brother, a Jew, and therefore is deserving of all financial reparations and food rations as given to any other member of the community."

Ahhh, now it was beginning to make much more sense to Gerber. Perhaps he just found out who the culprit was forcing this oblivious—and possibly guilt-ridden—man to come here today to testify. Aside from being ill-advised and easily manipulated, he wondered if it were also easier for this man to blame another—in this case Carl Katz—than to look to himself for not doing more to save his family. How hard it must be for him to live a flourishing life in England while learning of such horror befalling his closest of kin. Gerber had encountered many victims of wartime with these similar plagues of conscious. It was not unusual for survivors to struggle with their existence.

After seeing the Jew out with a polite handshake, Gerber quickly grabbed his hat and collected the typed account of the day's proceedings from the stenographer. Prosecutor Hoeffler had requested for Gerber to immediately report to him after the interview and inform him of his findings. With Schustermann returning to London on a flight early Monday, they would have to rush to get the testimony sworn in with the court.

As anticipated, Hoeffler jumped from his seat excitedly when he spotted Gerber approaching his office. Impeccably dressed, and looking as sharp as ever, he grasped the papers from Gerber's hands as though they were treasured items. Hoeffler would soon realize that it was nothing more than a heap of trash. To say that the policeman was not looking forward to the disappointment would be a vast understatement. With money tight, he and his family heavily relied on his employment. The Inspector resisted the urge to rub at his sore shoulder. He looked forward to eventually having enough money to purchase a mattress. His body felt bruised from sleeping on the hard floors beside his wife every night.

After several minutes of the Assistant Prosecutor reviewing the material, the Police Inspector couldn't help but wince in anticipation of the reaction. *He must be nearing the end of the report by now.* As if on cue, Hoeffler then slowly looked up from the papers to meet with Gerber's gaze. His clever eyes were open largely from what Gerber could only imagine was shock and dismay. This was most certainly not what he was expecting.

"I'm so—" Gerber began to apologize before being interrupted.

"Fantastic," Hoeffler interjected.

"I'm sorry?" Gerber replied, surely misunderstanding.

"This is fantastic news! I'll get the Judge on this immediately. If we are to get this sworn in officially on time, we'll have to get everyone in tomorrow, Saturday morning, latest. Good job, man! Get home and have some rest. You deserve it!"

With a firm handshake and flash of a white-toothed smile, Hoeffler sent Gerber on his way. He yelled to his pretty assistant over his shoulder to immediately get Bollinger on the phone for him.

"He'll know what this is concerning! Let him know we're prepared to move forward!" The secretary jumped at his command, and immediately turned her attention away from the bulky black typewriter upon the desk. She started dialing the numbers on the rotary with the receiver pressed firmly against her ear. Gerber heard her polite greeting into the line as he rounded the corner.

While the Inspector should have been happy—celebratory even—at the elated response to his findings, all he could feel was the distinct weight of his stomach turning in knots. It surprised him. He hadn't felt that sort of distress and angst in more than a decade. The same sensation experienced when he thought back to his time in the concentration camp as a political prisoner and enemy of the Third Reich.

He left the Landgericht building of the courthouse, and stood a moment in the sunny, cobblestoned square to decide if he should grab the trolley home. But the day was beautiful, and he thought it better to have some time alone to settle himself before taking on the chaos that was awaiting at home. Not only had the churning of his stomach not yet subsided, but right then, images of himself kneeling upon a cement floor flashed before his mind. Those moments when he'd look down helplessly upon his folded knees while awaiting a thrash to the head. The tips of polished black boots of a guard just in his line of vision, right before all befell to black. He barely felt those thuds as he crumpled seemingly lifelessly to the floor.

Missler Concentration Camp, Bremen, Germany. Existed from March 1933-September 1933.There were about 600 inmates in the camp, mainly communists. Unknown source.

Now standing alone in the center of town, Gerber held his hands to his ears as an intense high-pitched tone rattled through the fibers of his brain. His ears then grew numb with muffled frequencies echoing against the walls of his skull. He shook his head trying to clear it out. While his hearing was compromised—a result of the regular beatings endured from his duration in Bremen's Missler concentration camp—the ringing usually only occurred in moments of intense stress and/or exhaustion.

Just then an armed man bumped into him and whispered in a harsh tone, "*Kommunist* (Communist)."

"What?" Gerber asked frantically, fear clenching down upon the center of his chest.

"*Kommst du nun mit?*" (Are you coming along?) a woman repeated in clear language to a young child walking beside her. She looked towards Gerber curiously before rushing past.

What is happening? Get yourself together! Gerber urged himself impatiently. There were times when he'd fall into bouts of hallucinations, but they had only before occurred from dreams in the night. His wife would wake him carefully. She'd whisper to him softly that he was safe now. She'd wipe the sweat from his brown with the corner

35

of the sleeve of her nightgown, while assuring him that the Fascists were no longer in power.

As a communist, charged with high treason by the Nazi Party, he was detained at one time or another for a total of three years. But why was his trauma flooding back now? In the daytime? More than a decade since his incarceration? *Yes, definitely a good idea to take the longer walk home.*

Slightly embarrassed, he removed his hands from the sides of his head. As he turned left at the corner, he straightened his hat before proceeding in the direction of his home. He was given an apartment on *Keplerstrasse* 12. It was formerly owned by a Nazi Party member. He and his family received it as a consolation for his suffering as a political prisoner. This was a common practice by the Allies. They awarded former political prisoners, Jews etc. fully furnished homes as compensation for their hardships. However, just recently, that very homeowner came by and took back all his furnishings. Hence the sore shoulders from sleeping upon the floor. It was illegal for him to do so, and Gerber should have reported it to the housing authority, but Gerber had grown weary from his time fighting the Nazis. It was far easier to go along with them than challenge them. No matter the arena, they somehow always won. As the Allies' stronghold on their city had been lessening, Gerber noticed that the former National Socialists were growing in strength and confidence once again.

Perhaps that was what was bothering him right at this moment. The far-right regained control of the legal system, the media, most of the police force working today who had assisted the Third Reich agenda, and now those who served for crimes against humanity—like Nette—were being released with vengeance and retaliation in their grasp. Hoeffler, the Prosecuter, was one of the brightest men Gerber had ever known. If Hoeffler felt that the ridiculous testimony made by Schustermann was good enough to be admissible in court, then that spoke volumes: The Nazis were back in power.

If that were true—and it certainly seemed that way—then nothing had changed there in Germany with the loss of the war. There was no way, then, for Carl Katz, a Jew, to make it out of this alive. This trial was to be a lynching.

𝒞𝒽𝒶𝓅𝓉𝑒𝓇 𝒻𝑜𝓊𝓇
Friday, November 11th, 1938
Sachsenhausen

The entrance to Sachsenhausen Concentration Camp.

Carl's train gradually slowed as he neared his stop. He and the other men placed their hats upon their heads at the anticipation of their arrival. Peering out of the covered windows, it was hard for Carl to decipher his exact location. For the final leg of this journey, he had only seen indiscernible trees and tall grasses.

"You were ordered to shut those," a calm voice ordered Carl. *God Dammit!* He had told Moritz to warn him whenever Agent Parchmann approached. *The fool was given but one job!*

The *Gestapo* agent had been lurking up and down the train aisle ever since their departure from Bremen at 10 a.m. this morning. His quiet and severe presence scared Carl far more than the explosive or rash behaviors of some of the other agents.

"Ah, it is you, Katz." The slim man in tailored civilian clothing inquired, "How has it been going for you at the Beiser Company as of late?" The slightest of sneers grew expansive as it crossed his lined face.

Parchmann was, of course, referring to the sudden deportation of Carl's Eastern European business partner, Max Beiser. As the head of the department, "Actions Against Polish Jews of Bremen," Parchmann had suddenly, and without warning, extradited Beiser and his eight-year-old daughter, Etty, out of Germany, dropping them off at the border with only what they could pack in an hour's time. The horror of not knowing how his friend and child fared, weighed heavily upon Carl these past couple of weeks.

"Well, I—"Carl stammered, trying to search for an appropriate response to his captor's rhetorical question. So much so, that he didn't even notice the abrupt halting of the massive machinery.

Grabbing a hold of the seat back, Parchmann interrupted Carl. He leaned in a bit closer, to make sure the Jew heard every last word. "Now you will learn what it is to really work."

Fear instinctively flooded Carl's chest at the agent's menacing words. But before his mind could even decipher the nature of the agent's threat, Parchmann slowly and deliberately placed his hat upon his head. The edges of his fine, silver hair poked out from underneath. Maintaining his gaze with Carl, he unexpectedly shouted at all the men in the train.

"Raus! Schnell, schnell!" (Get out! Quick, quick!)

Carl jumped in his seat. With the curtains still pulled aside, he spun his head to peer out the window. The black lettering on the white sign on the platform read, ORANIENBURG.

Carl had no idea as to why they would be brought to this location train stop just north of Berlin. As far as he knew, there was nothing notable here. The Gestapo forced them off at the unnervingly quiet and empty station stop. They stepped off the low-lying platform before being led on a silent twenty-minute march through an unobtrusive town. After passing through some quaint family-style homes, a large cement gate entrance opened to an expansive paved clearing. Careful to avoid the small puddles of dirty, cold water, they funneled towards a large, three level, square building. Narrow, rectangular windows speckled its flat, white face.

As the men approached, they could see that all around the perimeter was barbed wire and observation posts. A cement block machine gun tower by the entrance had an armed man watching them. He kept the barrel of the assault weapon pointed in their direction. The center of the structure was carved out of the mammoth edifice. It served as the entrance to the concentration camp, Sachsenhausen. But first, they had to pass through an iron gate with the words *Arbeit Macht Frei* (Work Will Set You Free) written out in black lettering. Moritz walked along beside Carl.

"'*Arbeit Macht Frei*?' Carl, what do you think they mean by that?" he whispered.

"I don't know, Moritz," Carl whispered back, as he looked directly up at the man pointing a machine gun at his head. His heart began to pound a little faster.

Anchoring the base of the triangular-shaped, thousand-acre site, was the large, semicircular, roll call centered off the main entrance gate. They called this the *Apellplatz*. The men were being hurried there now, forced to stand within the high tension, electrified, barbed wire fence. White skulls painted along black wooden signs served as warning. While the thought hadn't yet occurred to Carl, he realized in that moment that escape would be impossible. His heart momentarily stopped and his breath escaped him as the gallows entered his line of vision. A singular roped noose swung in the gentle winds.

Moritz said what Carl could not, "Carl, is that—"

"Can't you run, you *Judenschweine* (Jewish pigs)!" one of the guards interrupted after their footing faltered at the horrific sight. A scowl ran across the guard's simple face at their palpable fear.

They hastened their pace and gathered into even rows of five. Many prisoners were already there when they joined. The new inmates were forced to remove their hats and not move.

As time began to pass, Carl wondered what they were waiting for. Narrow, primitive huts were lined just around and to the right of the area in which they were standing. With nothing much else to do, Carl speculated as to what they were used for.

During this stretch, the *SS* would come and go, and speak with each other here and there. All the while, the many Jews were forced to just stand perfectly still and at attention. They were warned that there would be severe punishments and harsh reprisals for anyone who moved or spoke.

Even though the hours passed, the men didn't want to tempt the guards to see if they'd keep their promise. They arrived at about 6 o'clock in the evening. He looked over at the large clock on the tower above the camp entrance. It read that it was nearly nine.

A tall, pale, otherwise unremarkable looking man sauntered over to their group. With his chin raised proudly, and his hands laced behind his back, Carl could see that he relished his position of superiority. Carl fought an urge to shake his head at his arrogance. He was the most decorated of all the officers, with a dark military suit and tie. His hat had a gold braid across the visor, and the German Imperial Eagle pin mounted on the front cap. He stood erect before the somber Jewish men to make his speech. He introduced himself as their *Lagerfuehrer* (camp leader).

"You probably know why you are here," he began, with his loud, exaggerated voice smothered in pompous audacity. "You are political vermin of the Third Reich and enemies of the Nationalist Socialist government. You do not know how to behave in accordance with the Third Reich, you will be taught that here. You will stay here for five years, and if you do not behave properly in that time, the time can be extended to twenty years," he announced.

There was an audible gasp from the prisoners. Some men directly in front of Carl—those from another transport—began to turn to each other to voice their concerns. He wished they had remained silent, as warned.

The Nazis marched towards them and raised their clubs. Carl squeezed his eyes shut in anticipation. They began swinging their weapons hard upon the defenseless men. The Jews fell to the cold, wet ground. They cowered at the relentless blows. Carl kept his face turned away. The thuds of batons colliding upon bodies pounded in his ears.

"Enough," the leader, impatient with the interruption, commanded the guards.

The subordinates dutifully stopped their attacks. When the Jews didn't immediately bound to their feet, the guards kicked at them with their mud-covered boots to rise. Carl dug his fingertips into the flesh of his fisted palms. Against all instincts, he forced himself not to intervene. He was quickly learning the new rules of Hitler's Nazi Germany. Nothing was natural, and all was forbidden. One of the men must have been struck in the head, for he was mostly unresponsive.

"Take him away," the commander stated, referring to the fallen victim.

The guards pulled the injured man by the arms and lifted him. The inmate's head hung limply. His hair was entangled with clumps of wet earth, while his feet dragged behind him. A bit of blood, and tracks from his shoes carved the surface where he had just lay. Carl silently prayed for him. He cursed to himself that there was nothing more he could have done. But he needed to stay alive. He needed to get back home to protect his family.

The remaining men stood there quite a bit longer. Their tired feet and aching backs given no relief. During this time Carl's mind would drift away—perhaps out of longing, perhaps out of escape. He left his young daughter more than a day ago. He knew she would have listened to his advice and taken her mother and grandmother to hide with his partner's, Max Beiser's, non-Jewish wife. She would be safe there. *She had to be,* he assured himself—pressing the fear that she, too, was captured from out of his mind. He didn't know if he could ever survive the loss of her—she—his only child.

One of the *Lageraelteste* (Senior Camp Inmates) must have seen the concern etched upon Carl's brow, for he came along beside him to whisper in his ear. Carl quickly stiffened at the approach. He shifted his eyes anxiously to see if any guards spotted them.

"Don't believe what the thug says, you won't be here for five years, you'll all be home again by Christmas," the man said quickly before hastily retreating.

There were a few moments of bated breath. After a few uneventful seconds passed, it appeared there would be no retaliation. Carl then relaxed enough to lower his shoulders. There would be no assault, and so he considered the man's words. While the message provided some comfort to Carl, it only confirmed his fears. He had no idea how to deal with this enemy. In these few interactions, not only did he not know what to believe, but more importantly, of what they were capable. He just knew he had to find some way to get back home.

The sky grew darker and the temperature colder, yet still the men stood. Carl folded his arms over his chest to keep out the penetrating chill from the increasing November winds. The huge watchtowers punctuating the outlying walls—those with machine guns pointed toward them at the ready—illuminated the night with enormous searchlights. This cast an iridescent glow over all as they lit the camp in an eerie semblance of day. The clock now read ten. Carl would soon find out what those long, narrow, wooden planked huts to the north east of the entrance were used for. But first, they were ushered to remove their clothing and bathe in the adjacent washing block. While threatened with a kick in the teeth if they didn't move quickly enough, the brisk movement felt good as it alleviated some of the stiffness in Carl's back.

He had to undress and hand over his civilian clothes. He threw them in a corner atop a giant heap and was only permitted to keep his shoes and a handkerchief. It had been quite some time—since his days in the service—when Carl was last ordered to stand naked before other men. He wanted to cover himself, or at the very least cross his arms, but he stopped himself from fidgeting. He had the sense that any displays of embarrassment or discomfort would only attract exploitation from the on-looking guards. Far more of an unfortunate and pressing matter was that Carl had to desperately make use of the toilet. He then resigned himself to the fact that he had no choice but to sit right alongside the man next to him. He took care to make sure their knees didn't touch.

He felt a moment of shame wash over him, but quickly ushered it away. Carl, in this moment, tried to suppress any otherwise natural sentiments of pride. But it was so hard. At this time of the evening, on Shabbat, he should have been home with his wife, daughter, and mother-in-law. They would be clearing and washing the dinner plates by now. He'd smile to himself, overhearing the chatter of the women in the kitchen, while seated in the adjacent living room. He'd be sitting in his favorite, forest green, leather armchair. The crystal ashtray on the side table next to his chair, holding a singular burning cigar within easy reach. Catching himself mid-fantasy, Carl suddenly stopped his longing for the comforts of home. Now was not the time. He must be present and have his mind sharp and strong.

After using the toilets, the men all had their heads shaved whilst instructed to lean over garbage cans. His strands of dark blonde hair fell atop the pile of those before him. While meant to strip him of his identity, he was instead relieved by this action. He couldn't quite explain it—but he felt that it alleviated his prominence. It helped strip him of his ego and pride, and therefore increased his anonymity.

As if in response to his observation, an *SS* locked his attention upon a conspicuous member of the group. The guard started spitting on him, while making the oddest homoerotic and lewd comments while he stood before him undressed.

"What's wrong, *Arschficker* (derogatory word for homosexual)? Since when don't you like being with naked men?" he shouted at him within an inch of his face.

When the fat man tried to cover himself with his arms, it only spurred the *SS* on more. "What's wrong with you, *bloeder Hund* (Stupid Dog), you don't want anyone to see your ugly body?"

Not wanting to be a helpless voyeur to this pitiful interaction, Carl turned away. But just then he heard a thud and the distinctive cheer of a young man. He whipped his head around just in time to witness the *SS* drive the butt of his rifle again into the side of the temple of the heavy-set Jew. He cried out in pain before falling to the floor. Tiny droplets of blood splattered upon the men standing beside him. Horrified, they looked down at the droplets in surprise. The *SS* did not abate his attack upon the fallen man. Moritz then shoved Carl aside, rushing forward to defend and intervene. Carl quickly grabbed at his arm to hold him back. It took all of his strength.

"No! Moritz! You mustn't!" Carl reprimanded in a harsh whisper, grappling with the man.

"But—" Moritz appealed, shocked at Carl's inaction, continuing to resist his restraint.

"No! Do you want to be next? Think of your wife and daughters," Carl interrupted, strongly holding onto Moritz's arm with all his might.

Just then another inmate did intervene. He had barely stepped forward before he, too, was dealt a mighty blow to the face—as Carl predicted would happen. The Good Samaritan crumpled into a heap on the floor, where the *SS* stood over him continuing their assault. The cracking of his skull echoed horrifically within the walls of that small room. Witnessing the horrendous assault upon the now two unresponsive men, Moritz quit his struggle with Carl. They stood there for a moment, dumbstruck, before turning their eyes away from the cruel and unprovoked brutality. Everything grew eerily still and silent, except for the relentless thuds of the butts of the rifles. Carl then released his grasp.

"There, Moritz, do you see *now*? That would have been you. And then what?" Carl whispered.

"But, Carl, shouldn't we have helped? Shouldn't we have done *something*?" Moritz pleaded.

"No. *We* have to stay alive. *We* have to get back to our families. *We* have to get out of Germany."

The portly inmate and Good Samaritan remained in heaps upon the floor. They were beaten so severely they were no longer recognizable. Buried under blood, lumps, and fractured skulls, their faces lost all distinction. Carl fought the abrupt rush of bile back down his throat.

"*Wegtreten!* (Dismissed!)" the guards breathlessly urged, having spent much of their energy attacking the unarmed civilians.

Carl, Moritz, and the other inmates returned to their task. The inmates turned their backs and stepped away as commanded.

"*Bringt sie weg!* (Take them away!)" Carl heard the orders bellowed, once turned away and at the next station.

The remaining men were then given old military uniforms to wear before they were each distributed a straw mattress and a woolen blanket. They were then led out and into a narrow building structure that was filled floor to ceiling with three-level wooden bunk beds. 350 men were assigned to each barracks, with 175 on each end. They removed, as instructed, their pants, jacket, and socks. Many people were already situated there when the new inmates looked for a good spot to lay their mattresses. Moritz and Carl managed to find a top-level bunk to share with others. Like a pack of sardines, they lay back to back. One of the political prisoners—a German communist—

already there long before, gave a friendly smile, and said, "Welcome! What took you all so long?"

"What do you mean by that?" Carl inquired, legitimately confused.

"Well, we have been expecting you for quite some time," he replied simply. It was too much to interpret as Carl was already far too overwhelmed by the day's events. He just climbed past the friendly inmate with Moritz close behind.

****

The days following all bled into one another. Every morning, the flashing of the bright, iridescent, overhead lights, told them it was 5 a.m., and time to rise. With their eyes struggling to adjust, they'd lift themselves from off their dusty, straw mattresses. Passing through the cold dark of early morning, they'd form a queue to receive their tasteless and lumpy porridge for breakfast. It splashed up from the bottom of the bowl. They were so hungry; it may as well have been soft boiled eggs and black bread.

Everyone would then go off to perform various forms of assigned hard labor, whether it be operating the cement mixer, or roof tiling, or the like. Their empty bellies never quite felt full. Days seemed endless as they were forced to work, hungry, under the gray November skies. At least the weather was mild for this time of year. Carl was thankful those gloomy clouds never produced any rain. Many would have easily succumbed to illness under those wet and cold conditions. Countless people were already coughing and groaning from the harsh environment. As the days and weeks passed, Carl's uniform started to hang over his ever-diminishing frame.

44

The barbed wire and observation posts of Sachsenhausen.

While certain inmates were in Sachsenhausen only days, they learned that others had been there for years. Sometimes, during the evenings, Carl's heart would stop at the unmistakable sounds of those committing suicide. Crashes and booms would erupt in a symphony of desperation and anguish. Those sorry souls, those who threw themselves upon the electrical barbed wire, saw it as the only surefire way to escape their hellish existence. The poor mangled bodies—looking more like scarecrows fallen from their posts than they did men—only strengthened Carl's resolve to survive.

On one evening, after lights out, Moritz whispered to Carl in the dark. Carl could tell by the words stuck in his throat, that Moritz was crying.

"Thank God Kurt is no longer with us," he said to Carl.

Carl lifted his head from off his makeshift pillow of folded trousers and jacket. He was in disbelief. Kurt was Moritz's son. When he succumbed to leukemia just six months ago, Moritz was inconsolable. Inge took his death awfully hard as well.

"Moritz—what do you mean? How can you say that?" Carl replied, whispering back and over his shoulder, shocked at his brother-in-law's confession.

45

"He would have been too weak to endure this. The *SS* would have surely beaten and abused him. I could never have borne to see that. It would have killed me," he responded through stifled tears before continuing. "There would have been no way I could have just stood by and watched. I would have intervened, and we would have both ended up dead."

It wasn't long before the shaking of Moritz's shoulders quieted. After his tearful confession, the men soon drifted off into their exhaustion-filled slumber. The persistent coughing and moans from the other prisoners often roused them, but they were accustomed to quickly falling back to sleep. A good rest was the only guarantee they had to surviving another day's work. Carl and Moritz were single-mindedly intent on making it home to take care of their families. When some from their transport were already getting released, like fellow congregant, Benno Schustermann, that, too, helped keep their spirits up, and their motivation strong.

Carl would not let the Nazis weaken him. Though at times it seemed impossible, he was determined to find some way—any way—to make it out of this alive.

𝒞𝒽𝒶𝓅𝓉𝑒𝓇 𝐹𝒾𝓋𝑒
10.25.1949
The Deposition

*Bruno Nette's mugshot for the Civil Internment Camp,
Riespott. Dated, February 2, 1948. Courtesy of Staatsarchiv Bremen.*

Bounding up the wide steps leading to the heavy wooden doors of the *Polizeihaus*, Bruno Nette did not feel his sixty-one years. Looking up at the high, multi-storied, stone-walled structure, Nette felt a sense of pride. This simple and pragmatic building structure embodied German efficiency and importance. Stepping through the entryway under the state's coat of arms, Nette felt right at home.

Barely past the doorway, the familiar smells of brewed coffee and cigarette smoke wafted through its halls. A secretary passed in front of him. She paused momentarily to give a warm smile before the clacking of her high heels led her down another corridor on official business. He had been released from the detention camp seven months ago. After four years of detainment, it felt good to be back where he belonged amongst the police.

Bremen's farewell of their police unit to the new armed forces.
Marching here in front of the city's town hall. April 1, 1935. Courtesy of Staatsarchiv Bremen.

Before he had a chance to continue on his way, a few policemen stopped him with polite, informal greetings. It seemed that they were also pleased that he was back. Here, everything appeared in its rightful place. These officers filling the station house, most of whom also served the Third Reich, were the same men who reported to him just a few years ago. He took a moment to reflect with pride on Bremen's very own 303rd Police Battalion. Even though it was not required of them, they volunteered to massacre 30,000 Jews in only a two-day period. They never shied away from serving their Fatherland nobly. These men were his brothers in arms.

Nette was pleased to see that the majority of those who participated still worked in this very building today. All the city's various police units, in one way or another, bore some responsibility for persecuting and annihilating those enemies of the state. Still dressed in their military-style, olive-green uniforms, it was easy for Nette to forget that so much had changed in the years following the end of the war.

He tugged on the lapels of his jacket and smoothed his hands down its front, almost expecting to feel the cool metal of a swastika fastened over his left breast. All that remained were the two small holes from where it had previously rested. *What a shame*, he thought to himself. Not only because of the loss of his position, but for the imperfection of his otherwise impeccable three-piece suit. *The Jews certainly know how to tailor a garment*. Nette was often gifted such articles before the end of the war in the hopes he'd spare their lives. It did work out for one of those tailors. Nette prided himself on that merciful act.

After a few more quick greetings and warm handshakes by various acquaintances, Bruno Nette arrived at the doorway of Charles Gerber's office. The Criminal Inspector quickly rose from behind his desk to personally welcome him. The Inspector had an eager and humble presence. He offered a quick smile while greeting his comrade.

"*Herr* Nette. Thank you so much for coming in," he said.

Nette replied with a brief smile through his thin, tightly pressed mouth. "*Guten Tag* (Good day), Gerber. Thank you so much for the invitation. It was very thoughtful of you to send your men over to my home to personally invite me to the station house."

Gerber gestured for Nette to take a seat, while he made his way back to his chair. "Yes. Of course. And how has your health been? Much improved, I hope?" Gerber inquired politely.

Nette was detained for four long years, the last spent in Riespott. Located in the industrial port section of Bremen, he was forced to perform various odd jobs, like moving boxes of metal in the warehouse. Surrounded by tall gates and wire, it was where Nette was required to reside under the suspicion of having committed crimes against humanity as a *Gestapo* Agent of the Third Reich. Although well-nourished and given adequate medical care, the normally lean man had grown even thinner as a result of the stress and anxiety of his detainment. While his second wife was permitted to visit him regularly, and he was even granted authorization to go home for holidays, he found his punishment to be undeservedly harsh. He even endured some heart palpitations and depression.

"Yes," Nette responded. "I have recovered quite well, now that I am back at home."

Just then, a stenographer with a pleasant demeanor entered the room to offer Nette some coffee, which he graciously received. He was truly flattered that the Inspector would share such a post-war treasure like this. Blonde hair neatly pulled in large curls behind her face, she served the two men before re-positioning the ashtray between them. With a smile, she softly closed the door behind her to offer some privacy before finding her seat perpendicular to them. Raising her pen to the paper placed before her, they were ready to begin.

"Thank you so much for coming in. Assistant Prosecutor Hoeffler really appreciates you helping with this case against the Jew, Katz. Is it okay if we begin?" Gerber asked.

Nette straightened his circular glasses and ran a hand over his thinning gray hair. Sitting straight in the chair across from Gerber's desk, he was more than ready to speak against the man in question. He had thought of little else since Katz's damning testimony during his denazification trial. Nette gave a curt nod as he placed his elbows upon the wooden desk and laced his fingers together in eager anticipation.

Gerber began, "Please, state your name."

Nette replied, "Bruno Nette."

"Date of birth?"

"December 22nd, 1887."

"City of birth?"

"Eisleben, Germany."

"Current address?"

"*Kirchbachstrasse*, Number 56, Bremen, Germany."

Gerber looked up from his notetaking to meet Nette's eyes. "Are you familiar with this case?"

Nette answered affirmatively, "I am familiar with this case and swear these words are the truth."

Nette had sent his son, Rudolf, to Katz's home before his trial a couple years ago. He had him request Katz's presence to testify on his behalf. These tribunals of denazification were an Allied initiative that attempted to remove those who had been members of the Nazi Party from positions of power and influence. There were five categories of offenders. It should have been an easy win for Nette in this inept, poorly executed American program. After all, the majority of the top positions of Bremen's Justice Department were filled with former Nazis. He wasn't even sure if there was one anti-Nazi active in the court system at all! But not only did Katz refuse to testify in his defense, he actually spoke *against* Nette, to his disbelief. For this reason, not only was Nette not originally categorized as a Level Five Exonerated Person, but he was classified as a Level Four Offender. This duplicity also prevented him from receiving a shorter sentence and caused a deep cut in his pension until his appeal hearing.

Katz's words to Nette's son would echo through the walls of his jail cell. "Get out of here," Katz had the audacity to say to Rudy. "All you *Gestapo* belong on the gallows for what you've done to us." The cold rows of huts in Riespott permeated Nette's resolve for justice—and today may just be the day for which he had waited so long.

"Please, go on with your deposition," Gerber politely insisted.

Nette reluctantly tore himself from his fantasies of retribution and continued. "Yes. From 1913–1945, I was involved in the police handlings. In 1920, I joined the criminal police force, and the last rank I held was that of Chief Criminal Secretary. On October 1, 1940, I was transferred to the *Gestapo* through the *Reichssicherheitshauptamt* (Reich Security Agency) from Berlin. I was in the Espionage Department. Then, on November 15, 1941, I went into the *Judendezernat* (Jewish Department). On April 27, 1945, I was arrested by British troops because I was *Gestapo* and was in different detention camps until March 15, 1949."

These last few words made Nette's mouth grow a bit dry. He paused momentarily to take a quick sip of the delectable coffee placed before him. Freshly brewed, it still steamed inside the porcelain cup. With the country desolate after the war and rations tight, he was grateful for this gift bestowed upon him. Only those with connections to the black market could acquire such treasure. He placed the cup down before continuing.

"My duties were to take care of necessary jobs due to the Nuremberg Laws (in 1935, these laws stripped German Jews of their rights to citizenship and so much more). My superior was the Criminal Commissioner. Until November 18, 1941, the contact person of the Jews to *Gestapo* in Bremen was Joseph Platzer. The contact person's duty was to take care of the Jews in Bremen, making sure they followed the ordinances of the *Gestapo*. After Platzer was transported to Minsk in November 18, 1941, Carl Katz became our contact person."

Gerber stopped his notetaking briefly to make sure the stenographer was gathering all of this testimony. Catching his eye, she nodded in his direction. Once confirmed, he gestured for Nette to continue.

"I, myself, had the best working relationship with Katz. I gave him a lot of freedom. When there was a decree from the Reich that items had to be taken from the Jews, I left that responsibility to Katz. Among those things were electrical appliances, furs, and the like. Katz did this work to the satisfaction of the *Gestapo*. For example, when there was

51

a question about which race or degree classification a person would fall into, I'd ask for his advice. It would involve questions as to whether a person was a full Jew, a half Jew who practiced Judaism, or a half Jew who didn't practice. These three categories would be subject to different ordinances."

"Yes, of course," Gerber acknowledged. He extinguished the butt of his cigarette in the full ashtray, before lighting up another Reemtsma. Nette declined his offering and continued with his story. He was just about to get to the incriminatory part, and was slightly frustrated with the Inspector's disruption.

"Amongst other things, he told me the names of many people of mixed races that weren't known to me. In my estimation, Katz was an Orthodox Jew who was the greatest hater of Jews who had converted to Christianity, mixed marriages, and those of mixed blood. All these categories he would denounce while sheltering the Orthodox Jews. Because I was on good terms with Katz, after he was sent to the concentration camp, Theresienstadt, I told the Camp Commander that he had made himself invaluable to the *Gestapo* and should therefore receive better treatment. Later on, I heard Katz had a major job in Theresienstadt. Katz came back from the camp healthy and with a wagonload of goods, such as typewriters, whereas others had barely anything at all."

Now sitting at the edge of his chair, leaning forward over the Inspector's desk, Nette grew a little red in the face. Images of his time in the labor camp flickered before his mind like that of cinematic film. Attempting to maintain control at the eruption of his latent hostility, he could not help but point his finger toward Gerber before releasing his final statement for the day.

"Due to my *former* relationship with Katz, I would never have brought up any of these things if it weren't for him giving false testimony against me. Therefore, Katz forced me to bring these accusations against him. But I would like to mention that this is not at all done out of revenge. My statements will be confirmed by the former Criminal Secretary of the *Gestapo*, Linnemann."

Breathless and red in the face, Nette, settled back in his chair. He took the square handkerchief from his pocket lapel and dabbed at the moisture collecting on his forehead. He was hell-bent on finishing up what he should have ended years before. He would make Carl Katz wish he had never survived the war.

Chapter Six
1939-1941
The Minsk Transport

Soegestrasse, Downtown Bremen, during the Third Reich. Courtesy of Staatsarchiv Bremen.

Carl Katz climbed wearily up the black and white tiled steps to the entrance of his home. Painfully aware of his undignified appearance, he ran a hand over his rumpled suit jacket front to smooth its surface. But to no avail. It had been sitting, wet, in a plastic bag, for the last several weeks during his detainment at Sachsenhausen. The smell was horrendous. As if things couldn't get any worse, it hung over his emaciated frame like a jacket upon its hanger.

His pretty wife, Marianne, stood before him to open the front door of 33 *Isartrasse*. When they met upon the platform at the train station just twenty minutes before, she tried to hide her initial shock at his altered appearance. As her gentle green eyes filled with tears at the man she wasn't sure she'd ever see again, none of that mattered. She'd get him cleaned up and fed as soon as they were home. All that counted was that he made it home alive. She had heard stories that many others were not as fortunate as she.

Just beyond the foyer, Carl spotted his sweet daughter eagerly awaiting him at the foot of the staircase. At first, Inge remained seated after their eyes met. She had no reaction at all, just a bit of curiosity danced across her bright, blue-green gaze at the stranger standing before her. *My God, she doesn't recognize me,* Carl realized. Embarrassed, he lowered his chin, and placed his hands over his bald head. The stubble from the clippers prickled his palm. A painful mark of shame he was gifted from the hands of his abusers.

He continued to walk into his home, and must have stepped further into the light, for he heard fast footsteps approach. He lowered his arms just in time to receive his young daughter. He caught her and held her tighter than he had ever held her before.

"*Vati* (Father)! You are back. Everything will be all right now." She spoke excitedly, her head still buried into his chest.

"Yes, Inge. Everything will be fine," he assured her. Unfortunately, he had no idea if, or how, he could fulfill that promise, as he followed her into the kitchen. He'd tackle that plan after a hearty meal and a good night's sleep. If they were together again, there were options.

****

As it turned out, it was much easier said than done to make everything right again for his family. As *Kristallnacht* ("The Night of Broken Glass," a term used to describe the destruction of Jewish homes and businesses that were carried out by *SA* paramilitary forces against civilians throughout Nazi Germany) portended, Jews were not only unwelcome in Germany, but now they were no longer even tolerated. A mad rush arose within the Jewish community to get out of Germany by whatever means possible. Some contacted relatives abroad, others visited the consulate offices of countries as far away as South America and Australia. There were even those who closed their businesses in the belief they would be able to leave. Carl's business partner, Max Beiser, was temporarily permitted to re-enter Germany from Poland in order to liquidate all his assets. This included the business he and Carl worked jointly.

They had always been close friends, but Carl would never forget what the Beisers had done for the Katz family on *Kristallnacht*—the day he was apprehended and later

54

sent to the concentration camp, Sachsenhaussen. He'd always remember how Max's Aryan wife had sheltered Carl's wife, daughter, and mother-in-law, for two days from the National Socialists in their very home. That his wife's Aryan sister—a member of Hitler's *Frauenschaft* (the women's group associated with the Nazi Party)—turned away a Nazi search party hunting for Jews, possibly saving the lives of Carl's women at her own peril. He wasn't sure how he could ever repay a favor such as that. At this time, all he could offer was his eternal gratitude.

Without the business to keep him occupied, and since the leader of the Bremen Jewish community, renamed the *Reichsvertretung der Juden in Deutschland Bremen* by the Nazis, had fled to the United States, Carl then willingly accepted the position of second in command. With the synagogue burned to the ground on *Kristallnacht,* communal meetings and all prayer services since then were being held in the home of his wife's cousin. With a different operation held on each floor, Carl devoted most of his time to caring for the elderly. He also knew the vice consulate of Ecuador very well and worked tirelessly with him to arrange for safe passage for his extended family to that country.

While Carl had requested visas for his own family as well, it was far easier for others to escape—whether because they were bakers, shoemakers, agricultural workers, or unmarried individuals, Carl found that quotas were much easier for others to meet. He knew some single men, for example, who took their chances to run off to Switzerland's border, only to be turned back again. Unfortunately, his brother-in-law, Hugo, who was one of those bachelors, couldn't make his escape because he was battling tuberculosis. This sickness occurred as a result of the government removing him from his job as referee to Bremen's professional soccer team, SV Werder. The cool and wet weather took a toll on his health as his new job required him to deliver coffee on his bicycle, no matter what the conditions.

Carl had his elderly parents, elderly mother-in-law, delicate wife, and a fourteen-year-old daughter to consider. He was given the option to send Inge out on a *Kindertransport* (an organized rescue effort that took place in the nine months prior to the war by the UK. They took in nearly 10,000 children and placed them in British foster homes, hostels, schools, or farms). Carl and Marianne then could try to get to England to work as a housekeeping couple, but there was no guarantee that they wouldn't be separated from their daughter. That was a risk he was not willing to take. Not to mention, who would take care of the parents left behind? Many other families were putting theirs in old folk's homes—coincidentally, those very people Carl was caring for right now in the center. But his conscience would never allow for that. It had also become obvious that he could never trust the government to take proper care of them.

Had he realized that this period within which to escape Germany would be so brief, perhaps he would have done something—anything—differently. Had he known what awaited the Jewish people in the coming months and years, he would most certainly have made more desperate attempts to get everyone out. However, in spite of managing those arrangements for his family to leave for Ecuador, it was not fated to be. Indeed, on the very day the family expected to collect their visas, Jews were no longer allowed to do so. Their fate was sealed.

As was customary for the patriarchs in those years, he had to protect everyone from the truth. He assured the others that he would figure something out—just like he always did. While he approached them with a calm resolve, and a steady voice, fear shook his heart. The painful reality was that there was simply nowhere for them to run. There was nowhere for them to hide. No sanctuary at all. While most countries were refusing to accept them in any numbers, Germany neither wanted them to remain or to leave, even if they could arrange to do so. He had seen firsthand from his stay in Sachsenhaussen that even if you were young, strong, and healthy in body and mind that it would still be difficult to stay alive. There was no way anyone in his family but he could survive a camp like that.

When he received a call three months later and was told of his father's passing, he hated to admit he was a bit relieved in the knowledge that Rudolf Katz was spared from whatever was to come next. But the fact that they hadn't gotten along for the last couple years weighed heavily upon his conscience. Surely the two of them could have handled things differently. Unfortunately, they were both cut from the same cloth—far too stubborn, and far too determined to have everything done their way. Carl just always thought there would be more time. *How foolish*! Carl reprimanded himself. After all, his father had a heart condition and his mother suffered from dementia. Now it was too late to ever make things right again.

On the train ride several weeks after the funeral, Carl held his mother's hand for a while. She looked sweetly into his eyes and patted his arm before looking back out the window. He wasn't sure if she even knew who he was in this moment, but he desperately wanted to believe so. He was thankful that she didn't understand that her husband had passed. For that pain to be spared, her son was grateful. They were now taking her to Berlin to go live with her daughter, Berta. In some way, things were too late for Carl and his parents, but he vowed in that moment to never make the same mistake again with his own family. He promised he would never let anything come between them.

During their short stay in Berlin, Carl's sister took a real liking to her niece, Inge, and even offered to care for her so that she may attend a two-year-long certification program in sewing. While it would truly pain Carl to be away from his daughter for any length of time, he knew it was the best thing for Inge. She had already not been permitted to attend school for more than a year now, and some time with friends her age would certainly give her a bit of normalcy. It would also be one less person for Carl to pretend to be strong in front of. Although a young girl of only fourteen, she was painfully bright and perceptive. He didn't know for how long he could protect her from their frightening reality.

Inge, 15, at a picnic during her stay with her aunt in Berlin, 1939.

Carl and Marianne spoke regularly with their daughter, and the cheer in her voice warmed his heart. Her stories of summertime picnics, and descriptions of the beautiful clothing she'd fashion from fabrics her mom would send over, was a welcome break from the sorry state of his community. He took his job caring for the elderly very seriously and worked tirelessly to provide them with all the supplies and articles of comfort they'd need to be at ease. With many of them being abandoned by their families, he took it upon himself to be the son, nephew, or brother that they were missing. He recognized that happiness had more to do with the affection and care from a friendly face or kind gesture than just about any medicine.

He was also glad that Inge didn't have to be a part of the procedure of having their home and belongings confiscated. Leaving behind all the memories and objects of their home on 33 *Isarstrasse* was gut wrenching and cruel. It would be far easier for Inge, he thought, to just settle into their small room in the multi-level house than to bear witness to all that she'd be leaving behind. In what was called a *Judenhaus* (Jew House) on *Legion-Condor-Strasse* 1, there were seven families with children, and five individuals, all crammed into a three-floored house. There were many other *Judenhaeuser* around town, created to gather local Jews and those from neighboring towns in order for it to be easier for the Nazis to keep track of them all, that is, to keep them all in more concentrated locations.

The Katzes were housed on the first floor. Upon Inge's eventual return from Berlin, the three of them would have to share just two rooms: one became their living room, and their other their bedroom, which had but one single bed. Inge would have no option but to sleep on a chaise lounge at one end of her parents' mattress. But despite that, Carl managed to find some joy in this harrowing situation. Just across the hall, there was the cutest little five-year-old boy living with his parents and two older brothers. With an impish smile, and a gleam in his eyes, the scrappy youngster would always dart in and around the entirety of the living space with a seemingly endless supply of energy. Always trying to get the others in the house to laugh along with him, he'd make silly jokes and faces. It worked all too well on Carl. He was completely charmed by this boy with the floppy brown hair. He even began playfully calling the young child August, like the popular circus clown of that time.

Carl and the young boy, whose actual given name was Rolf Frank, became the unlikeliest of pairs. He was a constant companion whenever Carl was not working at the old folks' home. One evening, after a long day's work, Carl sat in his living quarters to remove his shoes. Always at his side, Rolf broke into a fit of laughter at what was revealed. Right out of the top of Carl's sock was a hole with his toe sticking through! Quickly thinking, Carl had the child go to the kitchen for some vinegar and a piece of paper. Placing it upon the torn fabric, Carl told the boy to go about his day as the repair might take a while. Once the boy left, Carl replaced the broken sock with a fresh one, and shouted for the child.

"August! Come quick!"

"Coming!" the boy screeched before racing into the room. Upon colliding with the door frame, he caught his footing and, and stared in astonishment at the sight of Carl's foot.

"You did it! Thank you so much, August!" Carl exclaimed with a giant smile.

"Wow!" Rolf replied, just staring a long while at the magic and mystery of it all. While gawking down at the concealed toe, he whispered, "I performed a *miracle*!"

The child could be described by all who saw him as nothing else but a "cutie," but when you asked little Rolf Frank what he called himself, from that day on, he replied, "Rolf-Frank-and-August-Katz."

****

Carl was grateful for the bit of normalcy and cheer August afforded him, for outside the walls of the *Judenhaus,* it could be described as nothing other than chaos. With the Jewish people either moving into homes, losing their businesses, dealing with the uncertainty of sending their children away to foreign lands, the fear of what staying behind in Germany meant for those remaining, and the official start of WWII in September of 1939, tensions ran high.

His good acquaintance, Benno Schustermann, had a particularly more difficult situation than the rest—if one could believe that even possible. Upon Benno's return from Sachsenhausen, his non-Jewish wife, Johanna, had visited an Aryan lawyer and had all legal rights to his home and business turned over to her. She was now talking about divorcing him, which absolved him of all Aryan protection under the laws of the Third Reich. It was a trend in Germany for attractive, non-Jewish women to marry prosperous Jewish men. It saddened Carl to see that for some, when their marriage to a Jew was no longer an advantage, that they were quick to leave their men and children behind. As hard a situation as Carl found himself, he thanked God that those troubles were not his.

Within six months of the declaration of war, the local papers began to report the bombings of cities. It aggrieved him to retrieve his daughter from Berlin. For that one fleeting year, he loved the fact that she felt like a normal girl, leading a happy life, and was well on her way to achieving her dream of opening her very own Atelier. Unlike Carl, she had only known life under Nazi rule. Her school days consisted of lectures on Jewish racial inferiority, trips she was not permitted to attend, and school children being prohibited from playing with her. He was continuously and gravely concerned about how that sort of exposure would impact her self-worth. But he needed her close by.

"I'm sorry, Inge, but it is time for you to come home," he declared morosely into the receiver.

"Yes, Father," his dutiful daughter replied without hesitation. Her unquestioning faith in him only pained him further. He hoped to God he was doing right by her.

Carl didn't know exactly what protection he could offer, but it felt far better having Inge close. And life wasn't too awful for her back in Bremen, either—considering the given circumstances, that is. She was back home with her best friend and cousin, Ruthie (Moritz's daughter), and the two of them were even able to land an apprenticeship with

59

a local seamstress. Inge also got along quite well with the other members in the household. In some ways, it was a treat to live amongst so many other teenagers. Carl and the other parents would even allow them to play records and hold dances in the hallway upstairs. Carl smiled at those times in the knowledge that even with those cramped quarters, the teens could forget for a little while that a hostile world existed just inches beyond them.

L to R: Inge, Gunther Frank (Rolf's older brother), and Ruthie Cohen in the Judenhaus.

The Katz family visiting the Senior Living Home on Groepelingerheerstrasse, 1941.

On Sundays, he would take Inge to the old folks' home for visits. There she would be the daughters, and granddaughters of those that were left behind. The love and appreciation the Katzes would receive in return from the elderly filled their hearts. It gave them some much needed positivity on which to focus. Yes, after the initial shock and discomfort of all they'd recently been through, the Katzes decided that things weren't *so* bad, after all. Therefore, they were not prepared for the day when they received the letter in the mail from the *Gestapo* headquarters. All it said was that they should collect their things and that they all must go in two weeks on the *Sonderzug* (Special Train) to settlements "out east."

61

This notification of their forced departure hardly left Carl any time at all to prepare. *Two weeks? Impossible!* But he knew if anyone could get the job done it would have to be him. His wife and daughter prepared the personal baggage, like clothing for the winter, family photographs, and their prayer books, while he worked tirelessly to prepare for the community to live at these Jewish settlements. Of course, being November, it was nearing winter and they'd need portable heaters. A lot of them. Not to mention sewing machines, tools, nails, roof tiles, non-perishables, and other everyday essentials that were nearly impossible to find these days, but he managed to procure it all from the black market. Alas, through networking and utilizing his extensive knowledge of contacts from years in business, he amassed quite an abundance. There were enough supplies to fill an entire train car. Everyone was shocked. Perhaps no one more so than the *Gestapo* agents in charge.

But of no less importance to the move, was his little buddy's, August's, impending birthday. His birthday would fall on November 20, when they'd be at the settlement, and Carl just didn't like the uncertainty of that. He wanted to provide him with a proper 6th birthday celebration. So a couple of days before they were to be deported, the women prepared the food, and the teens brought down the record player, so that everyone could forget their troubles for a little while. August kept the family entertained and laughing, as always, while Carl placed the gift in the box for him in another room. Carl tried to stifle the emotion that gathered in his throat when he placed the *Judenstern* into the gift box (cloth patch in the shape of a Jewish star that the Jews were forced to adorn on their left breast jacket for everyone ages six and over. It was meant to identify and shame the Jewish citizens from the rest of the population). But despite his best efforts, a single tear did run down his cheek at the thought that this was the only present his little clown had wanted for his sixth birthday. He quickly wiped it away before he brought it into the adjacent room. The little clown bounced up and down in excitement at the sight of him. When August opened the box, and he saw that it was the star he had always wanted, he ran up to hug Carl.

"Thank you! Thank you! Now I look just like the rest of you!" he exclaimed excitedly, still clinging to Carl's arms.

Alas, that gratitude for something so horrendous only served to create more tears to well in Carl's eyes. Carl quickly released the child before he could see. He raced, though discreetly, into the bedroom to be alone. Marianne, spotting her husband's distress, hastily walked after him. She placed her hands upon her broken husband's shoulders and rested her face upon his turned back. She had never seen him this way. Her husband was never one to succumb to his emotions. But the sadness of this interaction with August was even too much for the capable Carl Katz to rationalize or contain. For the first time since their courtship, he allowed his wife to see him grief stricken. For the first time, he allowed someone else to care for him.

62

Chapter Seven
March 1950
Marie's Suicide

The main police station in Bremen.

Gerber sat behind his desk waiting for the next witness to arrive. He took an extra swig at his coffee-substitute to help ease his mind. He had conducted many interviews over the past few months. All these accusations against Katz, thus far, had been rather disquieting. The more he heard the testimonies, the more he became aware that the former National Socialists were still up to their old tricks. His night terrors, as a result, had become more and more frequent. His wife's soothing voice assuring him the Nazis were no longer in power, that peace had been restored, no longer seemed to settle his nerves the way they used to. Every cry for vengeance, every guilty conscience, every civilian's desire for monetary reparations that he was forced to record, was then treated as adequate evidence to denigrate the Jew. It appeared that in Germany, old habits certainly died hard.

63

A well-to-do woman, appearing to be in her mid-fifties, then approached his office. *Right on time.* As his secretary stood to politely take her woolen overcoat, Gerber placed his cup of bitter, warm liquid back onto the saucer. After a large intake of breath, Gerber then also stood to greet her. He hoped he could stomach this latest testimony better than he had the others. He wanted to be able to sleep tonight.

With a shy smile, the lady extended a delicate gloved hand to the Inspector. "Pleased to make your acquaintance, Officer," she said in a refined Bremen accent. Her shoulder-length brown hair was neatly curled under her navy, pillbox hat.

"Thank you so much, Mrs. Lange, for coming in. I called you in today to corroborate some claims former *Gestapo* agent, Bruno Nette, made against Carl Katz, concerning your late mother, Marie Huntemann," Gerber recited dryly. These days, he didn't even bother hiding his disregard. He had become disinterested in hearing yet another elaborate tale on how the Jew, Katz, was to blame for their misfortune. These false testimonies did little more than legitimize his lack of faith in humanity—as if all that he had experienced, seen, and heard during the World War hadn't already done that enough. He barely lifted his eyes from arranging the papers on his desk when he spoke to the lady.

"Yes, of course. But I'm not sure if I have that much information for you. Carl Katz really didn't have all that much to do with my mother's death," Henriette Lange explained, apologetically. Now *this* piqued Gerber's interest. He gestured for her to have a seat before he reclined back in his own.

"Oh? But are you aware that in Nette's deposition, he claimed that in 1942 Katz was the one who informed the *Gestapo* of your mother being Jewish?" He held his pen in his hand at the ready.

"Right. I heard that that was being reported, too," she said, while trying to make herself comfortable in the chair across from the Inspector's desk. She crossed her ankles beneath the wooden seat, and rested her hands upon her square purse, before continuing. "But I don't believe it to be true. You see, my mother identified herself as a Catholic, and was never part of the Jewish community. For this reason, Katz couldn't have known my mother. I believe her landlady, *Frau* (Mrs.) Radtke, was the one who denounced her," she explained to the policeman.

She looked right into Gerber's eyes while making these claims. At that moment, he didn't detect any deception in her steady gaze. He began to find her remarkably interesting—perhaps for no other reason than she didn't blame her misfortune on a Jew. Or was it because she was the first person he met that didn't seem to fear contradicting Nette? Maybe she would restore his faith in humanity, after all, Gerber hoped.

"Please, go on," Gerber encouraged.

"Years after my father died, she could no longer afford to live in her house on *Schillerstrasse* 53, in the town of Vegesack. So, when my brother helped sell the house to *Frau* Radtke in 1941, it was on the condition that she could live out her days there, receiving free room and board," *Frau* Lange reported.

The mention of Vegesack—yet again—pricked the Inspector's interest. This town seemed to be a location where a lot of reported offences occurred. It was also where Nette resided during the pre-war years after leaving his wife and children for another woman. It was quite the scandal in the day, Gerber remembered vaguely. He couldn't recall the details exactly, as he didn't know the man then. *Wasn't there a death—or a murder—of some sort?* Aye, he just couldn't recall. He marked his notes to remind himself to investigate this further. Right now, he needed to pay attention to the lady's story.

"Tell me, why do you believe it was the landlady, *Frau* Radtke, who was the one who denounced your mother, and not Katz?" Gerber asked, tearing himself from his speculations.

"Well, they barely lived together for a year before they had a big fight," Henriette Lange replied.

"When was this?" Gerber questioned, all the while writing furiously in his notebook.

"1942. You see, this was after they started transporting the Jews, like to Minsk, and *everyone* knew it was only a matter of time before the rest of the Jews would be transported out of the city. My belief, therefore, is that she wanted my mother out of the house, and to get rid of her for good. The *Gestapo* then did kick her out for being a Jew, so according to the laws of the time, she went to live with my brother. However, he didn't feel it was working out, so he put her in an old age home."

"One moment, please," Gerber responded, as he looked through his papers. *Yes, there it is, a list of all the addresses of Marie's four children's homes.* Just as he thought, these were all in nice areas of town. Certainly, any one of Marie's children had the space and means to care for her. Yet none of her children offered her the comfort of living with them. *Hmm…*

"Okay, so as far as you know, there was no connection with Carl Katz and your mother's fate?" Gerber inquired.

"No, that is not entirely true. His name was on the paper from the Jewish Community Center that was delivered to my family," she recounted to him.

"What did this paper say?"

"It was a paper declaring her a full Jew. My mother, my Aryan husband, and my Aryan sister-in-law would have to sign this as an official admission of guilt."

"I'm assuming she didn't sign it since she was a Catholic and raised you as Christians?"

"She didn't want to, no. But we thought she should. So, we all made her do it."

"I'm sorry, did you say that you *made* her do it? Why would you ever do that? Was she actually a Jew?"

"Umm… my siblings, our spouses, and I all thought we could get into trouble with the *Gestapo* if they really had proof that she was a Jew," Mrs. Lange stated, clearly avoiding the question. "We decided we didn't want to take that risk. That is why we forced her to sign the confession."

"And she did it? Without resistance?" Gerber reacted, incredulously.

"No, she was terribly upset about it. She even stated, 'If I sign this, I sign my death sentence,'" the lady recounted, choking a bit on her words. She averted her gaze down towards her shoes.

"But, as you said, you and your spouses wanted to avoid any possible repercussions with the *Gestapo*. By stating your mother is Jewish, doesn't that automatically put you and your siblings at risk? By virtue that if your mother is a Jew then you all are Jews? With all due respect, I must admit, I don't fully understand the reasoning." Gerber wrote all this in his notes.

He jotted down the question, *Motive?* in the margin. If Marie Huntemann was in fact a Jew, she successfully hid this fact for decades. There was never any proof, just a claim from some landlord that didn't want an old lady living in her house for free. The children could have easily kept her secret, thereby protecting her from harm, as well as themselves. None of this added up. All that he could tell for sure, was that this poor woman's children wanted to get rid of her—one way or another. *Well, that is it. My faith in humanity—after an ever so brief appearance—is lost again.*

"Okay, just to reiterate," Gerber continued, after Mrs. Lange didn't offer a response to his question about why she'd denounced her mother to the *Gestapo*, "Carl Katz's only presence was his signature on the JCC letterhead?"

"No, there was one other thing."

"Yes, what is that?"

"As you know, shortly after her confession, as predicted, she was notified that she was to be on the transport to Theresienstadt. At that time, they called it, 'The

Settlements.' Well, also as you know, rather than go to the concentration camp, she committed suicide by jumping into the Weser River."

Rather than go to the camp, or because the old lady's children didn't want her? Gerber couldn't help but wonder.

Mrs. Lange continued, "After her body was fished out, on July 25, my husband went to Katz's office to speak with him."

"You don't mean July 25. You have the wrong date," the policeman corrected her. It was well-known that the second of the two Bremen transports occurred on July 23. Katz would have been in Czechoslovakia on the 25th.

"No, I am 100% certain. How could I forget when they found my mother's body?" she interrupted him impolitely. Her voice was raised and shrill. "As I was saying, on July 25, my husband went to Katz's office whereby Katz said to him, 'She didn't have to do that, but perhaps she chose the better of the two options.'"

Husband is lying. Why? Gerber scribbled in his book. He marked it with an underline, before continuing the interrogation.

"Are you therefore accusing Carl Katz of willfully and knowingly sending them to be tortured, and possibly, to be murdered?" Gerber provoked her, trying to catch her in yet another lie. Even the *Gestapo* agents, like Nette, claimed that they had no idea what was awaiting the Jews at the camps. While Gerber didn't believe that to be the truth for one moment, he did believe the Jews had no idea. Why else would they go so obediently and calmly? Why else would they have prepared so many supplies for their new "homes"?

"My husband told me that Katz knew about the Final Solution through rumors and through 'enemy radio transmissions,' and also from 'whisper propaganda,'" Henriette Lange stated confidently.

Gerber placed his pen down with a sigh, and immediately rose to his feet to see the woman out. He had heard enough. The Jews' radios had been confiscated, therefore there were no radios at that time for the Jews to overhear any "enemy transmissions." This was yet another absurd claim by yet another horrible person. Germany was running rampant with them these days. What was interesting, however, were the last words she stated in her testimony. Every other witness also stated those exact last words in the exact same way. Obviously, they were being coached. *But by whom*?

Gerber never claimed to be all that intelligent, and those who reminded him of his meager 8th grade education certainly didn't contradict it. But was he really the only one that remembered that there were no radios, telephones, etc. for Jews to listen to during the war years? Did these people not realize that there were records of when the

Thereseinstadt transports occurred? Even if a kangaroo court were being held against Katz, they couldn't falsify information this much. *Could they?*

Done with the days' work, he pulled out his wallet from his inside jacket pocket. He unfolded some crumpled *D-mark,* wondering if it was enough to purchase the underwear his sons needed. If not, perhaps he could get an advance from his superior for this week's salary? His heart sank a bit at the realization that the truth of this case against Carl Katz just did not matter. It could not matter. With the death of his mother-in-law, resulting in his father-in-law's moving in, it just meant one more mouth to feed. One more person for whom he was financially responsible. Sometimes, the stress of it all just seemed too much. He didn't mention anything to his wife, but every now and then he'd get these odd bouts of shortness of breath. His heart would race, and he'd be forced to sit a while in a cold sweat until things calmed down.

They always calmed down.

But his instincts knew better. Although a man in only his early forties, Gerber feared something just wasn't right with his heart. With a fourteen- and a four-year-old son, he had better put his head down, shut up, and just do his job.

As he left the police station and walked the distance over to the Karlstadt department store for his sons' underwear, he just couldn't stop his mind from wondering. *What really did happen in Vegesack? Was Nette the one behind everyone's testimony? Was he trying to cover up something from his past? If so, how was he making all these witnesses come in to make false testimonies? Why did they all seem to fear him? What dirt did he have on them?*

God dammit! Why couldn't he just do this job and leave all this alone? He cursed himself upon realizing that, in fact, he just wouldn't—couldn't—let it go. He knew he needed to find out the truth.

Chapter Eight
1942
Treading Water

The teenagers from the Judenhaus excited and in line to go on the transport "out east" to their new homes at the "settlement." Rolf Frank's middle brother, Hans, pictured in the center of image.

Carl stood there a little while longer on the platform. The thick black smoke of the train filled the already overcast sky as it hauled everyone away to the settlements out east. He could barely make out the faces hanging outside of the train car windows. Yet still he stood. It was particularly hard to remain strong for little August, but he had to. For him.

While he kept an extended hand in the air to wave to them until completely out of view, Inge had already begun collecting a couple of loaves of bread from off the gravel. After a quick wipe of her sleeve to brush off any grime, she replaced them in the straw basket resting upon her hip. While she had successfully passed most loaves through the windows to Ruthie and her family, and to her Uncle Hugo, and to the Franks, some lost their grip in the urgency of their boarding.

A few more moments passed, and the train was now completely out of sight. All that remained were the overcast and stormy November skies of Northwest Germany. Carl lamented that there was nothing further he could do for his people now. He looked over at his daughter who had just seated herself upon a wood and metal bench. Like him, she was no longer looking after the train. Catching her gaze, he saw that, instead, she was looking upon all those across the tracks. Those German gentiles with briefcases or groceries, going about their usual daily business. The harsh damp winds picked up. Inge folded her arms across her body, yet still, she remained. He knew what she was doing. She was allowing those Germans on the platform to continue pretending not to have seen what had just taken place—and to continue pretending not to have known what just happened to the Jews of their city.

The look on his daughter's face was ghastly. Her tear-laden eyes were mixed with expressions of both grief and anger. He had never seen such a countenance on his otherwise mild-mannered, and cheerful, young girl. Yet there she was, with her brows firmly pressed together in stern consternation. Carl worried about how she'd manage without her constant companion, her cousin, Ruthie, for the short time until they all would meet up again. He had seen many in the community succumb to their despondency these days. Horrifically, some had even begun to commit suicide rather than leave on this transport. The emotional well-being of his people was not something to be underestimated. He had reminded his brother-in-law, Moritz, of this on the platform this morning while exchanging their final goodbyes.

"Remember what we did in Sachsenhausen. *Okay?* Play it smart, never trust anything the Nazis say, and always do whatever it takes to keep everyone safe," he stated sternly, while Moritz still avoided his gaze. He was nervously transferring his weight from one foot to another, wringing his hands. Carl could tell Ruthie's father was overcome with panic. *This is not good.* Carl needed Moritz to be resourceful and decisive at the settlements without having him there to rely on. His brother-in-law had to be the one to keep everyone out of trouble.

"Remember this!" Carl raised his voice, finally snapping Moritz to attention. Carl had only moments to set Moritz straight. The railway conductor was already blowing his whistle, signaling the train to fire up its engine.

"Hurry up! *Schnell, schnell!* The train is about to leave!" one of the *Gestapo* agents, Wilhelm Parchmann, shouted at them. Carl just ignored the commandant for a few moments further. He needed confirmation that Moritz was right in the head.

"I will. I will keep them all safe," he spoke while finally meeting Carl's eyes. They grasped each other's hands firmly in understanding. "Until we see each other again."

Carl prayed dearly that his encouraging words did the trick. He would find out soon enough. For now, there was simply nothing more he could do for his family.

Carl decided to leave his daughter on the bench for as long as she needed. After telling her they'd meet back at home, he turned to walk down the narrow cement stairway toward the street. He grasped the metal railing of the service entrance, but before he could take his first step, several *Gestapo* agents in charge called after him.

"Katz! How are you today?" a pleasantly featured, lean man, inquired smugly.

"*Herr* Linnemann, I am quite fine this morning," Carl replied optimistically, careful not to betray his resolve. He must be wary not to show weakness in front of the agents. He need not give them any ammunition. Linnemann could be unpredictable.

"Your daughter, Inge, is she well?" The officer nodded in her direction. His light-colored eyes shone a bit when resting his gaze upon her.

This made the hairs on the back of Carl's neck rise a bit. At seventeen years of age, Inge was certainly considered beautiful. She caught the attention of many men around town. But Carl most certainly didn't want her to grab Linnemann's. It concerned him that he even knew her name.

"This all went quite well, wouldn't you agree?" Carl asked the agent, cleverly redirecting this man's attention.

"Yes, indeed," Linnemann responded, readdressing Carl. "Speaking of which, we were all extremely impressed with how well you were able to organize and collect materials for the transport. I am sure that Special Agent Nette will have many jobs for you."

****

If given the choice, Carl Katz preferred to deal with Bruno Nette over the other two men, especially Parchmann. Everyone was terrified of Parchmann. After all, it was while under his "protection" where detained Jews would suspiciously "commit suicide" in their cells. Carl could sometimes sense that Nette had a wild, albeit explosive rage coursing just below his stoic veneer. But surprisingly, he found him easy to navigate. The occasional offering of cigarettes, a bottle of cognac, or even a used, but meticulously crafted suit, would be all it took to remain in the officer's good graces. That, coupled with Carl's efficiency in getting tasks completed, was enough to keep his temper from breaching the surface. The *Gestapo* agent, like most Nazis, was someone who incessantly needed to feel important and respected. If you knew how to play the game, then Nette was quite easy to get along with.

For these reasons, the *Gestapo* decided that the Katz family, only two days before departure, should be removed from the transport list. The *Gestapo* preferred working

71

with *Herr* Katz, and was so impressed with his organization and competency, that they decided it better to keep him in town. They favored working with him over the current JCC president, Joseph Platzer, because Carl was a full-blooded German, rather than Platzer who was Polish, and nearly twenty years his senior. In Katz's place, the *Gestapo* sent *Herr* Platzer and his wife to go to Minsk. With him now gone, Carl was appointed head of the JCC, and left in charge of those few Jews remaining in Bremen—namely, the elderly, and those of mixed blood and mixed marriages.

In addition to being the head of the JCC, and working for the old folks' home on *Groepelingerheerstrasse*, Carl had bureaucratic tasks to complete, like the *Heim-einkaufsvertrag*. This was a particularly distressing matter. It required him to take part in having the Jews sign over their property and belongings to the Third Reich. In return, they'd receive a home and an impending good and carefree future in the comfortable and cozy conditions of the "Reich old age home." This was a huge conflict for Katz—he wanted no part in what he feared were their dirty dealings. But what choice was he given? He had seen firsthand, at his time served in Sachsenhaussen, what happened to Jews who disobeyed Nazi orders. *But why have a Jew participate in Nazi dealings?* This question plagued him. Did the Nazis want it to appear that the Jews were involved in their fate? That they had a say in the matter? That they were not victims? That they were willing participants in their misfortune? Carl shook his head and laughed a bit to himself—as if anyone would ever—*could ever*—believe that. *The Jews holding power in this calamity—Ha!*

However, he recognized that he was fortunate enough to be appointed to this position. This advantage allowed him to further assist the community, as well as to keep his family safe until their own inevitable transport. Additionally, it worked out that this task could also be used as a tactic to keep Inge's mind busy and far from dwelling upon the recent loss of her cousin. Therefore, soon after, Carl had Inge also help the elderly fill out the paperwork. He reasoned that those at the home loved her so much, that it might be nice to give them an excuse to spend more time together. There was a blind woman named *Frau* Katzenstein, who treated Inge as her very own granddaughter.

"I am thinking you are my little Traute (Gertrude)," she would often say lovingly to Inge, while holding her hand. Inge would sit with her the longest. They always seemed to be by each other's sides, and always hand in hand. After *Frau* Katzenstein's family left her in the home to escape to America, Inge was all she had left in the world.

Having Inge attend to these matters allowed his daughter to remain under the watchful and ever protective eye of her father. She was far safer working under Nette than any of the other agents. While Nette found the bedding of Jews to be abhorrent, the other *Gestapo* agents were gathering more and more young Jewish women as mistresses. God only knows what the young women were forced to do to remain in their lovers' good graces. The over-protective father shuddered to even contemplate it. Carl's instincts, as always, proved correct, and he strictly forbade Inge from having any contact with those types of women. He needed his daughter as far away from that sort of trouble as possible.

****

Many more months passed as the days bled into one another. Life had become rather routine, and the Katzes got used to their new normal. Originally, they thought they'd be forced out of the city soon after the Minsk Transport. Yet here they remained, already nearing summer. Work with Nette was predictable, calculated, methodical, and precise. But one day, shortly after Carl appeared for work, Nette seemed very unlike himself.

Sitting across from him in his office, Carl couldn't help but take note of his slightly disheveled hair, and his wayward tie. Carl's suspicions were soon confirmed when Nette threw some paperwork upon his desk and crashed his coffee cup down. As the hot liquid spilled over the sides, it burned his hand.

"God dammit!" he exclaimed in a huff, immediately coddling his burn.

After gathering his assignment for the day, Katz quickly left the hostile agent, and his office in the *Gestapo* headquarters. He hated that place. It was right down the street from the *Gestapo* prison. Underground is where they had their holding cells. But really, the space resembled a medieval dungeon more than it did a penitentiary. He spent a night there himself a few months ago when one of his Aryan business competitors falsely accused him of not wearing his *Judenstern.* Carl was arrested by Agent Parchmann in the middle of Yom Kippur synagogue services—right in front of the entire congregation. Being led down those dark, narrow, stone passageways, he was unsure of what would happen to him. There were random rooms, with little more than a lightbulb clinging to a wall. Nothing but a chair placed beside it. He wondered if this was where they intended to torture him for the offence. But the guards only shoved him forward.

"Keep moving, Jew!" they ordered.

When they tossed him upon the floor of a small cement cell, he was relieved. At least they were not going to torture or kill him—for now. While that night occurred many months ago, it served as a horrific yet effective reminder to always be wary of the *Gestapo.* He visited the headquarters several times a week, yet there was never a time that the building didn't make the center of his chest grow tight.

Pulled back to his present task, Carl headed down the steps of the entrance on *Am Wall.* He wondered to himself who best to ask for information. He was certainly excited and intrigued. A bad day for the *Gestapo* had to mean a good day for a Jew, he reasoned. He turned towards the center of town and looked for a safe person to see if they knew of any news. Katz tried hard to quiet his hopes that perhaps there was a turn to the war.

Perhaps Germany was losing their favorable position? He had to try to find out what was making the agent so upset.

As luck would have it, he ran into an old acquaintance: Louis Neitzel. He used to live in the same town of Vegesack as Nette.

"Aye, don't even mention that man's name to me!" Louis Neitzel exclaimed all too loudly when Katz approached him on the matter. "That man has been after me for years—ever since I wouldn't sign a paper confessing my relationship with an Aryan woman. That bastard even punched me for resisting!"

"Please, please, not here. Come with me to my office. It's safer to talk there," Carl answered in a hushed voice, trying to coerce his acquaintance to match him in volume. This town was swarming with spies and informants. These days it was impossible to know whom to trust.

Neitzel agreed and looked a bit embarrassed at his foolish outburst. Katz understood, emotions were high these days. It tested the very limits of human abilities. To remain collected and calm always—no matter the circumstances—was perhaps the greatest challenge of all. To be safe, they walked to the *Judenhaus* on the corner of *Legion-Condor-Strasse* with barely a word uttered between them. They made their way toward the Schwachhausen part of town, and Carl and Neitzel took turns periodically looking behind them. It appeared that they were not being followed. You could never be too sure these days.

Once inside the main floor of the home, Carl led Neitzel into the office of the JCC. It was the room August and his family used to occupy. Even though many months had passed, Carl still half expected his little clown to come bounding around the corner— wild hair, and shirt untucked from whatever mischief he was getting himself into. Emotions caught in Carl's throat at the thought. There was just something about his purity—something about his goodness and innocence—that got to Carl every time. The thought of any harm coming to August simply broke his heart. He hoped to God that as bad as he knew the Nazis to be, that they could never harm a child.

Carl welcomed Neitzel into the main area of the room and offered him a seat at his desk. Before sitting himself, Carl peered down the hallway to make sure *Herr* Lisiak— the suspected *Gestapo* appointed caretaker of the home—was not there, before softly shutting the door behind him. Even in the *Judenhaus,* safety was not a guarantee.

"As I was saying before, Nette has been trying for years to get rid of me like he has some others from Vegesack," Neitzel explained in a hushed voice. Carl placed a small glass in front of his guest and one also for himself. He was careful not to interrupt the man.

"He's targeting me, my family, Marie Huntemann and her three sons, and others in town who know his secret." Carl unscrewed the bottle of Schnapps before filling each of their cups. He leaned in closely to gather every word. Neitzel continued in his quieted voice, "He already sent my brother, Arthur, away. He threatened me that I'd be next."

Louis Neitzel heartily drank some of the alcohol from the crystal. Carl joined him. His nerves certainly could use some settling.

"In fact, yes, that's probably it..." Neitzel continued. "Nette is probably in a bad mood because he wasn't able to get rid of all of us on that first transport. That and it's almost the second anniversary of her suicide."

"Whose suicide? What secret?" Katz asked, before placing his empty shot glass back upon its coaster.

"Nette's ex-wife killed herself after he left her for another woman a few years back. He took the older two to stay by him. He never gave his boys enough to eat. His children and ex were always hungry and penniless, they used to walk around town all skinny and bruised up from his beatings," Neitzel explained.

While this was not the news—specifically, that the war was ending—that Carl was hoping for, perhaps this bit of information could help him better navigate his well-being until then. It could only serve him well to learn as much as he could about his boss.

Neitzel continued, "He was the guilty party according to the law because he was living with the other woman while still married to the first. But you know Nette, he has something on everyone. He probably had some dirt on that lawyer or judge he used. All I know is, that one of their sons was the one who found her hanging. Right there, from the beam of her living area. The Nazis all like to pretend they're perfect, and he in particular, is a real stickler for the rules. This story makes him look bad. Not to mention, all the back payments he is responsible for. Anyway, he's been harassing all of us for years. If I had to guess his motive? He wants all repercussions and financial responsibilities to go away along with us."

Carl poured Louis Neitzel one last drink before thanking this man for confiding in him. As he walked him out of the office and to the front entrance of the home, they allowed their strong handshake to linger.

"Stay safe," Carl offered before they let go.

"You, too. Take care of that beautiful family of yours," Neitzel added, before straightening his hat, and walking out. Carl stood there, as was customary to a guest, until he was out of view. Louis only took a few steps down the cobblestoned streets before turning back towards Carl.

"Never underestimate Nette," were his last words.

That last bit of advice made the hairs on Carl's arms stand straight up. He soon found out that Louis was right to fear Nette, after all. A few days later, Neitzel was notified he was to be on the next transport out of Bremen to an undisclosed location. Nette stayed true to his promise, he always got his man.

Around that same time, the Katz family received that same notification.

Chapter Nine
Tuesday, March 21st, 1950
The Conspirators

Johanna stood by the register of her ground floor store. As she leaned against the counter amid the dresses on the racks, socks in their drawers, and underwear folded upon their shelves, her chest filled with pride. She was finally getting the shop, *Schustermann Vor dem Steintor*, back to its original glory. Standing there this evening, waiting for her friend to arrive, she pressed down a frizzy lock of salt and pepper hair, and straightened the hem of the skirt over her thick waist. At sixty-four years of age, this clothing store was exhausting for her to rebuild. But she was someone with an endless supply of passion and determination. She was a person who never shied away from hard work to get what she wanted.

Looking over her pride and glory, she could not help but reflect on how far she had come despite being dealt every disadvantage. Even in her youth, she was never considered attractive. Her crass demeanor was perhaps even less sought after than her looks, but she always managed. Depending on the circumstances, she knew how to be the most charming or else the most feared woman in the room. Using this unique skill set, she could always transform any given situation into a beneficial prospect. Therefore, she jumped when an opportunity presented itself in the form of a Jew named Benno Schustermann in Brussels in 1918. With his trusting nature, and an eagerness to please, she saw in him an advantageous opportunity. Yes, he may have been of an undesirable religious affiliation, but she could manage to overlook that shortcoming. With Benno, he had the means and temperament to allow her to chase her dream of running a successful clothing business. To attain that lifelong goal, she would do anything—even marry him.

It was nearing the 6 p.m. closing time, and Johanna was beginning to grow frustrated with her friend. She took out a satin chemise from a shelf, only to fold it again. As she pressed her hand along the lace trim of the fabric, she grew increasingly irate. *Emma should know better than to be late for our meeting.* As she went to lay the garment neatly back upon the shelf, Emma rushed through the door of the entrance. Johanna's watch read 5:55 p.m.

"So sorry, dearest Johanna! I am nearly late!" she exclaimed, with strands of hair still blowing in the cold March winds. The tips of her cheeks and nose, irritated and red.

"Don't be silly! What time is it?" Johanna exclaimed, while pretending to look at her watch. "I was so busy today, I haven't a clue of the time," she responded while approaching her friend to exchange a friendly handshake.

After presenting a few dresses that may suit Emma's tastes, Johanna Schustermann led her friend upstairs to the living quarters of her home. Without the luxurious area rugs to quiet her steps, the clattering of the heels of her shoes echoed loudly upon the wooden floors. She directed Emma past the kitchen, apologizing for still not having any furniture. Johanna and her late husband worked extremely hard together to grow their thriving business in Bremen, Germany. Up until the end of 1938, she and her husband managed to acquire quite a level of affluence. These days, she had to hustle and claw to simply make ends meet. It had not been easy for her to live so humbly after attaining prosperity.

Johanna invited Emma to have a seat on a chair in the living room and offered to serve her some *Kaffee Ersatz* with an apology, explaining that the real thing was still just so expensive and in short supply.

"Oh please, I can hardly recall the taste of actual coffee anymore. That would be perfect," Emma responded graciously to the offering of the bland-tasting substitute.

"As you know," Johanna spoke over the boiling kettle from the kitchen, "I have that big meeting tomorrow with the Police Inspector, Gerber, and I just wanted to catch you up and make sure we were still on the same page. After all, we could use any help we can get these days," Schustermann mentioned, while gesturing to her humble living quarters.

Once prepared, she walked in from the kitchen with the drinks in each hand. Placing them on the coffee table, the ladies waited for it to cool off before taking a sip. While doing so, Johanna absently drifted off for a moment rehearsing in her mind what she'd say at the deposition tomorrow: "*Katz, not Nette, is the one responsible for my husband's murder.*" *That should be simple enough,* she reasoned. *After doing this favor again for Nette, he'd have no choice but to keep my secret. That's it. It should be an easy win for both of us.*

"Oh yes, please tell me more about your arrangement with Nette. I am really worried about getting caught. As much as I can use the money, I don't want to go to jail for this!" Emma cried out, breaking Johanna from her contemplation.

This outburst concerned Johanna. She left the "coffee" sitting on the table and went to the cabinet. It would appear they needed something stronger. She returned with a bottle of Schnapps and two shot glasses. She couldn't let Emma ruin this for her.

Johanna needed the money, and Nette needed his revenge. Johanna was more than happy to give him a *Persil-Schein* (the brand name of a common cleaning agent used for shining surfaces) to scrub away his Nazi "stains." Emma needed to stick to the plan.

"I told you, I've already spoken to Nette about you and he promised not to dispute your story in return for your testimony against Katz," Johanna encouraged, trying to maintain her composure.

"Really? Are you sure he won't give me up? That's really all he needed? For me to say that Katz was the one that got the dentist deported to Minsk?" she asked nervously, cradling the now empty shot glass in her hand.

"That's it. Keep the story that Katz was the one responsible for his death and you're fine. Then the money will all be yours," Johanna confirmed.

Emma had been an assistant to a Jewish dentist named Ludwig Fuerstenthal for a few years before the war. The dentist was never married and had no children. Emma fabricated a story that she was his common law wife to inherit all his monetary reparations and assets. The dentist had no heirs who survived the war who could challenge her statement. The only ones who knew the truth were Nette and Johanna.

"But what about my *real* husband?" Emma whispered to her friend with concern. Referring here to the Aryan man she was married to since December 1942—the same time she would have still been engaged to the dentist in her made-up story.

"I told you! Nette will not contradict your testimony. *Don't you listen?* Just blame Katz for Dr. Fuerstenthal's death, and say it wasn't Nette. The courts will never find the truth."

"Okay, I trust you. I will do it."

"Perfect. Thank you, Emma, so much for doing this. You will not be sorry." It was getting late, and so Johanna urged her friend out of her home, but not before Emma promised to come back into the shop to try on those dresses she had her eye on.

"I will let you know how it goes with Gerber tomorrow. *Auf Wiedersehen* (until we meet again)," Johanna called out to her friend before closing the front door after her.

While she turned over the brass lock for the evening, Johanna felt a twinge of guilt tug at her side about what she had done all those years ago. Talking about those times was starting to weigh heavily upon her conscience. When Johanna was married back in 1921, she had every intention of being the perfect wife to Benno and doting mother to her son, Lothar. But the war years changed everything. When the shop on the main floor was plundered by the *SA* on *Kristallnacht*, she found herself inconsolable. It was in that moment that she realized that being the head of a Jewish household was a severe liability. As soon as her husband, Benno, was released back home from his detainment at the concentration camp, Sachsenhausen, she felt she had no choice. She immediately had him sign over his power of attorney to her.

"Do you think this will really help?" she remembered him asking her with those wide and trusting eyes.

"Of course. If everything is under my name, we will no longer be considered a Jewish household. This is the only way we can protect our assets," she recalled answering him ever so sweetly. He never could resist her charm.

Despite his reservations, he signed over all his legal rights to his wife's name that very afternoon. But rather than feel any remorse then, she was surprised at the first thought running through her mind: *you gullible fool.* She couldn't help it. As he pressed the pen to the paper to sign everything over to her with barely a protest, it made her lose any last bit of respect she held for her husband. She then realized that after nearly twenty years of marriage, she did not have the slightest bit of affection for this man. *All the easier for me to do what must be done*, she supposed.

In the weeks following, she kicked him out of the house.

Johanna then filed for divorce from Benno three years later in 1942. This act absolved him of all protection from the Nazis and enabled the *Gestapo* to discover her son's three-year Jewish school attendance. Shortly thereafter, both father and son were shipped out of Bremen to a concentration camp. She had a new chapter of her life to live. Johanna, a newly single, Aryan woman now held every privilege and opportunity available in Hitler's Nazi Germany.

Everything always turns out for the best. Johanna Schustermann sighed to herself, smugly, while scrubbing the used dishes in the sink. She quite enjoyed being smarter than everyone else. Now she just had to get rid of Katz. He was the only one standing in her way these days. She tried using her charm on him. She even converted to Judaism last year to prove her good intentions, but Katz wasn't having any of it. No matter what she did, he would not allow her into the Jewish community to get the reparations she was owed for being the widow of a Jew. Somehow, he saw right through her, and he let her know it. He was the one person she had ever met who was impervious to her ways.

With Nette on her side, however, she would prove to that arrogant and self-righteous Jew that she always got her way. She would blame Katz for the death of her husband and for the incarceration of her son. She would testify with statements like, "I was more frightened of Katz than I ever was of the *Getsapo*," and claim that he was a collaborator. She would slander his good reputation and say things like, "Katz was wild and liked drinking and the company of barmaids even after his marriage." With Nette more than willing to corroborate her lies—after all, she had helped clear him of all those offences and had shortened his sentence in doing so—Katz would be powerless in stopping her. That is all it would take for her to win.

As she placed the clean cups back on their shelves, she laughed a bit to herself at the challenge of it all. No man had ever survived being on the receiving end of her anger. She would show that haughty, sanctimonious Jew that he never should have underestimated her. She would reveal to Katz that he chose the wrong woman of whom to make an enemy. Finally done with the long day's work, she removed the apron from around her waist, and made her way to her room. Arranging the bedding on the floor, as she still didn't have the money to buy a proper bed, she couldn't wait to get a good night's rest before giving the damning deposition at the police station tomorrow. Katz may have survived the war, but he would never survive her wrath. She would make sure of that.

Chapter Ten
July, 1942
Final Days in Bremen

Carl had been expecting this notification for quite some time. He had his course of action prepared for months now. First off—he was responsible for making this as easy as possible for all those under his care. While delivering the news to his family, he had the women focus on how nice it would be when they would finally be reunited with their loved ones. That seemed to work—the women missed the family dearly this last year. As for the elderly residents in the home, he decided it best to withhold this information until the very last possible moment. Instead of their needless worry, he reasoned, let them enjoy their last Shabbats, birthdays, and holidays carefree. Carl, Marianne, and Inge made sure that these celebrations were more festive than usual at the home. With Carl as their manager, there was nothing for them to do anyway. He was the one in charge of all their belongings and was the one to make sure they had all the necessary medications.

He also found this a far easier transport to manage than the one to Minsk. All the equipment for the settlements he managed to acquire went on that last train. That should make it a far easier move into their new home, he speculated. An especially important advantage since he'd be resituating so many elderlies. All the Katzes had left to do was pack up their few remaining items of clothing, a soup spoon for each member of the family, and their prayer books and family photos. The Nazis had already taken pretty much everything else.

These were strange days. There was no time for Carl to mourn, revolt, or succumb—that is, there was no time for natural responses to his situation. If he didn't hold everything and everyone together at all times, he feared there was no hope. Everything rested upon his shoulders. He only prayed that his brother-in-law, Moritz, had also risen to the challenge in all these months since the Minsk Transport. Carl was not sure if he could console Inge and his wife if anything bad were ever to happen to Ruthie or his sister-in-law. He would find all that out in just a few days' time, now.

The Katz women all wanted to spend the final day in their hometown scrubbing the kitchens and bathrooms clean of the *Judenhaus*. One might find that to be odd, to voluntarily scour the porcelain tiles in a house about to be confiscated by the Nazis before they were all to be banished from it. But it made perfect sense to the Katz women. It saddened Carl when he realized that it was just an attempt for them to avoid any impression that they, too, fit in with the Nazi stereotype that they were just a bunch of "Dirty Jews." But this menial task seemed to keep their minds focused. While some of the others in their community were committing suicide upon receiving their transport notices, he allowed them to do whatever they needed to find some peace and comfort. Carl's wife was barely functioning these days. It became a huge responsibility for both he and Inge to keep her from falling into deep bouts of depression. Therefore, he encouraged the women to continue cleaning—no matter how inane it may be—if it helped them remain positive and have some semblance of control over their lives.

Even Carl had to admit, that sometimes it was all just too much to handle. In Carl's darkest moments of fear and contemplation, he'd seek the quiet and assuring company of his daughter. Now a young woman of eighteen, her calm and pleasant demeanor was sometimes the only thing that could offer him any solace. In the evenings, he would ask her to join him in listening to recordings of the comforting and lighthearted spirit of Mozart and the "Barcolle from the Tales of Hoffman" on the record player. That hour of peace sometimes felt like the only glue maintaining his fractured nerves. As Inge matured over the years, she was becoming more and more of a confidant and trusted support to her father.

On July 22, 1942, the day before the family was scheduled to leave, a transport of elderly Jews from Varel made a scheduled stop at the Bremen *Bahnhof* (train station). Their leader, *Herr* Wolf, had a serious problem, and was advised he should immediately seek Katz's counsel. Wolf ran straight from the train platform to the office of the JCC. He then explained to Katz that they took with them many coffins being as they were a transport of elderly. Within those coffins, the leader confided to Carl, they were smuggling large amounts of forbidden foods. He then proceeded to plead with Katz to help him sneak the potentially life-saving contraband into the settlements.

"You must help us not get caught. Our lives depend on it!" he begged Carl in desperation.

Katz had to think fast. They were all leaving the very next morning. How could he pull something off in such a short time?

"I'll figure something out. Go and take care of your people. I'll see you in the morning," he told him, without a clue of what he could possibly do to help. It was common practice for the *Gestapo* to search the transport trains and confiscate smuggled items. Carl had seen those sorts of things happen with the transport to Minsk. It was an absolute nightmare. The *Gestapo* had all the passengers empty their suitcases for hours as they searched through their belongings. The punishments for those who committed offences was harsh. Carl needed to devise a plan to ensure that all would run smoothly.

He understood that first and foremost, he needed to make sure Nette would be in a good mood.

****

Later that evening, Carl slipped a bottle of cognac into his briefcase, before kissing his wife goodbye at the door.

"You can't leave us," she said while grasping his elbows and looking pleadingly into his eyes, "not with *him* here," she whispered, while blocking his access to the door.

"Marianne, please, it's for the best. Linnemann knows I am coming right back. Just stay with Inge. He won't try anything," Carl assured himself as much as he did her.

If someone had told him a few days ago that he'd leave the house with Agent Linnemann alone at home with his daughter, he would have claimed they were crazy. Yet here he was, leading his wife aside so that he could meet up with Nette for a drink at a hotel lobby. As was always the case, Carl had been given no option. Forced to take a calculated risk, he wagered that it would be far more dangerous to have the smuggled goods uncovered, than it would be to leave Inge and the women alone with Linnemann for a couple of hours. As he charged down the stairs of the front entrance of his home, he prayed he was right.

Heading towards the hotel by the *Bahnhof,* Carl tried his best to focus on what needed to be said, but his thoughts kept going back to Inge. It irked Carl to no end to see *Herr* Linnemann make himself comfortable in an armchair in Carl's office at the *Judenhaus,* just as he may have done in his own home. Not to mention, it sickened Carl how the agent asked his daughter to serve him a cup of coffee. It took all of Carl's willpower to pretend not to notice how the agent's eyes followed Inge as she left the room.

Linnemann, overall, was pleasant in dress and demeanor. That fact only made his dealings that evening ever the more sinister. He was sent to this *Judenhaus* by the *Gestapo* to make sure that all the Jews who were leaving on the transport remained calm and orderly. Ironically, he was also there to make certain that nothing was smuggled in or out of the house. Before Linnemann arrived, his mother-in-law gave some of her fine serving ware to an Aryan friend for safekeeping. That, Carl had to admit, gave him a bit of satisfaction. It was a small victory, but he was more than happy to claim it.

Under an hour later, Carl finally arrived at the hotel by the train station, and spotted his acquaintance from Hamburg, Dr. Max Plaut, already out front. *Ahh,* he exhaled, *fortune will be on my side this evening*. Plaut was an attorney and appointed leader of the North-West-German-District of the *"Reichsvereinigung der Juden Deutschland."* More importantly for Carl that evening, he was an exceptionally entertaining storyteller. His presence would certainly help the meeting go smoothly. As Jews, they had to wait outside the hotel for Nette to arrive. They needed special permission to patronize a pub, as Jews were forbidden from entering dining establishments according to the Nuremberg Laws. A minute or two passed before he arrived, and after friendly greetings were exchanged by all, they each grabbed a seat in a booth. In that dimly lit bar, the three unlikeliest of comrades laughed into the night. As predicted, Nette was flattered that Katz gifted him that bottle of cognac. Desperately entertaining and joking to please his audience, Carl felt he was a jester in a circus that evening. But he had to do whatever it took to keep everyone safe tomorrow at the station—even if it required compromising his dignity. And as fate would dictate, his plan was working. Nette basked in the attention. *Could it really be?* Carl wondered, aghast. *Does he really think that we are friends?*

As though the night couldn't get any more absurd, Nette chose to celebrate the success of removing more Jews from their city with a bottle of champagne. *Yes,* Carl thought, *this man actually finds it appropriate to rejoice shipping out Jews with the very Jew he's transporting out the next morning.* As the waiter returned to serve the men their celebratory beverage, Carl entered a dark, introspective space. This may have very well been the last straw. After all these months of playing their game, he may have finally reached his capacity to repress his violent, albeit natural desires to harm this cruel and indifferent Nazi. Carl could easily grasp the bottle of champagne sitting at the edge of the table and smash it over the *Gestapo* agent's head without interference. As Carl watched the beads of moisture collect over the heavy glass, he contemplated if placing a massive lump on the left side of Nette's skull would be worth the trouble it would get him into.

"Here you go," Nette said to Carl, as he offered him the full glass flute.

"Katz?" he asked again when Carl did not respond. Carl, in that moment, was still contemplating knocking the agent back on his ass. However, after a very brief absence, reason reentered his thoughts. It would not be only he who would suffer the repercussions of that senseless act of violence—it would also be his family. They would be left without him there to protect them. It would also be that transport of elderlies denied of the necessary foods and suffering from *Herr* Wolf being removed as their leader. No, he knew then that he could not be so self-indulgent. Therefore, all he was left to do was smile graciously as he accepted the drink. As Carl drew in its sweet and bubbly texture, a searing pain pulsated over his right temple.

Shortly after a toast, the evening soon wrapped up. Carl felt he accomplished his goal of putting Nette in the most favorable of moods for tomorrow's transport. So, after

85

thanking him for their evening together, Carl, and his migraine, headed back towards his family at home.

Carl maintained a fast pace on that warm, July evening. He could not bear to leave his family alone with that hateful man, Agent Linnemann, for a moment longer than was necessary. The blocks seemed endless, and Carl began to sweat through his shirt. He removed his suit jacket and slung it over his arm. Usually he loved long summer evening walks, but on this night, it felt like he was completing a marathon. He pressed hard against the center of his forehead to help force the images of Linnemann harming Inge from his mind. His legs weakened at the strain of his speed, yet still he would not slow. Thirty or so minutes later, he bounded up the steps of the *Judenhaus,* and all but threw open the door. His wife peered out from the bathroom, with a scrubbing brush in hand.

"How did it go?" she inquired as he rushed towards her.

"Where's Inge?" he demanded, ignoring her inquiry. His eyes darted all around the main floor looking for confirmation of his daughter's safety.

"Inge? Oh I don't know. In our room I suppose?" she answered her husband to the best of her knowledge while he hustled past her.

"And the agent?"

"Linnemann? I'm not sure. He was around here a moment be—"

Carl did not need to hear the rest of her answer. It frustrated him to no end that he couldn't rely on his wife to stay by Inge's side at all times. That was all he asked of her. He could have done without a scrubbed floor this evening. But that was a problem for another time. *Where were they?* he wondered as he headed down the hall toward their living quarters. He desperately hoped his wife was wrong. But Carl's heart nearly stopped as he heard the unmistakable voices of the agent and his daughter—they were coming from the bedroom.

"Thank you, but my father would never allow me to do something like that," he heard Inge's voice explain.

Carl could not yet see what was happening, but as he stepped past the door frame, he saw the back of Linnemann's form. It took all his self-restraint to stop himself from tackling the man to the ground.

"What? What is it? What won't I allow?" Carl demanded breathlessly, only inches from where the agent now stood. Linnemann turned to face Carl at the intrusion. It was then that Carl finally spotted his daughter. She was on the floor. She was packing. She was safe.

"Hello, Father. Agent Linnemann was just telling me that my luggage will not be inspected, so I should be smart and put some money inside," she answered innocently, her expression inquiring after her wrongdoing. She placed the folded blouse into her valise.

Carl thanked him for looking after her, and, to Inge's surprise, encouraged her to heed his advice. Carl instructed his daughter to spend the last bit of nightfall sewing some bills into their pillowcases, before turning in for the evening. Katz was confident that Nette would be in a good mood the next day. Soon after Carl's arrival, the agent left the bedroom to prowl the other areas of the home.

It was a fitful and sleepless night for Carl. When he laid his head upon the pillow, the pounding of his heart filled his ears. But when he propped the pillows to sit upright in bed, he could no longer hear it, and it also helped alleviate the pressure from the throbbing migraine suffered since he had his drinks at the bar. Resting this way allowed him the unexpected peace of watching Inge and Marianne sleeping safely in their beds. He found himself thankful that at least for the next few hours, he had all those he loved most in the world securely beside him. He never wanted to forget the way Inge was curled up on her chaise, or the way Marianne always wore the most beautiful night dresses to sleep. These early hours made him appreciate all he had, and he was grateful. He never wanted to imagine a world where they'd be separated from each other or harmed. Enjoying the certainty of their safety—however brief—quieted his mind from fixating on whatever tomorrow would bring.

****

The very next morning came all too quickly, as the Katzes and the other residents of the *Judenhaus* rushed to leave their home, and city, behind. They each wore their finest suit as was customary for a day of travel, and had one suitcase as well as hand luggage stuffed with salamis, sausages, breads, and containers of soup. They were not told how long the voyage would be, so they were careful to pack as much as would fit in the bag. *Herr* Linnemann escorted the family and the others through the back entrance of the train station and onto the platform where there were already close to two hundred others, all Jews, also being transported. Everything was running smoothly, as far as Carl could tell. It appeared that his drink with Nette last night was a success.

There were a couple of people seeing off their relatives, but mostly there was no one left in the city for the Jews to say goodbye to. Inge mentioned to her father how sad it was when she saw an Aryan woman, Johanna Schustermann, forced to say goodbye to her Jewish husband, Benno, and their mixed-blood son, Lothar, on the platform.

"Yes, Inge, I couldn't imagine that. From now on, no matter what, we stay together. Do you understand? No matter what. What happens to one of us happens to all of us," Carl stated sternly.

"Yes, Father, I understand," she responded dutifully. But with the confused look present in her eyes, he realized that she was not actually sure what he meant by his harsh warning. It was evident, when she instinctively stepped closer to her father, that she was wondering why her father thought that the Germans would ever do that to their family. Carl had no intention of elaborating.

Upon entering the passenger train, they seated themselves on gray upholstered chairs that faced one another. *Herr* Linnemann also took a seat nearby. Finally, the train's whistle blew, the engines fired up, and they began on their way. As they left, the Katzes did not look out of the window at the city of their birth that they all sensed they were now leaving forever. There was no one for them to wave goodbye to, and mostly, they didn't want to see the faces of all the non-Jews standing on the platform who pretended not to know what was happening to them. Carl just sat there, stoically, looking into his daughter's eyes to reassure her and quiet her fears.

Once the train pulled out of the station, a man spoke aloud, "I hope she burns down along with that house."

"Sorry?" Carl asked Benno Schustermann, just now realizing who had sat beside him across the aisle. "Were you speaking to me?"

"No, I was speaking to my son about his mother, my ex-wife, Johanna," Benno exclaimed, with his face red with anger, and tears burning his eyes. His teenage son sat beside him, quietly, with his head hung low. "She divorced me, took everything I ever earned, and had me shipped off to this settlement along with our son. I hope she dies. I want her to burn down along with that house she stole from me. That was what I said."

Chapter Eleven
May, 1950
Is This All?

Chief Prosecutor, Siegfried Hoeffler, was frustrated. The other men, Inspector Charles Gerber, and former *Gestapo* agent, Bruno Nette, just waited in silence in their seats across from his desk. Hoeffler's face was red, his eyes fixated on a spot in the corner of the room. He nervously picked at the cuticles on his fingers as he decided how exactly to approach this matter.

"Is this all? Is this really all we have on him?" he finally asked of the men.

"I've provided plenty of testimony against Katz for you. I've given you everything you've asked for and more," Nette responded, incredulously.

Gerber laughed a bit to himself. Clearly Nette was living in the former golden era of Nazi rule. It would require a lot more these days to convict a Jew of wrongdoing than it did then.

"Plenty of testimony? Is that what you said? Have you even considered the sources?" Hoeffler countered in an exasperated tone.

"The sources?" Nette asked confused, removing the scarf draped around his neck. His body had suddenly grown hot. He'd anticipated a meeting where he'd be congratulated for his efforts to bring down their common enemy. He did not expect to be reprimanded by this insolent young man.

"Yes, the sources. Do you have anyone credible? You know, someone who isn't an idiot, delinquent, or thief?" Hoeffler clarified to the old Nazi.

"My sources are certainly credible people. All pillars of society. One Jewish journalist, a few well-to-do of mixed blood, some Aryans who were once married to Jews, then some witnesses—" Nette attempted to explain.

"Enough, enough. These aren't the good old days, Bruno," the Prosecutor interrupted.

Nette's left eye twitched at Hoeffler's informal use of his first name. He could feel his blood pressure rise with every pulse in the vein over his temple.

However, the Prosecutor was far from finished. "Everyone's lies can easily be uncovered by our town records. Not to mention, there are so many witnesses around the city who could possibly speak against us. The dental assistant, Emma Fernhomberg? Really? What about all the locals who attended her *actual* wedding during the time she claims to have been engaged to the Jewish dentist?"

Hoeffler was so frustrated, some spittle escaped his mouth. He quickly took out his handkerchief to dab at his lower lip. He needed to get a grip. The pressure to obtain a guilty verdict on Katz was certainly getting to him. After all these years of demotion, he finally earned back his place as head State Prosecutor. He would be damned if he'd allow his newfound credibility to be lost over this mess.

"Who would do such a thing? Who would dare speak against us?" Nette challenged the lawyer with a raised voice. He grasped onto the arms of his chair tightly. Police Inspector Gerber looked over at the older man's fisted hands. He wondered if he'd get to witness an actual scuffle this afternoon. Nette's temper, after all, was well-known.

"Oh I don't know—*anyone*? *Everyone* who wants to be in a favorable position with the Allies?" Hoeffler responded, sarcastically. "You know that this is a public trial we are preparing, don't you? It will be all over the papers. Any citizen who wants to attend the trial may do so." Gerber was still staring at Nette's physical reactions to Hoeffler when the Prosecutor suddenly turned his attention to him.

"Gerber—you are certainly quiet this afternoon. What do you say?"

Gerber startled a bit to his name being called. He weighed his words carefully before committing to a response. "I am afraid I do have to agree with you. These witnesses' stories are very weak, and I don't believe they will hold up in any authentic investigation or court of law. I believe the Americans may want everything legitimate these days."

Hoeffler was surprisingly pleased with the Inspector's response. Perhaps Gerber wasn't as dim-witted as he had initially thought. Employed to give the appearance of an unbiased and fair investigation, perhaps he would be of actual use to the case.

"So what do you suggest we do?" the Prosecutor pressed the police officer, while refolding his used handkerchief. He then leaned forward on his desk. The policeman earned his full attention.

"I don't know Katz personally, but I do know people. In my experience in this line of work—and in life, for that matter—I've never met a saint. That being said, there must be something he *actually* did to gain an advantage. We just have to find that something out. Perhaps the American occupiers are privy to information we lack."

Hoeffler sat back in his chair to consider these words. Yes, he had to agree—he never knew any man without sin. Perhaps they were not looking in the right places. Unfortunately, Carl Katz was a darling of the American occupiers. They put him in charge of Jewish ration distribution, he helped with government issued monetary reparations, and of rebuilding the Jewish community. If that weren't enough, the Allies also assisted him in restarting the business that was taken from him during the war. In just these past four years, by repurposing scrap metal, Carl Katz went from destitution to riches. Everyone heard of that elaborate wedding he threw in 1947. The stories of the abundance of food, wine, and music became legendary. The very food and wine that were gifted to those guests, those *Ost Juden* (Eastern Jews), meant less for the real citizens of Bremen. Hoeffler, and his people alike, found Katz's lack of consideration for Germany's impoverished inexcusable.

No one could have possibly bounced back on their feet so quickly after losing everything—not even a Jew, Hoeffler considered. He absentmindedly placed his hands to his lips to remove a last bit of pulled skin stubbornly hanging on to his finger tip. *After all, there were practically no others from Bremen who even returned from the camps alive, much less acquired riches so soon without any blood on their hands. How else could his prosperity be explained? He was certainly no angel.*

Hoeffler determined that he would just have to search harder. While Katz may have been beloved by some, his ostentatious behavior had to have resulted in enemies. He just needed to find them.

"Let's do it. Get every man you have on this case. Spare no expense. Contact the CIC (The United States Army Counter Intelligence Corps). We have to catch Katz and put him away for good," Hoeffler declared boldly to the men in the room.

Chapter Twelve
July, 1942
Arbeit Macht Frei

Nazi guards standing at the inner entrance of Theresienstadt.Terezin.
By Severoceske Nakladatelstvi, 1988. Image 6.

The weather grew increasingly and unbearably warm the further they traveled west and south. Marianne and her mother, *Oma* Rosa, put down the little fans they fashioned out of cloth napkins to cool themselves for the duration of their journey as they approached a station. Finally, they felt the train slowing down, as the engineer began applying the brakes, and then came to a complete halt. Everyone began crowding against the windows in an attempt to figure out where they were after the long trip out of Bremen. Carl made out a solitary sign atop a wooden platform that read: *Bauschowitz*.

"Bauschowitz?" Inge turned to her father and asked quizzically, "Have you ever heard of this place?"

"No," he replied grimly. "Never."

Those last words from Linnemann after the agent departed the train in Hannover rang in his ears. When Carl's daughter politely said, "*Auf Wiedersehen* (German for until we meet again)," to the agent before he hopped off, his response to her, smiling all the while, was, "If we ever do see each other again, you will find me hanging by my neck from one of Bremen's lampposts." Inge just found the statement odd and confusing. Carl allowed her to remain that way. He, on the other hand, became terrified at the implication.

When a painfully thin man dressed in tattered civilian clothing boarded their car to assist in ushering them all off, the reality that they were not being sent to the promised good and carefree future of the "Reich's old age home," and the comfortable and cozy conditions of the "Theresienstadt Spa" were confirmed. Carl always harbored suspicions—he knew very well never to trust anything a Nazi promised—but in that moment, he realized that he had greatly underestimated their capacity for harm. Carl would be careful not to make that same mistake again.

When that ragged helper cried out, "Leave your things here! It's a long walk. Don't take it with you. Everything will all be picked up and delivered!" Carl urged the women not to listen and to carry their bags of food with them. His instincts were confirmed when another painfully thin man, also in dilapidated clothing, boarded their train car and approached Katz.

"Don't listen to what you were just told," he whispered. "Take as much as you can carry with you."

Carl quickly, and discreetly, relayed the message to the others, and helped as many as he could off the locomotive.

Carl tried not to appear troubled by the implications of the helpers' appearances, but he sensed that Inge was not fooled. She knew him too well. He could tell she was about to voice concern about whether or not there would be enough to eat at the camps, so he shoved his wife's hand luggage under her arm to quiet her. He then told her to grasp a handle of a basket of food while he grabbed the other, and they each slung their own luggage over their shoulders respectively. Walking down the steps of the last connection to what was to be their former, comfortable lives, they then began their long march as directed while carrying the heavy load of food.

93

Marianne, meanwhile, was steadying her mother on one arm, and an elderly sister-in-law of *Oma* Rosa's, also on the transport, took the other. As the two old women stared at the seemingly endless path ahead of them, they became increasingly upset and flustered. Marianne did her utmost to comfort each of them, all the while doing her best to assure them that they could make it if they walked slowly. But under that already very hot, mid-day July sun, it became an excruciatingly long walk for all of them. Carl was not at all sure they would be able to make it to their destination, wherever that was. As Carl looked back at all those under his care behind him, he grew desperate. The *SS* all began yelling at the elderly to keep up. They hobbled on their canes, while some had already passed out on the road, and others simply sat upon the dirt unable to go on. Carl paused a moment to decide whose aid he should come to first. But there were just so many—*too* many. There were about one thousand confused, helpless, and desperate elderly in that march needing his assistance.

From Bauschowitz to Theresienstadt by foot. Like those pictured above,
the Katz family had to trudge by foot several kilometers to reach the camp that was to be their
residence. Terezin. By Severoceske Nakladatelstvi, 1988. Image 34.

"I said, move! *Schnell! Schnell!*" an *SS* commanded Carl and Inge.

What was he to do but march on? That fact sickened him, but he had no choice. Remembrances of his time in Sachsenhausen when a Jew disobeyed orders flashed before his mind. He knew he could never sit by while they beat one of his women. *Impossible.* And so, he and his daughter turned their backs on all those suffering behind them, and trudged on ahead of the others. Burdened by three pieces of luggage as well as the heat of the day, sweat soon drenched through their clothing. After about an hour following the dirt path with fields of long grass extending in every direction as far as the eye could see, *Oma* Rosa collapsed onto the ground suffering from an angina attack. Fortunately the *SS* in charge had moved further back in the line which allowed them the good luck to stop for a moment so that his wife's mother could take her pill. But there was no way she could continue on. What then? What fate would she meet?

Just then cattle trucks and tractors passed by their march, casting clouds of dust and dirt into the air. Carl, wiping his face of the muck, followed them with his eyes, and moments later witnessed the unimaginable. The SS began roughly piling the elderly into them! He couldn't allow that to come of *Oma* Rosa. She would never survive it in her state! But what could he do?

"There! Look!" Marianne shouted excitedly. She ran off into the fields before Carl and Inge had a chance to understand what set her off.

With a large smile, and in a highly uncharacteristic act of ingenuity and resourcefulness, Marianne ran back pushing a wheelbarrow she spotted discarded in the field. Although the grand dame, *Frau* Rosa Gruenberg was embarrassed, Marianne insisted her mother sit in it all the way to the entrance of Theresienstadt. None of the women noticed the alternative manner of transportation occurring just behind them. They didn't see what was happening to the elderly, and Carl made every effort to distract and avert the women's attention to keep it that way. They didn't notice the horrific images of the others loaded like cattle, packed together so tightly they could neither lie down nor sit. Those all forced to stand; exhausted, thirsty, women with tangled hair, and others screaming. But somehow, by some miracle of God, the women did not see any of it, and after maybe one hour later from that time, they could just make out the ghetto's looming structure appearing in the distance.

The place seemed enormous; with its outer gray and stone walls, it looked more like a fortress than the picturesque village they were promised they'd be going to. As they approached its entryway, and were being ushered in by the now several thin men and *SS* guards accompanying them, there was a large sign overhead with enormous black lettering: *Arbeit Macht Frei* (Work Will Set You Free). Despair and desperation suddenly overcame him, and he couldn't help but turn his head and look helplessly into his daughter's eyes. The first time Carl had seen those words at the entrance of

Sachsenhausen, he had no idea what they meant. But this time, when Inge turned to her father and asked, "What do they mean by that?" much like Moritz did four years ago, he knew exactly.

"*Vati?* What is it?" she asked him nervously when he didn't answer.

But he just couldn't bring himself to answer her—not when his greatest nightmare just came true. He was in a situation where he knew there was no way he could keep her safe—not from the conditions, not from the hunger, and certainly not from the physical abuse. As she looked innocently into the eyes of the man she depended on to always keep her safe, he couldn't bear to utter the horrific truth.

"I-I don't know..." he stumbled upon his words, before offering a thin smile, "we'll ask Ruthie when we see her inside."

He was shocked that he was able to pull himself together. But he would do anything for her. It seemed to work, as a bit of the fear passed from her eyes, while she looked towards the entrance in anticipation of being reunited with her beloved cousin. Once they passed beneath that sign, they could then see guards with weapons standing at attention off to the sides. As the Katzes followed the crowd, they were ushered into a dark warehouse-like building they called the "*Schleusenhaus*" (Floodgate House). Dimly lit, and with nothing but some long tables situated on rough wooden floors, the new arrivals were processed. As their hand luggage was rummaged through for contraband, they soon left with nothing having been confiscated, to be processed. There Carl and the others proceeded to give their names, ages, occupations, and then given their ID number. His was #VIII/I 676.

The rows of buildings in Theresienstadt.

As they stepped out of that warehouse-like building and onto the street of the "town" in which they were to reside, all breath escaped them. It was a desolate abandoned military base, with rows upon rows of two-story cement block buildings on either side, all painted yellow, with sloping brown-shingled roofs. The paint was all chipped and peeling, and any exposed wood was broken and splintered. They passed by a small marketplace and some storefronts, all of which appeared vacant or empty. But that was certainly not the worst part. It was the hordes of people—all dressed in rags, smelling like death, and so thin their cheekbones pressed harshly against their pale and yellowed skin.

"Carl…"Marianne stated in horror, as though she wanted him to do something.

But he ignored her appeal. There was nothing he could possibly say or do in this place. That was obvious. As bad as Sachsenhausen was, it was nothing like this. That was a prison, and for men. Here, women and children roamed the streets. They were *innocent*. It broke his heart when he saw a starving young boy approach him. *Is it August?* Another fear in those first few minutes was just then realized—that the Nazis were capable of harming women and little children. *But how could that possibly be?* He tried to reason with himself. But there was no denying the truth. The certainty of their situation just ran past him with muddy knees and tattered *Lederhosen*. The boy was not August. Carl was not sure whether to be relieved or fearful.

They were then led past a seemingly endless number of rows of cement block buildings, until their assigned *Blockaeltester* (block leader), *Herr* Comitte, announced, "Now we are entering one of the 'L' streets. We call it that because it is one of the long streets." After he led them a short way farther, he then told them to stop in front of a doorway numbered L308.

"This is where you will be staying from now on," he announced haughtily with his chin raised high. Carl estimated him to be at least his age. Carl didn't yet know him, but he already felt wary of this odd man standing before him in a brown jacket, equestrian pants and riding boots, with a bright yellow scarf draped about his neck. This Austrian accented fellow inmate then continued giving them their orders, "But the men must be housed apart from the women."

Upon opening a door to what would ordinarily be called at best, a hallway, *Herr* Comitte explained that this was now to be the men's "home." Aside from two windows facing the street, it was just a fairly large open space with a worn, wooden floor, and a small room off to the side.

Carl, Inge, and their grandmother were too shocked to express anything in that moment. The women then had no choice but to separate from Carl, as he went to assist some of the older men who needed help getting situated. The men milled about Carl in confused, dehydrated, and exhausted states, begging him for assistance. They'd ask him repeatedly things like, "Where's the nurses station?" or, "I think this is the wrong building. I requested a special facility for the elderly with a lot of amenities." Worse yet, when he helped them to a seat on the splintered wooden floor, with only their coats laid out to be used as mattresses, they'd express to him pitifully, "You have given me the wrong room. I ordered one with a balcony and view."

Carl desperately tried to comfort them and let them know that he'd be there to take good care of them, but when they needed to use a restroom, and they could only make it to the bucket placed beside them, Carl felt ill. Many others couldn't even make it that far, and soiled their clothes. Carl needed to take a moment. He needed some fresh air and a minute to clear his head and think. He stumbled to the light of the doorway, afraid he would pass out. He clung to the wall for balance, and tried to take deep breaths, but the air outside was not much better from that inside. Almost as if she had known his distress, Inge was just outside waiting for him. She had left her mother and grandmother to rest in their private attic that the *Blockaeltester,* Comitte, had set aside for young, pretty girls like herself, and went to see if her father could use any help. Carl decided he would concern himself with that lascivious old man later—first things first.

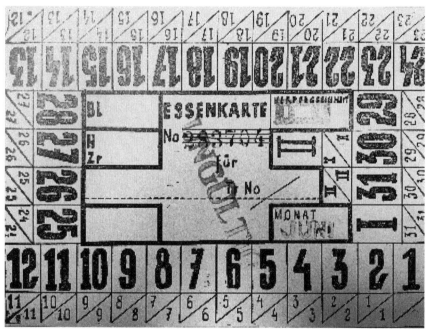

Carl's actual food ration card.

"Yes, come with me," Carl told her. "The men need to wash themselves. Help me pump some water into these pails." After he had distributed a bucket of water to each inmate, he had to deal with the next pressing matter of importance. He again turned to his trusted companion, Inge. "The men are all too sick to leave their makeshift beds. Let's go and collect food for them from the kitchens." Their *Hausaeltester* (house leader), *Herr* Loewenthal, a Czech Jew, distributed ration cards for food and bread portions to those who were strong enough to eat. Carl was given those as well as a food bowl for each of his own family members, and a large metal pail.

"Great idea, Father. Also, then we can look for Ruthie. Maybe we will see her in the dining hall," Inge responded excitedly. She and her father then each grabbed one side of the handle and walked as directed towards the barracks.

The bowl given to the Katzes for food, as well as the four soup spoons each member brought with them from home, with the initial "K" on the handle.

"Yes, Inge, that is a good idea. I like the way you are thinking." He did actually. Her looking at the bright side of this garish situation was far better than his current state of mind. He knew it would do him some good to spend time with her. The camp kitchen was a large three-story structure, with arched windows facing onto a courtyard. To get to their destination, they had to pass among many inmates, and although Inge kept searching, they were unable to spot Ruthie or any of their other relatives. By the time they reached to where the food was being doled out, there was already a long line of people standing outside the kitchen window with their ration cards in one hand and a spoon and pot in the other.

As they came closer to that window, they could see a man punching each card. The cook at the window filled each pot with soup. Carl and Inge quickly realized that the soup would have to do, as it turned out to be their only meal for the day. They stared down at the murky, brown broth. Nothing else was being served. Turnips and potatoes were chopped into cubed pieces in the soup, but they were clearly not very fresh by their dark color and mushy texture. They were so hungry, however, that they didn't think it tasted all that bad. Inge ate upstairs with her mother and grandmother, while Carl ate amongst the men after he served them all their rations.

Sitting upon his makeshift bed of jackets and rolled trousers as a pillow, he struggled to keep his meal down amongst the smells and filth of the men and their overflowing pails of waste. He realized it would only be a matter of time before serious diseases and infections would begin to spread. Their luggage never did arrive—in fact it never would—and they had nothing clean to change into and no proper baths in which to sanitize themselves. With the camp's harsh conditions, inadequate food, and no medical services, he realized that there was simply no chance for those he cared for to survive. All he could do was his best to keep them comfortable for however long they had left.

Although it was obvious to him, it did not seem quite as apparent to his women just how in danger *Oma* Rosa was living here amongst them. Her angina attacks were coming far more frequently since their arrival, and it seemed like it was taking her increasingly longer to recover. Her other daughter, son, and remaining grandchildren, were nowhere to be found in Theresienstadt. She was growing despondent wondering after the health and well-being of her family. Carl and the rest would constantly try to reassure her with words like, "I am sure they are somewhere safe and together. Just like we are now," but it did little to calm her nerves. She spent most of the time in her "bed" upon her laid out coat and purse as a pillow. The bones in her back and shoulders were constantly sore and aching from resting upon such an unforgiving and hard surface. Marianne would often stay by her side, commiserating, and also too depressed to complete her assigned job of caring for the elderly women of L308. As far as Carl could tell, the camp required everyone to be useful and contribute in its running in an organized and orderly fashion. It was too early to say for certain, but it couldn't bode well for his wife to never show up for work. He would then be forced to have Inge do her mother's special assignments after she was done with her own shift at work for lecherous, old *Herr* Comitte in his office at L407.

The Katz family was in trouble. That much was obvious. Carl needed to devise a plan if there was any chance of their survival. *Any* plan.

Chapter Thirteen
1942-1943
Trying Times

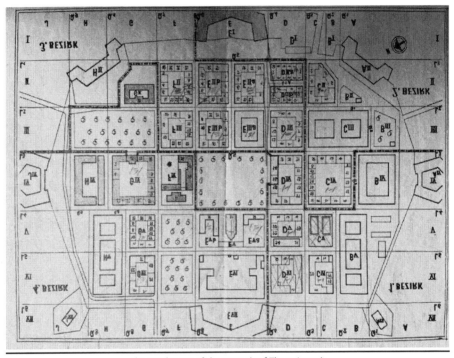

The Katz's map of the grounds of Theresienstdt.

On August 2, 1942, roughly two weeks after they arrived in Theresienstadt, *Oma* Rosa said she was not feeling well. She remained lying down all that day, and Marianne urged her daughter to fetch her some breakfast before she headed for work that morning. After taking her pills, Inge gave her grandmother a quick kiss on the cheek, as she did every morning, before running out the door.

"See you later, *Oma*," she said, in her usual happy and cheerful manner.

Inge then stopped by her father before leaving for the day. He was glad she could catch him before he left to speak with the Camp Commandant's Office about requesting extra mattresses and blankets for the elderly inmates arriving from the additional transports that month. Carl had already managed to provide the items for those from the original Bremen transport, along with extra soap and further changes of clothing from the "clothing warehouse," but there was just so much more they still needed. As appointed *"Hausaeltester,"* or "house leader," there was little more he could do, but from past experience, Inge's father always exceeded all limitations and possibilities. Inge then expressed her concerns to him about her grandmother's health.

"Hmm. Okay, I will be sure to check in on her throughout the day," he promised Inge.

"Thanks, *Vati,*" she answered, before giving him a quick kiss and turning to walk on her way towards the office.

"And Commite? How has it been working for him these days?" Carl called after her.

She turned back to him, and rolled her eyes a bit at the mention of his name before answering, "Oh he's never around me very much anymore—thank heavens. I hardly interact with him at all."

He exhaled with relief before replying diplomatically, "Very good. Have a nice day at work. See you when you get home."

Herr Commite enjoyed certain privileges, had more flexible free time, and a comfortable office job, here in the camp. Therefore, when Carl casually mentioned that it would be a shame for Commite to lose said privileges over any reports of misconduct, it didn't take much more than that for the man to understand the heavily implied threat from Inge's father. Everyone knew that Carl, even in this short time, was already in good standing with many of the Theresienstadt officials for his good work ethic, and competent organizational skills. Since that heated conversation, and even though they worked in the very same office space, the *Blockaeltester* had almost no further interactions with his daughter.

Unlike Inge, most young girls were here without their families, or anyone at all for that matter, to watch out for their well-being. It wasn't unusual for Carl to catch Commite striking up hushed conversations with other young, pretty girls from the camp. As Carl patrolled the streets for wandering, lost, elderly inmates struggling to find their ways back home before their evening curfew, it was not unusual for Carl to catch *Herr* Commite whispering to a young lady in the shadows and alleyways of the ghetto. He shouted out to them to disband and return to their quarters. They usually listened to his order—at least for the time being. It seemed like most everyone could benefit from a conscientious community, and a compassionate leader. Part of his job, Carl then realized, would have to be advocating for those under his protection from wrongdoers. Although with the seemingly endless influx of transports—in July alone the camp rose from 21,304 all the way to 43,403—he had to accept that he'd fail far more often than he could ever succeed.

At around lunch time, he went up to the attic where his women lived to check on *Oma* Rosa. His wife ran to him as he stood at the entrance of the door.

"Carl, Carl. Thank God you are here. I just don't know what to do! She is not getting any better!" Marianne cried out in desperation.

"Okay, let me have a look, and see," he spoke calmly, trying his best to quiet her nerves. His mother-in-law wouldn't benefit from overhearing that sort of panic.

Carl went to look over at his helpless mother-in-law, lying feebly upon her straw mattress. Marianne then returned to her place by her mother's side, and held her hand. *Frau* Gruenberg looked frighteningly pale, and her breathing was rapid and shallow. She was damp with sweat, and when he placed his hand to her forehead she felt still and cold. She barely looked at him, but instead focused on the lightbulb dangling from its cord directly above her. If there was any chance of saving her, Carl knew he'd have to act fast.

"I'll be right back," he said before sprinting towards the door.

"But where are you going? Please don't leave us. I am scared," Marianne pleaded after him.

"I'm going to look for a doctor. I'll be right back. I promise." He spoke from the doorway before rushing out.

He ran to the infirmary—if you could even call it that—as next to no medical services were provided. The only one there was a dentist he knew from Hamburg. He would have to do. He rushed back to their attic over L308 with the dentist. They entered the room, he went over to examine the patient, and placed down a small bag of medicines he had managed to smuggle with him when he first arrived into Theresienstadt.

Carl was surprised, but in those few minutes since his departure, she seemed to have worsened. Her eyes were more distant, and she began to mutter quiet, inaudible words. After a few brief questions, and a short examination of the patient, the doctor's face looked grim. Carl didn't need to hear the official report. He just thanked him for making it over so rapidly, before shaking his hand and leading him out the door. On his way out, the dentist turned back and placed a couple of pills in Carl's hand before saying, "These may make her more comfortable."

When Carl went to rejoin his wife, she was confused. "Why is he leaving? What did he say we should do?" Marianne pressed him.

Carl then took her in his arms, and held her tightly. Understanding, she collapsed into her husband and cried softly into his chest before pulling back away to spend those last moments with her beloved mother. Hand in hand, she sat beside Grandma Rosa with sad resignation. Marianne ran her fingers through her hair, neatening a wayward curl, and straightened the pendant of her mother's necklace. Even in the camps, it was very important for *Oma* Rosa to appear well-put together and presentable. Before Rosa took her last breath, she smiled a bit in the direction of that lightbulb dangling from the ceiling. Marianne, in that brief moment, felt joy. She believed it was her father that her mother smiled at before she left this earth.

Rosa Gruenberg
1874–1942.

Carl stood over her for a moment, before taking out the kippah he kept in his interior suit pocket. Placing it on top of his head, he closed his eyes tightly, and sung out, *"Yitgadal v'yitkadash sh'mei raba b'alma di v'ra chir'utei!"* The wailing of this ancient and mournful melody officially proclaiming the loss of her mother made Marianne cry out as it pulled on her heart. Carl, pushing through a lump of emotion collected in his throat, then continued with the "Mourner's Kaddish," knowing it by heart, as he had repeated these lines far too often in the year since his father's passing.

May there be abundant peace from heaven, with life's goodness for us

and for all thy people Israel. And let us say: Amen.

May the One who brings peace to the universe bring

Peace to us and to all the people Israel. And lest us

Say: Amen.

With those last lines it was concluded. Carl stood a moment longer, honoring the life and loss of such a beloved member of his household. But not for too long, as he had to leave to make for the necessary preparations. Although he had only been there two weeks, he was well-versed on the funeral arrangements at the camp. He left Marianne there as the acting, "Shmira," or as the person elected guardian of the body prior to its burial, to notify those in charge.

A little while later, after all tasks were completed, Inge came bounding through the room after seeing the sign hanging on the door of her house. In bold block lettering, it simply stated, DEATH. Carl, while still holding Marianne, allowed his daughter to grieve her final goodbyes over her grandmother's body, now covered. She knelt beside her with her head in her hands, weeping over her repeating the words, "No, it cannot be." Shortly thereafter, four men arrived with a wooden plank on wheels, which two men pulled from the front, and the other two pushed from the rear. Two of those men rolled Oma Rosa onto a board and then carried her down the stairs. After they placed the body on the wagon, they needed to make several more stops to pick up others who had also died. Those bodies were also put on the cart—the same cart used for delivering the bread.

Carl, Inge, and Marianne all followed the cart, but they were the only ones. Oma Rosa was apparently the only resident with any mourners to pay their respects. Once the men neared the walled gates leading out of the ghetto, they couldn't allow the Katz family to go with them. That was where the family made their final farewells before the wagon disappeared from sight. Then Carl put his arms around both women and led them back home.

"But you cannot be here," Marianne said to her husband, as he went to sit down next to them in their room.

A painting of Inge's attic that a resident gave her as a gift.

"What else can they do to us?" he asked, as he began to make himself more comfortable.

That evening he felt defeated, and lost, and overwhelmed, and helpless, and truly saddened. He permitted himself to feel that way as he held his women close to him all that night. When he was assured by their shallow breathing that they were asleep, he too, allowed himself to shed a few tears over the loss of such a kind and innocent soul.

He knew he only had those few hours to mourn, as with the light of day, he'd have to again be everyone's rock, everyone's shoulder to cry on, and everyone's problem solver. As he squeezed those he loved a little tighter, he did try to press the fear of how he'd keep them all safe from creeping in. More tears fell as the guilt of his failing Grandma Rosa pressed down upon the center of his chest. He failed them all with the loss of her. Looking up to that splintered and worn ceiling above him, he vowed to her spirit in heaven, that he would not fail her again.

****

During the months immediately following her passing, the daily lives of Carl and his family continued much as before. It left little time for mourning for him and Inge. They had to remain strong, that is, stoic in order to endure life in Theresienstadt. But Marianne, on the other hand, was not quite as resilient or philosophical as Carl and their daughter. Taking the loss of her mother hard, and with the harsh conditions and inadequate food, Marianne was often far too sick to work. Inge had to cover her evening work details more and more so as to ensure that her mother would never be flagged as unproductive. As concerned as he was about his wife's weakness, he was equally, if not more troubled, by the resolve of his daughter. Although initially relieved at her mental toughness, he found this replacement of her natural innocence and optimism concerning. The naiveté of her wide, blue-green eyes had all but left these days, replaced by an unnerving distant and closed expression.

Although anyone who didn't know her would remark that she appeared sweet and pretty, the ever so detectable narrowing of her eyes haunted Carl. This predicament was only further confirmed when she hardly reacted to the loss of her favorite patient, *Frau Katzenstein*—the blind lady she'd always stay hand in hand beside for hours while still in Bremen. She simply wrote her name in her small leather notebook where she recorded the first and last names of each one in Theresienstadt from Bremen, who had died there. Most of them had been in the camp alone, and this was the only way she could think of to honor them, that is, to retain some record of their existence and of their death. This act was highly prohibited, but Carl allowed her to perform this hidden act of rebellion. He encouraged Inge to honor her grandmother, the first name in this book, in this way, followed seven names later, by that of Lina Katzenstein. He realized Inge was becoming merely a shell of her old self, therefore, if this small act of defiance helped her resolve or process some of her anger and grief, then he greatly encouraged it.

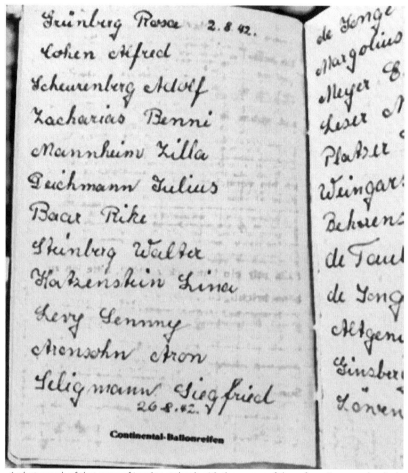

A photograph of that page of Inge's notebook with the names of those from Bremen who died.

As the transports kept arriving from Cologne and other cities in Germany, there were ever more elderly persons, many having been evacuated from nursing homes. Many of these new arrivals were placed in an enormous barracks, called the Kavalier or "Gentleman" Barracks, which not only housed them but maintained one of the camp's large kitchens and housed the mentally ill. To Carl's surprise, one day a man sent by the Jewish Council of Elders, all appointed by the Nazis to run Theresienstadt, Engineer Elbert, by name, approached him asking whether he would be willing to leave his current job as a *Blockaeltester* to manage the entire Kavalier Barracks.

"You seem like a good organizer," he said to Carl. "I have a good job for you."

Carl knew that when the administration made a request, it was really more of a command that couldn't—nor shouldn't—be refused. The camp was structured in an odd manner of self-administration, a combination of different "national" (Czech, German, Austrian, etc.) and "ideological" (Zionists, Czecho-Jewish) streams. This self-administration was headed by an Elder of the Jews together with a Council of Elders, and a Central Secretariat beneath which various departments administered life in the ghetto. Those leaders initially planned to convert Theresienstadt into a productive economic center to therefore avoid deportations; however, they were unaware that the Nazis already planned to deport all the Jews. While they didn't know it then, the majority would be sent to extermination camps. The unique style of self-government in Theresienstadt gave birth to a sophisticated system of departments. While the ghetto fell under the authority of the *SS*, but with only thirty or so members present, they were actually thinly represented. The Nazi presence was largely absent from the ghetto's day to day actions. Therefore, the actual job of running it was in these hands of the Jewish administration: the *SS* controlled Theresienstadt, but the Jews were the ones responsible for administering it.

When Carl reported to the Kavalier *Kaserne* on his first day of work, he could see that it was a far cry from what he was used to managing. While the elderly in L308 existed in subhuman conditions, with the majority of them dying from diseases caused by starvation, it was nothing compared to what he'd be facing now. It was a giant and primitive warehouse that remained nearly pitch black no matter the hour of day or night. Previously used for storing potatoes, the rooms were all narrow and deep, sometimes with only a singular window to offer any ventilation at all. To make matters worse, if that were at all possible, the administrators were directed to save electricity, so only one light bulb dangling from the high ceilings was ever permitted to be lit. The sick and elderly, all bumped into each other as they wandered aimlessly through the hallways—hitting against the damaged walls, and stumbling upon the uneven stoned flooring.

There was dirt and dust on every surface of the dwelling, and Carl thought it would be impossible to keep these areas clean, where a minimum of twenty people would stay crammed in every room. His head spun at how he could even sanitize the people themselves, as it was obvious by their shaved heads that lice had taken over the residence. The struggle against infectious diseases was perhaps one of the largest struggles for Carl as a part of the Jewish self-administration. The difficulties in overcoming this were increased by the constant fluctuations in population, and even once survival and immunity were acquired, there were new arrivals bringing fresh diseases with them. The most common in this barracks, nicknamed, "The Home of the Old and Incurables," were Typhoid Fever, Scarlet Fever, and Encephalitis.

In this overstuffed home of approximately 3,000 men and women, the worst area had to be that of the insane asylum. Although they were locked away, you could still

109

hear the haunting cries coming from the other side—those sorry souls strapped into straight-jackets. They were hidden away from all others, but you could still make out their piercing screams and haunting melodies of their sad songs. One in particular, an older man's moaning of *Bei Mir Bist Du Schein* (By Me You are Pretty), sent shivers up Carl's spine. Thankfully, doctors and nurses were assigned to handle them, so his interactions with them were severely limited. Considering all these aforementioned horrid conditions, Carl assumed many others, despite their better judgement, had either refused to work there, or were simply incapable of the overwhelming task. He would be smart and use that as leverage, or as a bargaining chip, for extra consideration to his family when the time came.

As he returned to his room late that evening, he went to check on those he had been caring for these last several months. For the most part, these were all the original people from their transport from Bremen. Inge, Marianne, and Carl had all formed loving relationships with the residents. While the family couldn't control very much of their conditions, they were always available to offer a smile, a word of encouragement, or a compassionate ear. It served the women well to be around people that were so loving and appreciative, and it particularly helped Marianne that many had fond memories of her mother to share with her. Marianne had grown painfully thin since Grandma Rosa's passing. Although they had all lost a considerable amount of weight, Marianne's jaw and collarbones were noticeably protruding beneath her skin. She was beginning to look more and more like the elderly she was appointed to care for—with their frail bones, and translucent skin. This frightened both Carl and his daughter terribly.

Around this time, transports out of Theresienstadt started increasing. No one really knew where they were going or why they were selecting certain people and not others. All they were told was that they were going somewhere "out east." While no one knew for sure, they estimated that it couldn't be something good, considering their prior experience with being loaded onto trains heading east to an undisclosed location. Long lines of the elderly, sickly, and unproductive were periodically herded down the streets to their trains to be taken away. No one knew for sure what their fates would be, but all wondered if it would be to their deaths.

Inge was growing increasingly tired these days. The lack of food, emotional stress of losing her grandma and worrying about the welfare of Ruthie, and not to mention the extra hours she had to put in covering her mother's shifts when she was unwell, all contributed to her exhaustion. But she had to do it. Her father desperately needed her to find the strength to keep going—for what would become of her mother if the truth were ever to be discovered? Would she be one more of those pitiful souls being marched out of the camps to meet God-knows-what fate?

****

By the late springtime, Carl was finally faced with the request by the Council of Elders to become the official *Gebaeudeaeltester* (building leader) of the entire Kavalier *Kaserne*. It would require him to be on call twenty-four hours a day, to remain on the premises at all times, and to live in a room directly above it. As horrible as that would be, it would also take him away from all those he had been caring for this past year. He simply couldn't be as available to them any longer. On his last day, they were all so heartbroken to see him go. Some even wrote sweet poems as a tribute to their gratitude. A fellow inmate had Carl choke up when he wrote that he felt Carl cared for him like a father, yet he wished him good fortune and that, "... a gentleman belongs in a gentleman's barracks." As much as it pained him to leave, Carl was aware that to turn down this position could endanger his and his family's lives. However, when he realized that few others could execute the assigned job, it gave him an opportunity to bargain. He requested that he would only do it if his family could remain together. Thankfully, that was a simple enough request, so that very evening, after finishing dinner, their one meal for the day, they moved to a room in that building.

As they made their way down to the end of a very long and dark corridor on the second floor of the barracks, Carl couldn't help but notice that Inge was a little different this evening. Her steps appeared lighter and swifter, and her eyes seemed as though there was a bit more life in them. As she threw her few belongings onto one of the bunkbeds of their tiny room, she didn't even seem to take much notice of the sparse conditions, or of the muffled screams and groaning of the insane situated just directly beneath them. Carl was intrigued, but he didn't want to ask. He waited for her to confide in him. As though she sensed his curiosity, she sat upon the mattress, and exhaled loudly.

"Mom, Dad, I think I met someone," she declared simply, as she tried to suppress a smile.

Chapter Fourteen

1943
A Bit of Light in the Darkest of Nights

Schmuel Berger (center), in a photo with his friends taken before the war.

Carl was quite pleased to see his daughter's old happiness return. He was also very surprised—after all, there was certainly no shortage of suitors for his daughter's affection. Everyone from the kitchen staff, to a worker in the lumber yard, to even the boy from Bremen, Benno Schustermann's son, Lothar, all pined after Inge. But she was simply disinterested. The once sociable girl was largely removed and isolated even in this densely populated prison. She'd have pleasant, albeit distant conversations with those she ran into, but largely remained close to her parents when finished with work. Carl missed how his daughter would excitedly speak about her days' events with him.

These months she just sat silently hovering over her bowl of mush at dinner time, with her eyes out of focus and settled on a spot just before her. Nearly a year after their arrival, Inge's temperament had begun resembling those inmates that had resided there for longer. Therefore, whoever this boy was to bring about such cheer to his daughter, must be someone special.

"I'd like to meet him," Carl commanded her, over their breakfast of their bread ration and a hot cup of *"Mucka Fug."* The cook called it coffee, as he handed them this steaming liquid, but it was unlike any coffee they had ever drunk. While it may have been brown in color and hot, it tasted like it must have been made from corn.

"Of course," Inge responded, surprised, while spreading an ever-so-thin layer of margarine over her last bit of crust. She would never have dreamed to go out on a date without first gaining her parent's approval.

Inge ate very slowly across from where her father was seated—this was all she would be permitted to devour until the next thin slice of bread she had been saving for her lunch. After consuming his own portion, Carl wished her a good day, and then headed just past the window of the Kavalier's kitchen—an enormous structure which was responsible for feeding 10,000 inmates of which he now also managed—and into the adjoining entrance of his "office." He took one last look up at the beautiful sunshine of this fine spring day. As he let it cast its warmth over his upturned face, he smiled a bit—*at least the sun was one thing not under Nazi command.* He then entered the dark, cavernous space, as he was welcomed with the usual groans and whimpers of those who suffered. He greeted them all with pleasant good mornings, and handshakes, as he tried to make meaningful eye contact with each and every one. This small act helped to remind him of their humanity, and they of their own. It was easy to only see them as masses, as sufferers, as those who only had a short time left. Why then connect? Why then form relationships? Carl desperately held on to his interactions—even if it pained him. To rid the patients of this decency would only result in yet another act of violence for them to withstand. He would be damned if he held any part in their misfortune.

Carl looked through the reports of those assigned to making rounds examining every last surface. They'd inspect all bedding structures, and make notes of those he'd need to have repaired. They also went to the bathrooms to inspect all plumbing fixtures and pipes to make sure they were in good working order. Carl needed to make sure the roof wasn't leaking, that the cleanliness of rooms was passable, and would serve as mediator to roommates not getting along. The hardest job of all, however, was the daily headcounts of inmates. This was of particular importance to the Nazis. Katz was responsible for giving this number to the Jewish administration, to the *Zimmeraeltesten* (Room Elders), in the Magdeburg *Kasserne*. If he was off by a count of even one, all food rations would be withheld from them. This was no simple task however, as it would require all inmates to hold still in place. While some were bed-ridden, many others would roam the hallways and rooms in confused and non-functioning states. One couldn't explain to them the purpose, much less restrain them all from moving. The whole process was so frustrating and burdensome.

But just as Carl began to grow irate at the situation, a young girl, who must have been around Inge's age, with long reddish brown hair, and a pale complexion, passed by him with a bucket of human waste in tow. While Carl's work was exasperating and tiresome, it took little more than a haggard nurse like her to remind Carl of his privilege. These poor women, who were mostly untrained, were the ones who were really doing the hard labor.

Another yet walked into the sick room that the first girl just exited with cleaning equipment in hand. If their jobs weren't awful enough, the real danger these nurses faced was in contracting the highly communicable diseases that they were in contact with sometimes for up to eighteen hours a day. They hardly had proper disinfecting cleaning materials, protective clothing, or any distance at all for that matter. Of course, it was not unusual for any one of them to fall ill, resulting in their own loss of life. Carl reminded himself of their heroic jobs whenever he began to feel sorry for himself. These young girls were truly the valiant workers of the barracks.

Despite the numerous obstacles, Carl did manage to get most of his work done that morning, and as it neared lunchtime, a messenger came for him.

"The Elders need you to come in to speak with them at the Magdeburg Barracks," the young girl said before returning from whence she came.

Carl hung his head at the news. Nothing good ever came from being called in for a meeting, "Uh, yes... yes, I'll be right over," he replied after her, barely able to form the words.

Despite all the efforts of the Council of Jewish Elders and the camp-ghetto inhabitants to make the best of the atrocious situation, their orders all came from the dreadful Nazis. As he headed over to the nearby barracks, the building housing the offices of the different departments of the Ghetto's Jewish self-administration, as well as the flats of some of the leading office holders, he felt himself grow short of breath. As he approached the tall rectangular, three-story structure, he wiped a bit of sweat from his brow before entering. He met with the man placed in charge of making horrible, unimaginable decisions, before leaving the building with the dreaded paper in hand only a few minutes later. Carl couldn't even bring himself to look upon it.

He went back to his office at the Kavalier Barracks, trying to avoid interacting with any of the inmates. Of course, that was next to impossible. Some called after him when he attempted to slip past, disappointed at his evasiveness. But how could he smile at them? How could he pat them on the shoulder and inquire about their health? How could he do any of that when he possibly held their very fate literally in his hand? He slammed the paper face down upon his desk, and then slumped heavily into his chair. He pulled out a ration of bread from the drawer beside his leg, and unwrapped it—careful not to lose any of the margarine that may have stuck to the paper. As hungry as he was, he could barely taste the food as it slid down his throat into his ever-empty belly. Picking at the last crumb that fell upon his shirt, he turned over and read the names off that list.

****

Later that evening, Carl left his office to go to the kitchen window on the outside of the building. Inge was already there with a shovel in hand, waiting for the truck with the potatoes to arrive. She was standing very straight, and looked excitedly around her, offering brief hellos to passersby. She seemed so happy this evening, so much like the girl she was before arriving at this dreadful place. He paused a moment before taking a step further. He needed to see her smile. He needed to feel that sense of joy at his daughter's happiness in order for him to shed the pain of all those he'd lose on the next transport out east. He also didn't want to infect her with his sorrow. He wanted her to stay like that—in that state of perfection—for as long as she could. She, however, felt his gaze upon her.

"*Vati!*" she shouted in his direction, and then waved with a smile. That was all he needed to feel like himself again.

"Coming!" he answered her, and hastened his stride. The truck just then pulled up on the street in front of them, and dumped all the potatoes on the ground before their feet. He grabbed a shovel and joined his daughter.

It didn't take too long to haul all the potatoes over to the cellar by the kitchen. He felt sorry that Inge had to cover this job for his wife yet again, but the physical labor actually helped clear their minds. Part of Inge's office job responsibilities was to report all deaths to the authorities. She was in charge of a registry containing the names of all the inmates from their district of the camp. It was called the *Standmeldung* (position indicator), which listed all the names of all the men, women, and children and in which houses they were. She had to list in it every new death that had occurred the previous day (usually one or two per house) and all visits any inmate made to the infirmary. She was then to give this detailed compilation back to her superiors in the office, and it eventually made its way to the *Judenaeltester* (Jewish Leader), who would then turn this over to the German commanding official. These days it seemed that the death rate within the ghetto accelerated so dramatically that the Germans had to build a crematorium in the south side of the ghetto. This crematorium had to be capable of handling nearly 200 hundred bodies a day. Yes, though tired and hungry at this time,

115

occasionally this sort of mindless physical labor served to free them from the distressing thoughts. However, Inge didn't appear very troubled by much of anything today.

"Dad, remember that young man I was telling you about?"

"Yes, of course."

"Well, his name is Schmuel. Schmuel Berger. Anyway, he stopped by my office at work today, and asked me if I'd go out with him on a date tomorrow after work. Would that be alright with you and *Muti*?"

"Of course, go have fun. Make sure you bring him by after. I'd like to meet this young man."

Carl smiled in her direction—she seemed really excited to be going on that date with the boy she mentioned, and was eager to get herself ready and introduce him to her parents. Like any typical young girl, she was more concerned with what she should wear than anything else in that moment. Of course, she didn't have many options, so after she finished her shoveling, she said a quick goodbye to her father before running over to the *Kleiderkammer* (Clothing Warehouse). With her ration card in tow, she pleaded for something—anything—she thought would be appropriate. Finally settling upon something nice enough, she felt she would look pretty in a new skirt and blouse.

****

The next morning, the day of her actual date, she even fastened a cluster of artificial daisies made out of felt gifted to her by one of the elderly she looked after, before leaving for work.

Before curfew that evening, Carl and his wife met Schmuel when Inge brought him to the door as promised. Standing just at the doorway, he was tall and slim with a fair complexion and green eyes. He held himself with confidence, and shook Carl's hand with self-assurance.

"Nice to meet you," he said in heavily accented German.

"You are Czech?" Carl asked

"Yes, I had been a student in Brno (the second largest city in Czechoslovakia), in hopes of becoming a doctor before I was sent to Theresienstadt. Prior to that I grew up on a farm in Velky-Rakovec, a small Czech town, with my parents, two brothers, and five sisters." He quickly recited this resume to her father, apologizing for his broken German.

"Wow, that is quite a large family you have. Are they here with you as well?" At this question, Schmuel hung his head and lowered his eyes. For the first time he appeared vulnerable, allowing Carl to get a better glimpse into the young man's true nature.

116

"No," he answered his date's father, "I don't know where any of them are except for my younger sister, Perla. She is the only one here with me."

In their brief interaction, Carl recognized in this young man a quick wit, and a strong character. Eastern European Jews also held a reputation for being quite tough in both body and mind. In Carl's estimation, they were the most well-equipped to survive the harsh conditions of this camp. Not to mention, the young Czech men all received the most favorable jobs in the ghetto.

"Do not worry," Carl responded with kindness and assurance, "I am sure they are together and well, just like we all are right now."

From that night on, Inge spent nearly every evening with the young man from Czechoslovakia. It turned out that Carl was right in assuming he had a good job. He actually worked in one of the bakeries. When he picked Inge up for their second date, he tried to gift Marianne with a small loaf of bread. The Katzes refused it, suspecting that it had been stolen.

"They give us extras," Schmuel claimed, "and we usually eat them in the bakery. Please take this, if not for you then for your mother," he said directly to Inge, while gesturing to Carl's wife from just outside the doorway.

In that last statement, it was evident to Inge and Carl that Schmuel noticed Marianne's ever-diminishing frame and hollowed eyes. It frightened them to realize that her condition was also so apparent to strangers. Carl nodded to Inge to accept the generous offering, for his wife's sake. However, it carried the burden of the full understanding that more for one only meant less for another.

"But what about you? Don't you need this for your own health?" Inge still implored, as she held the bread in her hand.

"Ahh, don't you worry about me," he said with a flash of a smile and a wink. "I am strong like bull."

She chuckled at his silly joke, and the young couple went out on their date, for what Carl hoped would be an enjoyable evening. Inge would later recount to her father how they'd spend time with Schmuel's friends, and that she got along well with his sister. In those two hours between work and curfew, Carl noticed that Inge found herself enjoying life again. For that reason alone, Carl felt entirely indebted to that young man. The Czech inmate granted her a more tolerable existence, as looking forward to her evenings with Schmuel and his friends allowed her an easier time enduring the workday. Now the daily burden of recording all the names of the dead was no longer the primary focus of Inge's day. In Theresienstadt, where so many died each day, Carl noticed his daughter becoming more positive and remembering what it was to feel alive.

If that weren't enough, Carl could finally relax a bit in regard to caring for his women. That little extra bit of food made quite the difference in his wife's energy and well-being. She was able to show up for work far more, which made her more "productive." In addition to that, it felt good to have this bright and capable boy looking after his daughter's well-being. There were many rumors of wrongdoing to young girls like her in the camp. Around this very time, Carl had discovered that a certain influential inmate left a young girl pregnant. How a man who should know better could manipulate a young woman frightened Carl to no end. He shuddered to think about how the young mother would fair with no adequate nutrition, and no passable medical care. It was truly a crime—but Carl was thankful this was no longer something he needed to worry about with his daughter. He could tell that Schmuel's intentions were pure, and that he prioritized the entire Katz family's safety—even to a fault.

****

Over the months of their courtship, Carl began to really get to know his daughter's boyfriend. Carl understood how Schmuel was a young, and brave, and heroic man, who was tired of being alive just to avoid death. He empathized with how he was weary of scrambling for scraps of food, and worn-out from discovering just how skinny one could become before their hearts would give out on them. He and Schmuel alike were both sick and tired of looking upon the walking skeletons; their eyes bulging in despair without even a trace of humanity remaining. The men found that being a witness to such degradation of their people was unbearable. Therefore, Schmuel knew he could confide in her father, when he rapped on his office door that fateful afternoon.

"*Herr* Katz, might I have a word with you?" the young man requested respectfully, standing just at the doorway with his hat in his hand.

"Absolutely." Carl was startled. His thoughts immediately went to Inge's well-being.

"Do not worry, this has nothing to do with your daughter," Schmuel stated quickly, noticing the fear flashing in his eyes, "well, not really." Carl offered Schmuel the seat opposite him, and asked him to further explain.

"I want to do more. I need to do something—anything." The young Czech spoke in barely a whisper, and gestured to the space around him.

"Go on," Carl stated, intrigued. He leaned in closer.

"An opportunity to form an armed resistance presented itself to me while I was still living in the Sudeten Barracks—and I must admit, I was captivated."

Carl straightened up in his chair at the mention of retaliation. He had often thought that if he were a young and single man, he undoubtedly would do the same.

"I was approached one workday by a Willy Groag, a *chaver* (a Hebrew term meaning friend) of the Makkabi-Hatzair movement. In hushed tones we sat in the shadows of the alleyways, and spoke of a covert operation in very short words. I was told that I would be notified when more information was to follow. Until then, Groag required me to acquaint myself thoroughly with the building's architecture." Schmuel paused a moment as they heard footsteps approach the door. When they continued past, he went on.

"In the days that followed, I had very little trouble doing so in the rooms that were available to the bakery workers, however the other areas posed significantly higher risk. But, highly motivated, I eventually succeeded in surveying nearly every other room of the bakery complex. I broke through wooden walls reinforced with barbed wire, and then quickly closed those gaps again before anyone could detect any wrongdoing—just like an experienced burglar who hadn't left the police a trace of a clue! I penetrated corridors built into the ramparts which surrounded the ghetto. I even drafted blueprints and maps of the areas I discovered and presented it to the organizer, Willy Groag."

"Are you crazy?" Carl exclaimed, before lowering his voice. "You mustn't leave any evidence!"

"Well, yes, you are right. Willy reacted in quite the same way, actually. 'Are you insane?' he shouted at me, before crumpling them in his hands and shoving it back against my chest. He then leaned in closely so that I could not misunderstand a single order. The visor of his cap bore into my forehead. He then said to me, 'Destroy these immediately. You are not to put anything on paper—everything in the head! Understand?' In that moment, I understood the severity of the situation. Of course I comprehended the risk, but I didn't really integrate its peril until that very moment. Not until I saw the fear coursing through Willy's eyes, and felt the heat of his angry breath in my face. Anyway, this next part involves you, *Herr* Katz. As you are someone I greatly trust for support."

"Yes, what is it? How can I help?"

"He told me to think of a few strong men I trust. He required that they have to be brave and not afraid of a good fight. Naturally, I thought of you. When this armed resistance happens, we're going to need everyone to battle against these *SS* ruffians with everything we got." He looked into Carl's eyes, with bright optimism and strength.

"Schmuel, my fighting days are long behind me. In the shape I am in now, I may prove to be a liability more than an asset."

Schmuel's shoulders turned in a bit, and his gaze was cast down in disappointment. But Inge's father hadn't finished.

"I will offer you this: I will recruit good men willing to join you, and I will also support your cause with material, information, and anything else you may require to pull this off."

"Thank you, sir, you are very kind," Schmuel said before he rose from his seat.

"One last thing," Carl warned. "Please keep Inge out of all of this. If anything were to happen to you, she'd be much safer knowing nothing."

Not that he needed it in this moment, but Carl couldn't help but remind Schmuel of the brutal nature of this uprising against their Nazi oppressors. Schmuel instinctively clutched at his stomach as the reality of the likelihood of his not surviving was voiced. But Carl could see that that sensation soon passed, when he raised his chin with pride. Carl understood precisely: Schmuel should have perhaps been more fearful at this precarious situation, but when you have nothing to lose and everything taken from you, you become the most deadly sort of opponent.

"Of course. She will know nothing of this," he assured the protective father, and shook his hand on it.

Both Carl and Schmuel heard rumors that the communists in the camp were simultaneously organizing a similar resistance movement, and when the day arrived, that they would fight both separately and together to eliminate their common enemy. Schmuel expressed that he had a lot of faith in his leader, as Willy Groag was a lieutenant in the Czechoslovakian army before his arrival in the ghetto. Unfortunately, you were never entirely sure of who else could be trusted. One never knew if there were moles and informants in the midst. With starvation and the threat of imminent death at every turn, it would be of no surprise that people would do whatever it took to secure any extra piece of bread, or a promise to have their names kept off a transport list.

Carl called over one last time at the departing Schmuel, "Keep your eyes and ears open. Be wary of any and all suspicious behavior." With those parting words, Schmuel nodded assertively in his direction, before placing the hat upon his head and rounding the corner. Carl then got up from his desk, and approached the window to watch Schmuel exit the building. He looked around to see if anyone had followed him to their meeting.

Carl then jolted as he saw two young lads run up to his daughter's boyfriend. His instincts had proven correct, Schmuel was being tailed. They had been waiting for him to exit this whole time. Carl pressed himself against the paned glass to see if he could overhear what was happening.

Chapter Fifteen
Autumn 1944
Schmuel's Resistance

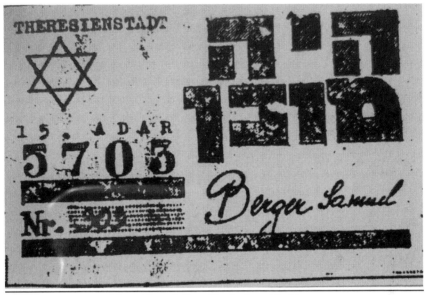

Schmuel Berger's ID card for the Armed Resistance.

Unaware he was, in fact, being surveyed, Schmuel rushed out of Carl Katz's office in order to not be late to work at Block A IV. He was looking forward to how he'd later spend his evening before curfew with his beloved Inge. In about a month's time she would be celebrating her 19th birthday, and he wanted to prepare something extra special for her. He knew he wanted to figure out some way to bake her a cake, and he needed at least this much time to find the right person to barter the right goods or service for it in return. The young lover thought to perhaps ask his friend, Turek, as he sometimes had extra white flour. *Ah, yes! Also Tevlovic!* He worked in the Nazi gardens. Perhaps there was some way he could smuggle a flower inside the camp for her? *No, on second thought, he shouldn't. That could cost us all our lives...*

"Schmuel!" A boy of thirteen or fourteen shouted after the young man. He clearly didn't know this child as he kept walking past despite his name being called. But then the boy cried out to him again.

"Schmuel Berger!" he repeated while further approaching. He shoved something into Schmuel's palm. The child leaned in close, and looked right into Schmuel's startled eyes. He whispered urgently before running off.

"Read it when no one sees you. Hide it so no one can find it. In case of danger, destroy it!"

****

Schmuel ran upstairs to his *cumbalek* (attic space where he resided) to read the card the boy placed in his palm. He grew faint, and felt his breathing go shallow as he read the surface of the paper. In the Hebrew writing it read, "Be Prepared," and Schmuel's number, 303, indicating his address in the ghetto. "How could this be?" he wondered to himself aloud. *How could they have put this information in writing, with my very name on it!* If this card would have fallen into the hands of the enemies, it would have meant torture to the death for all involved—and in this case, for Schmuel in particular. He paced the area of his room for a while to try to regain his breath and slow his heart rate. But the questions just wouldn't leave him: *Why would Willy have done this to me?*

Schmuel had no choice but to leave this matter for another time, as he was nearly late reporting to work. He raced down the steps of his attic, all the while wondering who he could depend on. However, there were a few of his friends he trusted with his life, and so he decided to try to run into them today to ask them if they knew anything about the card. He did eventually find them, but curiously, the resounding answer was no. That helped him relax a bit. However, Schmuel just didn't know what to think, and he had no choice but to leave it for another time. Also curious, was that he never saw or spoke to Willy Groag again after that afternoon's meeting.

But Schmuel, nonetheless, was quite excited at the prospect of his retaliation against the oppressors of his people. Theresienstadt was surrounded by fortresses like the one where his bakery was situated, fortified with ramparts and broad trenches, and in his daydreams in the times following, he imagined them as battlegrounds. While he mindlessly wet the loaves of dough with lukewarm water and placed them on the wooden planks for baking, he fantasized of all those who would fight along beside him. As the baker arranged the raised dough onto the shovel to put into the oven, his imagination wandered as he visualized giant tanks rolling in to quell their uprising. The *SS* units employed by the Germans, armed to the teeth with machine guns, who would undoubtedly shoot wildly after them all, killing as many as possible.

It was no surprise that Schmuel predicted this sort of brutality from the Nazi forces. After all, it was around this time, towards the end of August, 1943, that a transport of 1,200 children, aged ten to thirteen years old, arrived at Theresienstadt from the Bialystok Ghetto in Poland. They reported to some detainees, like Schmuel, of the brutal slaughter of the Jewish people of their town by the *SS*, with the cooperation of the local people. Schmuel listened on with horror as the children recounted the gruesome details of the story. He learned that some Jews planned and executed a revolution there, too, but the Police Regiment 26 (largely composed of Ukrainian collaborators) and other German forces crushed the uprising.

With his mouth gaping, Schmuel and the others removed their caps and placed them against their hearts when they were told of how the townspeople were assembled at the marketplace. Tears collected in the corners of his eyes, when the children, starving and dressed in rags, some even bare footed, told about how the murderers surrounded them from all sides and wouldn't stop shooting until nobody was left alive. Then they spoke about the gas chambers used for mass murder. Schmuel found it impossible to believe something like that could exist, but when the children refused to assemble to take a shower with screams of terror, he and everyone else had no choice but to believe every word they said. Schmuel would later find out the fates of the other 25,000 Jews, who were not murdered then and there, but were all deported to the Treblinka and Auschwitz-Birkenau death camps. Schmuel's fire in his heart grew greater after hearing the tale. There was no way he could allow his uprising to fail.

When Schmuel later told Inge's family of all that he heard, they didn't want to believe it. They couldn't believe it. Yet Carl was very quick to catch on. The women, on the other hand, preferred to think that these must have only been rumors. Or else, Inge just told this to her mother so as not to upset her. Although admittedly difficult to completely grasp as the conditions described were beyond all realms of comprehension, it did offer them a few clues as to the fates of those deported from the camp. Carl seemed oddly reserved in this moment and didn't say much of anything at all.

"Dad, have you heard anything like this? Have you also caught such rumors?" Inge asked her father, wondering what he was thinking.

"Me? No, I'm at work all day. I never hear much of anything at all," Carl responded cautiously.

In truth, along with talk of resistant movements growing in the camp, this news from the child inmates only heightened Carl's fears. Schmuel understood Carl's odd reactions well, as he, too, was faced with the same realization: The uncertainties of what would happen to all those involved, and now even more so, of what would happen if the movement would, God forbid, fail. They would both pray to God, now more than ever, that the insurgents would succeed, and that Schmuel and his conspirators would remain

123

unharmed. But these were desperate times, and there were no guarantees of much of anything these days.

****

But for many months, nothing happened. The summer came and went, and then so did the fall. Over the coming months and into the new year of 1944, the hardships of the ghetto only worsened. And once summer approached, and the advancement of the Soviet troops and the invasion of the Western Allies in France were transpiring, it served to support the Nazi plans to rapidly exterminate their Theresienstadt prisoners. By September of 1944, in one month, 18,402 prisoners were transported from Theresienstadt to the death camp, Auschwitz-Birkenau.

But despite the dire situations for all, Schmuel managed to remain much focused on his love affair with the beautiful, young Inge. They'd wander the avenues together, pinky finger in pinky finger, and talk of their plans for their future when the dreadful war would end. She'd laugh and smile up into his eyes, as she spoke about how much he'd love to take evening walks in the Buergerpark in her hometown of Bremen, Germany. She described Ruthie to him in great detail, and had him agree that it would nice for them to go out on double-dates with her and her special someone. Although Schmuel would try his best, and actually preferred to avoid talk about life after the camps altogether, he just couldn't deny his girlfriend of her much needed escape into that fantasy world. A domain where everything was in its rightful place, where all those she loved most in the world were alive and thriving, and one where she was free to pursue the life she chose for herself.

In truth, Schmuel was far more practical. He felt it was only a matter of time until one of those transport lists had his name on it. Many of his conspirators had already suffered that fate, and he had this overwhelming dread that he would soon be next. Those accomplices of his were told that they were being transported out on "work details." He wasn't so sure that was the truth. By now he knew far better than to trust anything a Nazi promised. It was probably just a lie so that they would all go willingly and not cause too much of a scuffle. He wondered, instead, if word had caught on of the resistance. What if instead of cleaning up the city streets of rubble from Allied bombings, they were sent out to those extermination camps those children described? What if all that was waiting for them when they jumped off the trains, was a queue into a gas chamber? No weapons had been stockpiled for their uprising—neither makeshift, nor any smuggled into the ghetto. *What was taking so long? The time to act is now!* Schmuel was ready for his fight. All he needed was the word, and he'd be out there combatting with everything he had in him.

At the end of September, he finally did receive the notice he was waiting for. But unfortunately, not the one he was hoping for. On a warm evening on September 24, before curfew, Schmuel was acting very differently.

"What's bothering you?" Inge asked.

"I have been informed that I must go out on the next transport," Schmuel replied as he stared at the ground.

"But you are so productive," Inge pleaded, as she placed both of Schmuel's hands in hers, holding on to them tightly. When he said nothing further, they gathered each other into their arms, and clung to one another for as long as possible.

As it turned out, word had gotten out of the planned uprising of the young men. This transport had nothing to do with a lack of productivity like it had in transports past. Schmuel's suspicions were correct and were now being realized—the authorities had learned of their plans. He and 2,500 other healthy, young men between the ages of twenty and forty were scheduled to be deported along with him to the death camps out east. It appeared that the punishment for their disobedience was now to be doled out.

Chapter Sixteen
Late 1944
Fighting for the Family

Carl tried to ignore the despair in his young daughter's behavior. He'd pretend not to hear the stifled cries in the dark of the night, as she'd lie with the envelope from her beloved. Inside she placed the delicate pink petals of the rose he had given to her as a last gift before his transport out. The paper would crackle as she would touch them ever so softly with her fingertips, awakening her parents despite her best efforts. There was nothing as bittersweet as Schmuel's final display of love and rebellion when he jumped over that fence into the Nazi garden filled with wild roses just behind the bakery to pick for her the "most perfect flower for his most perfect girl," as he said, ever so wickedly, while sifting through the bushes behind the high, locked, wrought-iron gate.

The petals of this rose Schmuel risked his life to obtain for Inge
that have been preserved to the present.

"But they'll punish you," was all she could think of to say in hushed tones.

While that was absolutely true, the fact that this man would willingly risk his life as a display of his intentions and affections for her, was something that would keep her hopeful and optimistic for however long it was until they would meet again. Or at least, that was what Carl hoped. He couldn't shake the tales of those young children from the Bialystok ghetto and the camps where those cattle cars were most likely destined. He knew now, almost for certain, that there was no chance for his daughter to ever see her boyfriend again. But he would never allow her to think that—not for a moment. Before passing through the room they shared In the Kavalier *Kaserne*, he straightened the photograph of Schmuel he encouraged Inge to display over her cot.

"Thanks, Dad," she stated softly, eyes still swollen from the night before when she was ravaged with dreams of Schmuel standing in line and starved half to death—unrecognizable as he resembled a skeleton far more than he did the proud and handsome man she had known. She had images of him with a shaved head while dressed all in rags. The air was thick with black smoke and ash. She woke up that night in a panic, and cried out. Her father ran beside her and held her in his assuring arms tightly.

"Don't worry about him," he'd say repeatedly, until her breathing slowed, "he is just working hard cleaning rubble from Allied airstrikes on German cities." He'd then pull her from him, to look directly in to her trusting, upturned eyes. The room was nearly pitch black except for a bit of glow from the searchlights entering though the narrow window above her bed.

"That is good news, don't you realize?" Carl rationalized with his distraught daughter. "It can only mean one thing—the Germans are losing, and this war will soon be over."

Without Schmuel in the camp any longer, Carl worried terribly about his daughter. Without him, Carl knew, Inge felt like her life no longer had any meaning; from one hour to the next, from one day to that succeeding it, she simply no longer had anything to look forward to. Those short dates before curfew were all she had to hope for; the only things that enabled her to get through the day.

The transports out of Theresienstadt were steadily increasing, and unlike the ones with Schmuel, these appeared to all be filled with those deemed "unproductive." In Theresienstadt, everyone seemed to be ranked on their usefulness. This meant that for those like Carl and Inge, fortunately, ranked high, while others, like his wife, ranked at the very bottom. While it wouldn't be all that surprising to find Marianne's name on a list, Carl nonetheless prayed that between he and his daughter's efforts, that his wife's absence from work was largely unnoticed. This fantasy was short-lived, however, the night he had to sit before his wife and daughter and explain to them that Marianne's name had been posted for the next outgoing transport.

"Isn't there someone you could speak to?" Inge pleaded with her father upon her single mattress. After all, he was very influential in the camp.

"No, it's impossible to bargain," Carl replied sternly.

Although he understood Inge's reasoning, he resented the presumption that he had any control over who went and who stayed in the camp. He had been overwrought with grief that he couldn't ever assist those under his care. They would come after him relentlessly, with tear-filled eyes, offering him tons of things they could never possibly fulfill, in the hopes that Carl could grant them the option of staying. His prying their desperate hands off his jacket sleeves would haunt him for the rest of his days.

"I'm sorry," he apologized to Inge for his harsh response.

She couldn't have known all he had suffered these past years. She was not unlike any other he'd deal with on a weekly basis who was trying to save someone they loved. He went on to explain, more patiently this time, that the time had come.

"Although I am a leader of sorts in this ghetto, it doesn't provide enough influence on this matter," he responded truthfully. "Even the 'Prominents' aren't exempt these days."

Some of them, too, had been transported along with those considered worthless. Carl's initial reservations when he declined that more elite position which included better housing and more food rations, now made some sense. Whereas everyone thought he was insane to decline such an opportunity, he was relieved his instincts had served him well. More and more of those "Prominents" who had received status positions or favorable treatment along with their families, had by then also been sent to the "east."

"Whatever happens, we must all stay together. That's what we decided from the time we first arrived," Carl reminded the women through clenched teeth. Inge and Marianne sat down before him upon their straw mattresses and hung their heads.

He couldn't believe what he was then about to order his daughter to do. "Inge, tomorrow, go to your factory supervisor, *Herr* Freiberger, and submit your written request to be included on the next transport."

She raised her chin and looked upon her father with shock. She stared at him silently with her mouth agape. Carl quickly averted his eyes. Even though it was their greatest chance of survival to stay together, even though he had promised himself all those years ago when his father passed away that he would never again ever let those he loved become separated, it took all his strength to utter those subsequent damning words to his beloved child.

"Carl, No!" Marianne began to argue before Carl abruptly interrupted her. He cleared his throat loudly for a moment, and loosened the tie around his neck before continuing with his head lowered. He could not bear to look either of them in the eyes.

"And I will go to the *Judenaeltester, Herr* Murmelstein," Carl continued, "and submit my request to be on it as well."

He then brusquely removed his jacket and shoes to turn in and sleep before anything more could be discussed. The conversation was over. After declaring that all those in his family would have to willingly be put on what was most likely to lead them to their deaths, his women remained dumbstruck and lingered in place for a while, before they did the same.

Perhaps Carl should have offered a wise word before resigning, perhaps he should have hugged them all closely through the night. But he couldn't. He remained the entirety of the evening just looking up hopelessly at the cracks in the ceiling above where he lay. And when the light of the early morning creaked through that tiny window, he hopped out of bed, quickly got dressed, and left for work. Not a word was spoken between any of them.

****

The very next morning, Inge went directly to her supervisor's office to do as her father decreed. She had tried to express to her father last night that she was actually in favor of his decision, as she couldn't imagine being separated from her parents. But he wouldn't allow her to speak last night or early this morning. She had never before seen her friendly and warm father ever before behave so detached and cold.

When she arrived at *Herr* Freiberger's office early that morning, he wasn't there, so she borrowed a pen and wrote a note requesting to be placed on her mother's same transport. Her hands were shaking as she folded the letter that was perhaps her death sentence.

Carl had instructed Inge the previous night to meet at the *Judenaeltester's* office, but it was virtually impossible to reach it. A mob had been forming; that is, all those who had been selected to be on that next transport, and who were trying to get more information. Carl spotted Inge's face in the crowd, and lifted his hand to gesture her to come over. Inge spotted him flagging her, and each began edging their way towards each other.

"Did you speak to *Herr* Freiberger?" Carl asked his daughter when they finally joined.

"No. He wasn't there, but I did leave a note on his desk."

129

"Good," Carl replied, and turned away, before Inge could detect the pain he was certain was held in his eyes. "I am still waiting for Murmelstein to come to his office so that I may leave my notice with him." Carl was standing right beside the door to the *Judenaeltester's* place of work.

Just then, Carl heard an increase of excitement and raised voices by the crowd. He turned his head and caught sight of a bullish built man pushing through the people. Benjamin Murmelstein then appeared right in front of where Carl now stood, with his ever-present scowl etched upon his brow. Through his small mouth and thin lips, he began shouting out at everyone to step further aside so he could make his way back into his office. People on all sides yelled questions at him, all of which he ignored, saying only, "Please be patient," as he had just met with the Nazi commandant.

It was then that Murmelstein noticed Carl, and whipped his round face towards him in his direction. Through squinted eyes he huffed, "Katz? What are you doing here? You're not on the list." He looked confused.

"I want to be with my wife," Carl replied, sounding adamant.

The *Judenaeltester,* obviously displeased on hearing that, quickly ushered Carl into his office. He had to leave Inge, however, outside, still obviously shaken from having left that paper with *Herr* Freiberger, the one that would seal her fate.

Before Carl even managed to take his seat, Murmelstein began arguing with him, "Katz, you can't volunteer to be on that transport. I need you here."

He was a man around the same age as Carl, and also used to being a community leader both before the war and while inside the ghetto. While many resented his rough and intolerant demeanor, as well as his ruthless implementation of Nazi policy, Carl understood all too well this man's conflict, and the love-hate relationship some in the camp would have for him. His actions were simply necessary to avoid the Jewish prisoners being exterminated. For this reason, Carl understood that the *Judenaeltester* in the room with him, relied on Carl to help him maintain things as best as possible and for as long as possible for those still remaining in the ghetto. He counted on people like Carl to make sure whatever meager food, or other amenities they received, was because they were productive. Moreover, their labor was valued by the Nazis. After all, their forced toil provided the Germans with jewelry, and uniforms, as well as other benefits at practically no cost—whatever it took to have this camp survive and remain operational.

"We all need you here to make sure that Theresienstadt continues to run productively, you know this," Murmelstein repeated once more when he realized that Carl wouldn't consider separating himself from his wife. The two men just sat for a few silent moments across from each other. Looking into one another's eyes with the shared understanding of the circumstances and the roles they were anointed to play, as only these two men could.

With compassion in his sorrow-filled, blue eyes, Carl explained further, "We decided a long while ago that we would all endure the same fate together whatever it may be." He then exhaled loudly, as the guilt pressed upon the center of his chest. "Besides, my daughter, Inge, has already left a note on *Herr* Freiberger's desk. Please see that all of our names are on that transport list."

For several bated breaths, the *Judenaeltester* reclined behind his desk and pondered what to do. His gaze remained fastened upon Carl, while he linked his fingers and rested them upon his belly. He let out a deep sigh, and sat back up in his chair, when stating his proclamation, "I will see that Marianne's name will be removed from the list."

"No—that's not necessary, I was not asking for that favor, I actually..." Carl hesitated. *Did he misunderstand?* Carl wasn't bluffing, nor was he using any sort of negotiation tactic. After all, what if—God forbid—Murmelstein would then be forced by some quota to send someone else in Marianne's place? No, he was the one who had to be placed on that list.

"Nonsense. We can't lose you. Not now," the *Judenaeltester* explained. "We would suffer too many repercussions from your loss. Especially all those under your care." Murmelstein, although having a far from diplomatic reputation, somehow exactly understood Carl's dilemma and reasoning, not to mention what Carl needed to hear to convince him to stay. It worked, for Carl immediately exhaled in relief at the good news that he could simultaneously keep his family and all those thousands of people directly under his care from harm. But before Katz could take even a moment to thank the man before him, Murmelstein issued him a stern warning that Inge still remained in great danger.

"You had better hope that *Herr* Freiberger hasn't seen Inge's letter, for he may not think she is as valuable as you are to me," he warned.

Carl jolted up in his seat, and thanked Murmelstein with a hurried, but sincere handshake, before rushing out the door of his office. As soon as he spotted his daughter, who remained right where he left her minutes before, with both determination and dread, he looked straight into her eyes.

"You must get that note back," he declared. But Inge just stared back at her father, trying to understand why he was ordering her to do it.

"*Mutti* is off the list," he explained. "You've got to get your note back from Freiberger." Yet still she stood there in a frozen state of panic. Her blue-green eyes wide open and still.

131

"RUN!" Carl shouted at her, as all self-control and resolve left him. It worked, as it snapped her out of her trance, and restored her senses. Inge spun around and quickly ran down the hallway. Carl watched after her as her heels kicked up the back of her skirt, and she grabbed at the wall's bend to stabilize herself as she turned the corner and out of Carl's view.

With his back pressed against the wall, Carl felt his knees give out on him as all strength left his body. He slid down onto the floor, and pressed his hands hard against the dirty travertine. His head felt light, and he tried to focus upon a speck of dirt, desperately attempting to maintain his consciousness. His heart pounded through the front of his sweat-stained dress shirt, and his vision fluctuated with each thud as it beat. He removed his hat, and loosened the binding of his tie from around his neck. The other inmates, still all gathered around the outside of the office, would bump and stumble over Carl as they continued to seek information from the Elder, but neither he nor they gave it any regard. Each was too focused on far greater matters than a man slumped upon the floor in grief. After all, everyone there this morning was dealing with matters of life and death.

Several more minutes passed, and Carl forced himself—somehow—to get back onto his feet. He couldn't let Inge find him like this. No matter what was to be the determination of the family's fate in the next few minutes—he needed to be strong, for her. He remained leaning against the wall however, as his knees trembled far too intensely for him to be confident in their stability. He saw her frame just about to turn the corner back to meet him, and he quickly took the end of his tie to wipe at the sweat collected in beads upon his forehead. He couldn't bear to see her face, and what expression it bore. However, after a few moments passed, when he saw the tips of her shoes placed directly in front of his, he knew he had to look up at her and accept his fate—whatever that was.

As he lifted his gaze from her feet, he saw that her hands were hugging her torso. Her whole body was visibly trembling. Her face was pale and her eyes were wide open. They, too, were shaking. He didn't know what it felt like to have his heart stop beating, but he thought it happened in that moment. Everything became still and quiet, and an intense ringing flooded his head.

What have I done? he repeated in his mind over and over again. *My darling, Inge. No.*

Through his spinning thoughts, he heard her speaking at him, but he couldn't make sense of any of the words. He just couldn't get past the hatred he suddenly felt for himself in this moment. Instead of caring for her, he was the reason she was going to die. *How could I have done such a thing?*

Chapter Seventeen
February, 1945
The Innocent Children

In an affluent home in a nice part of town, *Gestapo* Agent Bruno Nette all but ran to his front entrance. Today he was expecting a very special visitor. Upon opening the door, Nette took a moment to look upon his youngest son standing before him on the stoop. The agent could see in the boy's still-childlike face that war had certainly taken some toll on him. Yes, his eyes undoubtedly held the unmistakable knowing of someone who has lived—of someone who has seen things. Looking him over now, Bruno Nette couldn't help but feel a sense of pride that this perfect Aryan specimen was born of his own flesh and blood. Alfred Nette was tall, strong, and classically handsome. Along with his fair complexion, and blonde hair, he was also gifted his father's attributes of self-discipline, determination, and a strong sense of duty to his country.

Still dressed in his soldier's clothing underneath a belted overcoat, Nette wondered if he ought to hug the child. It had been quite some time since Alfred left to fight the Allies.

"Guten Tag," Nette's son said formally, resolving the matter with an extended hand.

"Good to have you home, son," Bruno stated resolutely. Nette grabbed at his son's hand firmly and looked him straight back in his eyes. Yes, that was a far more comfortable greeting than an embrace for these two.

Nette then had him step in from the cold, and gestured to his son to grab a seat in the parlor. His second wife stood politely outside the entrance of the room.

"Welcome home, Alfred," Marie stated uncomfortably while wringing her hands.

"Guten Tag, Tante Mieze." Alfred stated these words through pressed lips. He could barely bring himself to look at her. After all, she was the reason he spent all those years of his childhood penniless and starving after his father abandoned them. Alfred could not so soon forget how Marie—or *Tante* Mieze—as he was instructed to call her, had stolen his father away, and with him, all their resources. While she spent the day enjoying good fare and parading around in fur coats, Alfred's mother suffered backbreaking labor and menial tasks to support the family after his dad left them with nothing. Yet no matter how much his mother toiled, it never seemed enough to put an

adequate amount of food on the table. However, this current wife kept the pantry door locked, and had her new husband beat his kids when they snuck in for sustenance. Until Alfred became a soldier, he had practically forgotten what it was like to go to bed with a full belly.

"I'll go make some tea," Marie stated. Before she hastily left the room, Alfred couldn't help but notice the enormous diamond ring upon her finger. He wondered if it was a new gift from his father.

"How long can you stay home?" Bruno turned his attention back over to his son, attempting to divert the blatant hostility in the room.

"Not long at all. This is only a short leave. They need me back out there," his son declared strongly, leaning back into the armrest of the upholstered chair. He looked about the room at his father's lavish furnishings—a seized spoil from a prominent Jewish family. With the extravagant area rugs and heavy draperies, it was certainly a far cry from the small space in the basement he had shared with his mother.

"You must listen to me," Nette declared in hushed tones, and leaned forward towards his son. "I know a man—a farmer. Now, I already discussed it with him, and he'd be willing to hide you in his barn until the war ends."

"Are you joking?" Alfred shot up in his chair. A look of disgust narrowed his eyes, and curled his lips at his father's suggestion.

"Don't worry about it," Bruno attempted to explain.

"I will not desert Germany. Not in its darkest hour! *Where is your loyalty?*" Alfred raised his voice. Marie was walking into the room with a tray of cookies, but upon hearing the escalating discussion, she decided it better to hurriedly exit back out.

"Listen, Alfred, I don't think you understand. Germany is losing the war. It is only a matter of time. Have you seen Bremen? It's all in shambles—just like every other city in Germany. You must think with your head. Now, go to this farmer," he said while pulling a folded piece of paper from the inside of his jacket pocket with the name and address, "have him burn your uniform, and just hide out there. No one will know."

While Nette never pretended to be a loving, attentive, nor caring father, here was an opportunity to do something right. While he fell out of love with his late wife, Alfred's mother, she was actually a good woman. She didn't deserve how hard he'd beat her for all those years. Here was his chance to honor her memory by finally taking care of their youngest son.

Alfred abruptly stood up from the chair, and walked directly to the front door. As he opened it, his father called after him.

"Alfred? Where are you going?"

With disdain in his eyes, Alfred looked back at the man he detested—at the man he held responsible for his mom's suicide. At the individual he blamed for being haunted with visions of his mother hanging from her neck by a beam in their living room.

"You should be denounced to the *Gestapo* for what you have just said," Alfred exclaimed before slamming the door behind him.

Later that day, Nette tried to shake off the wretched feeling of his interaction with his son. He couldn't let his mind go to the thought of possibly losing a child. Oddly, in that moment, as he walked to his office, he was flooded with thoughts of Katz. He wondered if, by now, he had suffered the loss of his child. *Yes, what was her name, again? Inge?* Yes, that's right. Inge must surely be gone by now. *I wonder, however, if she managed to die before her father?*

Once seated at his desk, Nette did what he always did to take his mind off of things, he buried himself in his work. Nette pondered the Katzes' fates as he leafed through the names on the papers atop his desk. Now that the war was ending, it was time to finish off every last bit of business. Since he was put in charge of the *Judendezernat* (Jewish Department) of Bremen, that meant getting rid of any remaining Jews—more specifically, those who did not directly serve his interest. In this case, this included two little girls ages two and five, as well as a seven-year-old boy. He needed to finalize the details and paperwork of these Jewish children to go on the next cattle car, unaccompanied, to the concentration camp Theresienstadt.

Chapter Eighteen
May, 1945
How to Face the Day?

"Vati!" Inge now yelled at her father, after he didn't respond the first few times. "Did you hear me?"

Standing outside of Murmelstein's office, still propped against the wall, Carl finally brought himself to look Inge directly into her eyes. *What perfect thing can I say or do to make something—anything—better in this moment? Is it even possible? When nothing can ever be right for us again?* he lamented, as the reality that he was the cause of his daughter's demise left him paralyzed with grief.

"Vati! Look. Look what I have in my hand." Carl tore his gaze from hers as he did as he was told. There in his daughter's delicate fingers, held right before his eyes, was a folded piece of paper.

"Is that…" he dared ask her.

"Yes. I got my note requesting I be put on the transport back from *Herr* Freiberger's desk. He never saw it. We can all stay. We are safe!" she stated firmly to her father.

****

Life for the Katz family in the days immediately following that fateful transport returned, more or less, to the way it had been. Except for another change in residence, and yet another new job for Carl with much more responsibility. He was now assigned by the *Aeltester,* Murmelstein, to the role of *Innere Verwaltung* (Central Management). He was now responsible for overseeing what went on in all the buildings in the ghetto where Jews were housed. Because of these responsibilities, the family was moved to the Magdeburg Barracks.

That was the very same building where all the Jewish officials and managers appointed to run Theresienstadt as well as the "Prominents" were housed. Because many higher-ranking inmates had recently been shipped out on transports, numerous vacancies needed to be filled, and that was the reason Carl was selected. It was definitely an improvement in living conditions for Carl and his family. In place of their single bare room in the Kavalier Barracks, they now had considerably more space. There was even a couch and a table. But, most importantly for his daughter, she now had her very own bed all to herself.

These few months remaining in separate living quarters certainly likened their chances for survival. And by May 1945, nearly three years since they entered under the archway of the sign that read, *"Arbeit Macht Frei,"* they all managed not to succumb to any of the diseases that ran rampant throughout the camp from cramped living conditions. And on an evening when they were fortunate enough to be able to share some extra bread from Inge's new job working in a bakery, they suddenly heard the unmistakable sound of machine guns firing. The loud noise resounded through the courtyard. All three of them immediately jumped up and rushed to the hallway. Likewise, most of the others in that barracks did the same. Soon, those hallways were packed with people, all pushing to peer out the open archways facing the courtyard, to see what was going on.

Voices could be heard outside of people screaming and shouting, and machine gun blasts from round after round of gunfire kept roaring away. The light from the explosives burned their eyes. Carl then realized what was happening. He did not share it with the women, but he had understood in recent weeks that it was the intentions of the Nazis to murder them all. In these recent days, he learned from the new transports of inmates that mass extermination was part of the Nazi plan from the very beginning.

These latest inmates, dressed in rags, smelling of death, and stumbling about like corpses, entered as a result of the Germans emptying their Eastern European camps to avoid the Allied liberation forces. The Nazis sent their prisoners on death marches to other camps, from places called Buchenwald and Gross-Rosen, to those closer to Germany, like Theresienstadt. Approximately 15,000 such prisoners arrived there in the last weeks of April, almost doubling the population in the camp. The prisoners, appearing more like skeletons than humans, were in very poor mental and physical shape, and, like the Bialystok children, refused disinfection fearing they would be gassed. They spoke of these camps where clouds of dust from the burning bodies the Nazis had deemed "evidence" blocked out the early morning sun. They were all so thin and frail, that it seemed a slight gust of wind could easily topple their remains. They were not only starving, but also infected with all sorts of diseases, like lice and typhus. Carl found them particularly terrifying, perhaps, for no other reason that they lost all semblance of humanity.

Carl, rather than becoming overwhelmed with their horrific appearances and information, just focused, instead, on the reports that these people were moved there to avoid the invading Allied forces. That meant that the war was clearly almost at its end! He just had to keep everyone alive for only a little while longer!

But, as the roaring of enemy fire became deafening the closer it came to their doorway, he placed his arms around his daughter and wife, and said, rather solemnly, "Let's go back to our room and wait."

137

Barely a word was spoken between them, as his wife and daughter did exactly what he instructed. There was nothing left for them to do. No great act of determination, or grit, or adaptability, or faith, was going to save them from a gun pointed directly between their eyes. Unfortunately, they all understood that this was the beginning of their end. And so they remained, sitting quietly, just the three of them, about their small table and holding each other's hands, as the deafening gunfire and barrage of screams continued unabated.

"This may be our final hour," Carl announced with tears welling up in his eyes, "but there is no other way than this that I would rather spend it than being with the both of you."

Chapter Nineteen
April, 1945
Fighting in the Cities

September 18 1944, 206 Lancaster bombers of the Royal Air Force
attacked Bremen's center of town and destroyed all of it
within a mere 20 minutes. Photo:Magnus Iken, photoarchive SKB-Bremen.

Gestapo agent, Bruno Nette's, face grew hot before the impenetrable flames of the raging fire, yet still he remained. The air was thick with black smoke, and the fumes of burning gasoline started to make his head grow light. He reached into his left breast pocket, and removed the handkerchief square folded ever so neatly from its place. Shaking it out, he pressed the cool linen up against his mouth and nose. This prevented him from inhaling any of the ash of the burning documents. He sighed to himself, and his heart felt heavy at the loss. *After all these years, after all this work. Everything I had dedicated my every waking moment to in these past few years, reduced to piles of ash,* he lamented, feeling quite sorry for himself. Another agent then came up behind him, and placed a strong hand on his shoulder.

"Nette, you need to step back. You're too close!" Wilhelm Parchmann shouted into his ear in order to be heard over the roaring of the flames.

Nette probably should have done as he was advised, yet he remained steadfast. Those shaming last words his son spoke to him ran through his head: *"Where is your loyalty?"* he scolded his father. *"We cannot desert Germany in its darkest hour!"* Despite Nette's outrage at Alfred's insolence, Nette was proud of him. He had often thought he was perhaps too harsh with Alfred during the early years of the boy's life. He certainly didn't hold back as he struck him repeatedly with the end of his belt, for he'd be damned to raise a weakling of a son. Perhaps, however, he did too well a job of it. In this instance, Alfred should have accepted defeat and hid out in that barn for the remainder of the war. It was only a few short weeks after his son returned to the frontlines, that he was shot dead—just as Nette had forewarned. He was not yet eighteen. In his son's memory, Nette was determined to stand with Germany, just as Alfred had wanted.

A large covered truck pulled in front of them, and his comrades all began scurrying towards it. They appeared to him like little children, running away in a heated game of Cat and Mouse. Special Agent Nette shook his head in disappointment at their behavior. Why, just days ago, he and the other Nazis were posting fliers on every lamppost, or else shoving them into the palms of the Hitler Youth still too young to serve, and not fortunate enough to have taken shelter in the Black Forest. These papers declared it everyone's duty to stand fast and fight for their country. Yet here was the last of the magnificent, superior, Aryan race—scampering for their lives while the children, elderly, and women of their city fought the very war they were now abandoning.

It was shocking how quickly life could change. How did he and his men go from world domination to cowardly surrender in a mere matter of months? Why, it wasn't all that long ago that he acquired his position of utmost authority. Up until a few weeks ago no one would dare deny him any command; whether it be cognac, cigarettes, suits, false testimonies, divorce, anything at all! Within a moment of his request, all orders would be satisfied. In fact, he most enjoyed being the man who decided who was deemed worthy to live or die. It was—now this may sound a bit grandiose—like he was some sort of living God in this city. *Is that too large of a statement?* Perhaps so. *Perhaps I ought to be a bit more modest,* he considered. But… if one were to objectively think about it, he *is* part of a group that is ruling the world. He caught himself in his musings, and couldn't help but grimace at the sad realization. He corrected himself—that *was* ruling the world.

As the other *Gestapo* agents jumped into the back of that wagon, all records and evidence of their devious dealings burned behind them. The canvas tarp of the vehicle was hastily pulled down to better conceal their identities. Even the most heavily feared Agent Parchmann, was among those who couldn't flee the falling city fast enough.

"Nette! Come with us!" Parchmann yelled, poking his head out from the back of the truck. The driver fired up the engine. Nette didn't dignify his call with a response. Parchmann then, ashamed, pulled his head back from view.

The truck's tires screeched over the dirt and rubble of the once immaculate city streets of Bremen, Germany. It was hard to discern the road from the dumps of debris from toppled buildings as the truck made its escape. Piles and piles of wreckage were all one could see in every direction. Everything else that could possibly be burned was now burning. Wartime bombings had begun hitting the city more and more since 1940. However, they were initially delegated to the port and on shipyards where the U-boats were docked, but since the evening of September 18, 1944, 206 Lancaster bombers of the Royal Air Force attacked the center of town and destroyed it all within a mere twenty minutes. By the time the roaring propellers of those silver birds retreated back into the clouds, 2,070 buildings had been destroyed, 618 civilians were left dead, 1,193 were wounded, and 30,000 were left homeless.

Everyone thought Nette was crazy to stay behind. But the agent felt he was far cleverer than the others. When he saw that Germany was fast losing the war these past months, he began doing favors to those full-blooded Jews, converts married to Aryans, and the Jews married to Aryans still residing in the city. He offered them his protection, and kept them off the transports out to Theresienstadt during Hitler's rush to exterminate the Jewish race, also known as his "Final Solution." There were dozens of residents of Bremen that swore they would vouch to the Allies about the kindness Nette showed to the Jewish people. Furthermore, there would be no one left alive to contradict his best informants, the convert, Karl Bruck's, nor any of the other Jews' testimonies, and all damning evidence of the true insidious role he played as a *Gestapo* agent was being incinerated in the yard just beside the *Gestapo* headquarters.

Now standing there alone, he looked around as he waited for the fire to finish consuming the little that still remained. However, there was nothing much to see. The Allied Infantry already left the majority of Bremen's beautiful, historic, and stately buildings as grotesque skeletons looming overhead. It appeared almost as if they were so thin and frail, that a slight gust of wind could easily topple their remains. There also seemed to be a perpetual cloud of dust looming in the air persistently invading his lungs and stinging his eyes. *Those animals. Where is your respect? Where is your honor? These are cities, not military strongholds!* he uttered to himself. Catching sight of the tops of

141

shoes in where the city center used to stand, he cursed at those responsible. *These are not soldiers you are murdering, these are innocent civilians!*

Later that day, when his work was done, he took his wife, Marie, to sleep in their shelter. Yet when he closed his eyes, he'd be startled awake by the heavy sound of gunfire and exploding bombs from the ample fighting just outside the city lines. And yet, the next morning, as he did every prior morning, he'd awaken thinking it was all a horrible dream. He only had to look outside, however, to see the clouds of dust blocking out the early morning sun.

Nette had a decisive plan about what he would do the day the invaders would ultimately enter the city: he'd wait on the steps of the *Gestapo* headquarters proudly. He'd wear that fine three-piece suit, the one with the vest, which the Jewish tailor crafted for him in exchange for his life. Or perhaps, better yet, he should instead dress in the moss green policeman uniform to appear as though he were of a lower rank. And while those arrogant, fresh-faced, young British boys held their rifles at the ready, marching through town in rows, smug faces gleaming, as the deafening clanking of the Sherman tank chains barreled over the fallen rubble of his once majestic city, he would face them with his chin held high.

Nette never imagined that he would have to orchestrate his surrender to those subordinate forces. He never imagined that the great German army could lose the war. However, it was now time to face the reality.

Chapter Twenty
Fall, 1945
The Guilt of a Survivor

Bremen's Jewish Community Center at 17 Osterdeich.
Jewish life took root again there after the war
in what was a residence requisitioned by the Allied forces.

Carl darted up from unconsciousness to the sounds of gunfire and screams. It was dark all around him, and he could not make out anything definitive from the shapes of the shadows in the room. Sweat soaked through his nightshirt, and his breathing was so rapid and shallow, that it made his chest ache. Confused, he jumped to his feet and crouched against the wall for protection. But after a few minutes of silence and inactivity, he realized that all was still. It was only a dream. A bit embarrassed, he then shot up to his feet. It was nearly four months since the fighting at Theresienstadt took place. That is, four months since the Soviets liberated the camp, yet still he was plagued with this recurring nightmare.

On the fifth of May, 1945, the Soviet troops approached from the east to head towards Prague on their way to confront the Germans. When the *SS* realized they couldn't hold out, Commandant of the camp, Rahm, and all his guards in Theresienstadt, tried to flee. Some scattered German military units that remained clashed with the Soviet forces in the vicinity of the ghetto. On May 8, 1945, the Soviets officially liberated approximately 30,000 inmates.

Their liberators cleared out all of the Germans and assumed official responsibility of the ghetto. As all of the inmates lined Theresienstadt's streets to welcome their rescuers, the Russian soldiers marched through in orderly rows along with their military vehicles. Everyone shouted, "Thank you!" and cheered them on. Music played, and young couples danced in the streets.

Carl, shrugging off that horrid evening when he anticipated his execution, went to get his wristwatch laying at the side of his mattress. *It must be nearing morning*, he figured, holding it to the light of the window. He read the face—it was nearly 5 a.m. *Good enough*, he reasoned, as he went to splash his face with water, and get ready for the day.

It was still very dark out as he left his residence to head over to his office at 17 *Osterdeich.* The cool early morning air and brisk walk was just what he needed to clear his head. He hated his new job. The endless lists of names of those who hadn't survived piled up in stacks on his desk. The shrill jingles of the telephone ringing never failed to make his heart stop. It seemed that the calls made to ask if he had any information on missing relatives were endless. He despised the sounds of the voices on the other end of the line as he told them of the definite deaths. The grief, the screams, the sobs he was subjected to as he confirmed their worst fears—that yes, their mother, their child, their brother, or else their friend were, in fact, all murdered.

At least the office space was beautiful and clean and unharmed from the Allied assaults. It had only been a couple weeks since he left the concentration camp, Theresienstadt, and he was still adjusting to civilian life back home in Bremen. After three years of horrific living conditions, starvation, and death in masses, he wished he could enjoy his surroundings more. The Allies relocated him to a beautiful area of town, on *Georg-Groening Str.* #80, and only a short walk from the magnificent, bucolic Buergerpark. He couldn't remember the last time he had seen trees or flowers, or smelled the fresh air of a garden. He'd walk those familiar paths of its grounds daily, but as much as he tried, his body just couldn't appreciate it. He hoped it was just a temporary condition, for it was experiences like these that made him contemplate why he bothered surviving if he could never again enjoy life.

Turning the corner to his destination, a large Star of David graced the entrance of the stately new home of Bremen's Jewish Community Center. He felt his chest swell at its pristine face. There was no graffiti, nor fliers, nor brown shirts there to defile it. There were no slogans denying a Jew's entrance, or any threats at all upon it. *Is this possible? Is the Nazi presence really all removed from the city? Am I really free to live as a Jew once again?* If the clean face of this estate were any indication, then yes, it appeared so. This then made Carl smile a bit to himself. Maybe he would be okay after all. He then passed the stoop of its enormous, wooden, arched doorways. He went through this stage of emotions every morning. He couldn't help but distrust that life could ever again be good.

Interior entrance of the new JCC, 1945.

Once through, he passed by the magnificent wide, oak stairways, and the grand, carved, wooden mantles of the home's multiple fireplaces. His footsteps echoed loudly as he crossed the herringbone patterned flooring towards his office. No one else had yet reported to work. Grabbing a seat behind the desk allotted to him, he looked through the papers that he hadn't yet gotten to the day before. He was desperately searching for information on his family. So many were still missing. He was conflicted with wanting to know what happened to everyone, yet scared to death to find out. With the exception of a few interfaith couples who were sent to the camp only a couple of months before liberation, it seemed that so very few from Bremen survived. *That can't be possible, can*

145

it? After all, he didn't return to Bremen for nearly four months after its liberation. He insisted on staying behind to ensure that everyone under his care was well enough to make their own journeys back home. Perhaps Moritz and Ruthie and the rest of the Cohen family were doing this as well? Perhaps his sister was also too busy caring for others, and he'd hear good news from them any day now?

A friendly face poked his head into Carl's office a couple hours after he arrived.

"Carl!" Karl Bruck greeted him merrily, behind circular glasses, and a broad smile.

"Good morning!" Katz answered happily; he was truly pleased to have his former colleague working alongside him. Carl was so grateful that this man, a Jew who was converted and married an Aryan, was somehow able to be spared from going to the camps. He was truly a friend, as proved when he was the only one from home who was willing to house the Katzes after liberation. Even though *Herr* Bruck didn't know their condition, or whether they were infected with diseases, he selflessly offered to have them live in his home with his wife and two young children for the first two weeks of his return.

Karl Bruck at work in the office of the JCC, 1945.

"Get any sleep last night?" Bruck inquired with concern.

"Nah, not yet. But I'm sure once I get tired enough, I'll have to." Carl shrugged.

"Well, let's hope so," his friend responded with empathy weighing in his small, morose eyes. He turned to leave when Carl called out after him in the softest of voices.

"Are the Americans leaving you alone these days?" Carl whispered in a hushed tone. Oddly enough, Bruck was under heavy investigation by the US Intelligence occupying Bremen. They'd frequently make unannounced visits to his home. They suspected him of having secret alliances, and believed he had served as an informant for the Nazis. "Absurd," Carl would often remark in response to the allegations at questioning. He was even working at the community center to aid in displaced people, and the distribution of rations! *What sort of Nazi sympathizer would ever do that?*

"Unfortunately, no," Bruck proclaimed. "They always show up at my door at the oddest times. But what can I do? Thank you again for testifying on my behalf. I am very grateful," he replied solemnly, before his lean frame exited the room.

The offices of JOINT (American Jewish Joint Distribution Committee) and HIAS (Hebrew Immigrant Aid Society) were set up on the main floor of the spacious, Allied requisitioned, three-story building, as well as a synagogue. With the main activity at this time centered on reconnecting survivors with family and friends, Carl was also in the fortunate position of being the first to learn of any survivors. One such happy occasion was to take place this very afternoon. Richard Frank, the head of the household of the Frank family that lived with the Katzes in the *Judenhaus* was coming to see him today! While the whole family was so pleasant, Carl really couldn't wait to see his little clown, August. Why, he must be ten years old by now! Would he even be able to recognize him after all these years? Carl desperately hoped that whatever he lived through in the Minsk Concentration Camp didn't erase his joyful spirit or that impish grin. For Carl, that little boy was such a ray of light in an otherwise bleak and dark time.

"You're being called down, sir," his secretary, Martha, stated as she broke him away from his contemplations.

"What is it now?" he asked impatiently. He was used to being the mediator to those who never felt they were given enough food, or by those non-Jews who felt they too deserved rations because they had a best friend who was a Jew, etc.

"It's Lothar Schustermann, he has a question for you," the friendly young secretary responded, as she shot him a polite smile. "He's probably just wondering if Inge will be attending the dance this weekend," she said and giggled, before leaving the office.

The young, good natured Martha was an acquaintance of his daughter, and always tormented Inge about all the suitors Inge had pursuing her. She'd often tease, "If it's not the Americans, it's the English, if it's not the soldiers, it's the local boys—how about leaving some men for the rest of us single girls!"

147

The office of the secretaries. Martha is seated on the far right.

But poor Inge only had her heart set on one man. She even worked alongside her father so that she'd have faster access to locating family members like Ruthie, as well as lost persons like her Schmuel. Even with all the reports of the horrors of the war, and the very certainty that he couldn't have possibly survived the camps "out east," she still refused to give her heart to another. While Inge placated her parents and friends by going to dances at the synagogue with one of the American soldiers, there was no doubt to anyone that her heart only belonged to another.

"I'll go down and meet with Lothar now. Thanks, Martha. Did he say if it was regarding his father?"

Martha shook her head "no."

Carl wondered what the boy needed. He was happy to help with any request. Lothar was transported out of Bremen with Carl to Theresienstadt along with his father, Benno. However, the boy's dad was shipped out of the camp, and no one had heard from him since. All assumed he didn't survive. But maybe he had some good news?

"Lothar! How are you this morning? Did you get everything you need?" Carl asked with a smile and pat upon the shoulder after he met with him downstairs on the main level.

"*Guten Morgen* (Good morning), *Herr* Katz," Lothar replied while holding the bowls and papers filled with Velveeta cheese and other grocery items he was entitled to. "And how is your daughter? Is Inge here today?" he asked cheerfully, while looking around.

Carl sighed. He had hoped Lothar had news of his father, but it was just as Martha had suspected, he was just inquiring after his daughter.

"She'll be here a little later. Come back this afternoon," Carl responded impatiently. He turned to retreat back to his office, a bit annoyed with the unnecessary interruption.

Lothar Schustermann and Inge dancing at a party hosted by the Katzes in June, 1946.

"Uh, one other thing," Lothar called after him. Carl turned back around to face him. "My mother, Johanna, was wondering if there were some extra rations she could have because, you know, she is a widow to a Jew."

Carl felt his face burn up at this request. He sensed the anger begin to boil deep within the depths of his gut. That mother of his, Johanna Schustermann, was no grieving widow. She, an Aryan, divorced her husband when it no longer served her station well. Once she acquired all his belongings, as well as retracted his protection under Nazi law,

Benno and their son were transported right to the camps. Carl wouldn't soon forget what she had done to his friend, nor of those words Benno spoke behind tear-laden eyes as they were leaving the Bremen train station to Theresienstadt together: *"I hope she burns down along with that house she stole from me."* In his friend's honor, he responded swiftly to Lothar's request.

"No." Carl, with his hands now held in fists, left to go back upstairs. He already felt a bit remorseful about how short-tempered he was to the boy. He didn't deserve that. He'd be sure to make it up to him later.

"She won't like that answer from you," Lothar stated uncomfortably at Carl's back.

Carl paused in his steps. *Is this a threat?* It certainly sounded like a threat.

After all these years of living as a Jew under Nazi rule, it would take a whole lot more than a frightened boy and a shrew of a woman to intimidate him. Carl then regained his pace, but perhaps stomped a little louder than usual up those stairs. Carl had no patience for women like Johanna. Now that the war was over, suddenly everyone claimed to be either descendants of Jews, or friends of Jews, or saviors of Jews, or worst of all, the grieving widows of Jews. Perhaps if more time had passed, or if his work didn't involve the constant reminder of how many innocent Jewish lives were killed by the Aryans, then he would have a little bit more patience when dealing with opportunists like Johanna. Alas, this was not the case.

Carl walked to the large paned window in his office. Resting his arm upon the sill, he looked out at the panoramic view of the Weser River. A few leaves had just started to turn on the trees lining the banks. People rode on the adjacent trails on their bicycles, while others walked hand in hand. He wondered if they were reunited couples who found each other after suffering years of horrors. This made Carl smile. Few were as lucky as he. He had not yet heard of one other family unit where all the members survived. Looking out upon the tranquility of the water as it reflected the early morning sun, Carl was reminded of how blessed he truly was. This helped to calm him before whatever ugliness he would be faced with in the coming day. It was not enough, however, to prepare him for what he was about to hear.

Just after lunch, his secretary alerted Carl that his friend, Richard Frank, was here to see him. Carl didn't wait for Richard to enter, but instead rushed to the door to greet him. It was hard to recognize Richard. He was emaciated, and his skin had a sallow pallor. His eyes seemed to have recessed into their sockets under his full, dark brows, and there was no shine or luster permeating. The grin Richard flashed upon seeing Carl was deeply lined and forced. After a warm and enduring handshake, Carl looked around for little August, but he was nowhere to be seen.

150

"Where's August—I mean, Rolf? He didn't come in with you here today?" To say that Carl was disappointed not to see his little buddy would be a vast understatement. He had been looking forward to this reunion for years. He even had a special magic trick in mind that he was going to perform for the child. Carl hoped Rolf hadn't yet outgrown magic. But upon mention of the child's name, Richard almost collapsed in on himself. His narrow shoulders hunched forward, and he swayed a bit on his feet. Carl rushed to lend him a steady arm.

"Are you okay? Do you need a seat?" Carl then took Richard's arm over his own shoulders, and while leading him to a chair in his office, called out to Martha, "Please, get him a glass of water. Now."

Once seated, Martha placed a drink in his hand. Carl waited a few moments while his friend held a hand to his head. Richard was so frail, and his once dark curly hair was still cropped short against his scalp, as per camp protocol. He didn't appear at all unlike those Carl cared for in Theresienstadt. Even though liberation was several months ago, some inmates had a harder road to recovery than others.

"Do you have anything stronger?" Richard inquired, with a raised glass.

Carl soon had a pit in his stomach, and thought it best to prepare a drink for himself as well. He didn't know what Richard was going to say, but he sensed it could be nothing good.

Fence surrounding the Minsk ghetto. Unknown source.

151

Richard's hand trembled, and tears leaked from the corners of his eyes. He had not yet even said a word. Carl's heart sunk. *Where was Rolf?* was all he could wonder, as images of his bright eyes shining beneath that mop of dark curls danced before his mind.

"Me and my oldest son, Gunther—you remember Gunther, right?" Carl nodded his head, of course he did. Richard then continued, "Well, we were assigned to a heavy work detail, while Rolf and my wife did light work, and my middle son, Hans, also had it pretty easy." He broke away into a smile, and shook his head a little bit. "Now I know Rolf was your favorite, but that Hans is also quite the charmer." Carl's chest grew tight at the past tense used when he spoke of Rolf. *It must have been a misstatement. Right?*

"Hans instantly became everyone's friend—even to the Nazis! They loved him! When he wasn't pushing around lorries, they had him polishing their boots. That whole time, Hans had them in stitches with jokes and stories—if you can imagine that." The smile suddenly left Richard's lips, and his face grew dark with shadows. "If it weren't for Hans and how well he got on with them, the two of us surely would never have survived."

"What do you mean the two of you?" Carl blurted out against every better instinct. He didn't want to hear more, yet he needed to. He needed confirmation that Rolf was okay. *If the guards liked Hans enough to spare his life, then surely they must have fallen in love with Rolf! No one on earth could possibly resist his impish grin—not even a monstrous Nazi,* Carl rationalized as he tried to soothe his fears. He got up to pour himself and his friend a little more Schnapps.

"But one day, Gunther wasn't feeling well. So Hans offered to come with me to cover his brother's shift—you know, so no one would know he was missing." Richard's hands started to then shake so violently that he had to place his replenished cup down. He started fidgeting nervously, and began rocking in his seat, as he continued. "Usually, after work is done, we'd go back to the ghetto—what is now called the Minsk Concentration Camp—but on this night, things were done differently."

"How so?" Carl inquired, all the while nursing his near-empty glass.

"Well, we had to stay out overnight. But we could hear everything. Carl, I heard *everything!*" Richard raised his voice, as his crying then became uncontrollable. Carl didn't know what to do.

"Richard," Carl stated softly, with his fingertips pressed hard into the grooves of his cup, "what did you hear?"

"She was screaming my name! I could hear her scream for me but I couldn't get to her!" Richard blurted out, spittle landing upon his chin.

"Your wife?" Carl asked, placing a supportive hand upon his friend's trembling arm.

"Yes, my wife! Of course, my wife! I'm sorry, I'm sorry, I don't mean to yell at you," he apologized, while wiping his chin with the back of his sleeve in embarrassment.

"Of course, don't even think of that," Carl said dismissively, while handing him a napkin. "Richard, why was she screaming?"

"They had these wagons driven into the camp. While Hans and I were locked outside of the ghetto, they piled everyone into them, and then they gassed them. Everyone. That night they gassed my wife, my oldest son, Gunther... and my little one, Rolf." Richard took the napkin and placed it over his face to hide the tears flowing down his cheeks, to hide the anger glowing red upon his face, and more than anything else, to hide the shame that he didn't do something—anything—to save them. "My boy—he was so small. He wasn't even seven!"

Carl felt himself grow numb. It was all simply unimaginable. His hearing clouded over, and he thought he then heard Richard describe that there was thumping on the walls of those wagons, because some had survived the poisonous gas, and that is why the guards then threw in grenades to finish the job, but he couldn't be sure. He was just trying—desperately—not to visualize little August packed in and scared, clinging to his mother, as those Nazi scum filled his lungs with cyanide. But he just couldn't escape it— he couldn't run from the imagery of little August huddled into his mother's chest as she screamed for Richard to save them. It wasn't until he heard the name Ruthie mentioned, that he snapped out of his trance.

"... I didn't see it but that was what I was told," Richard concluded.

"What? Did you say, Ruthie?"

"Yes, your brother-in-law, Moritz, his wife, Frieda, and their daughters, Ruthie, and Mary, were among those that same night who were taken out to the woods."

Carl shot up in his seat at the mention of good news. "Taken out to the woods? Were they released? Did they get out?" His voice rose with nervous anticipation.

"No, Carl, no. Weren't you listening to what I just said?" Richard looked at him curiously before continuing. "They were taken out into the woods—to the mass graves—where they were then all shot and buried," Richard repeated.

Before Carl had even a chance to react, before he could even warn Richard to never again speak a word of what happened to Ruthie to Inge or to anyone else, he heard his daughter's voice directly behind him.

"Dad?" was all she said, as she looked at him dumbstruck. It was too late.

"Inge, I'm so s—" Carl started to say, while staggering up from his chair to grab his daughter and pull her into his arms. He was terrified of how she would take this news of

153

her best friend's murder. He wasn't sure if there would ever be any way he could console her. As strong as she was, he knew her well—what if she couldn't ever survive this knowledge? But before Carl could finish his apology of her young cousin's murder, Inge broke out into a smile. *She hadn't overheard the news!*

Curiously, there was a letter in her raised hand.

"I just got this," Inge stated excitedly.

"W-What is it, dear?" Carl stammered, trying to collect himself from the shock of all he just endured.

"It arrived today. It is from Schmuel! He is alive!" Inge shrieked.

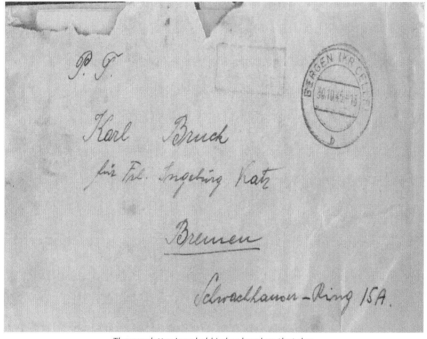

The very letter Inge held in her hand on that day.

Chapter Twenty-One
April 15th, 1946
Wilhelm Parchmann

Former Gestapo Agent, Wilhelm Parchmann's, mug shot, taken in April 1946.Staatsarchiv Bremen.

The truck bumped hard against its front wheel axel when it crashed into a rut in the street. Wilhelm Parchmann turned his head disapprovingly at the man beside him. While much of the debris from the bombings had been cleared off the main streets, the beloved city of Bremen was still completely in shambles.

"Hey, I'm trying," the driver replied gruffly at his passenger.

"I know." The agent sighed in resignation. "I know you are," former *Gestapo* Agent Parchmann said as he settled back into his seat, and next to the farmer who had so selflessly hidden him on his property this past year since his escape.

It had been quite some time since Parchmann fled the city in the back of that military truck. The evidence of all his fine work floating in the wind in ashes behind him. He wondered if the scrap of paper that had fallen upon his jacket sleeve that afternoon was something concerning himself. Something regarding all those Jews, like Carl Benz, whom he disposed of in the jail cells whilst framing them as "suicides." Or maybe yet, paperwork showing his direct involvement with sending all those young couples and their children to their slaughter in the Minsk Concentration Camp. He chuckled a bit to himself at that one. It shocked him to no end at how naïve the people of Bremen preferred to remain even when in the most obvious of circumstances.

The car turned toward *Osterdeich*, so that the Weser River was situated along the passenger side. Parchmann was grateful for this brief tour of his beloved city before surrendering to the CIC. Even though he was positive he'd get nothing more than a slap on the wrist for his crimes, there could be processing time before he would be released back out into society. He leaned against the door of the truck to place his forehead close and up against the window. He missed the flurry of activity of a city like Bremen. The solitude of the farm, while comforted by its familiarity, reminded him all too much of his upbringing in Wohle.

"It's right up ahead," the farmer alerted his passenger.

"Ah, yes." He smiled gratefully toward his collaborator. "Thank you so much for this excursion."

As promised, the tall white walls of the sports complex shot straight up along the northern banks of the river. The Weserstadion was a sacred place. Perhaps the only thing he loved more than his work for Germany, was his team, SV Werder. Never a weekend would pass without him watching a game. Lost amongst a sea of emerald green and white banners, was where the otherwise controlled and grim man would let loose. He'd rise to his feet as the famed striker, Matthias Heidemann, swerved around rival Hamburger SV's defense. He'd jump up and down, arms raised, shouting, "Goooal!" as, without fail, Heidemann kicked the ball right through their wall of defenders and into the net. Oh, how he missed the roar of the crowd, and the pride of Bremen! After a brief disbandment after the fall of the war, he couldn't be more pleased with their performance in the Northern German Championships these past weeks.

Soccer players in the Weserstadion. As part of the air defense in 1939, there were a total of three anti-aircraft towers like the one in the middle of the picture. Source unknown.

But to his shock and dismay, he saw the most horrendous sight.

"No," he declared firmly, pressing a palm against the cool glass. "What are they doing?"

By "they" he was referring to the American soldiers defiling his stadium. They were all collected, making themselves at home, playing an impromptu game of football, their favorite pastime. Why, he even spotted a Negro G.I. playing amongst them! As they slowly drove past, the young, fresh-faced occupiers, with their bright white smiles and clean uniforms, even attracted the attention of young German girls walking past.

American soldiers playing a game of football in the Weserstadion, 1946. Source unknown.

"They renamed the field, Ike Stadium," the farmer informed his passenger, while shaking his head at the desecration of it all.

"What does that mean? Why do they want to call it that?" Parchmann responded, still unable to shift his gaze from this unthinkable vision. Before they turned down a street, he had just caught sight of a group of heavy-set Negro soldiers holding large brass instruments, and bass drums.

"They renamed it after their General, Dwight D. Eisenhower." At this, Parchmann shot his head around to stare at the farmer incredulously, his mouth gaping open.

"Yup, that's how it is now. I've heard that the troops have been competing in track-and-field, playing baseball, and American football here ever since the occupation. If you can believe that."

Parchmann had seen enough. "Let's just head over now. To the CIC headquarters."

After a short drive, they pulled up close to the former Hotel Zur Post, near the main train station. Parchmann directed him to stop a couple blocks away. The former agent of the *Gestapo* had promised to protect the identity of the man who had come to his aid all these months in the countryside at his farm only two hours or so from Bremen, and didn't want anyone to spot him.

"*Viel Gluck* (Good luck)." They shook hands firmly before he exited the car.

"*Vielen Dank* (Many thanks). For everything," Parchmann replied, and with a great sigh, stepped out and onto the familiar gray cobblestoned streets of his old stomping grounds. But for some reason, in that exact moment, right before he was to take his first step towards the CIC headquarters, he felt this thunderbolt of fear jolt up his spine. It was so strong, in fact, that it made him lightheaded, and forced him to stumble over to the side and into a passerby. He felt a strong hand upon his shoulder, and a loud voice at his side.

"You all right there, pal?" an overly friendly voice speaking English inquired.

Once Parchmann gathered himself, he looked over to the origin of the offensive, informal greeting, only to see a toothy boy with a rifle slung over his shoulder. Incredulous, he wanted to demand an answer from this child as to why he would assume that he spoke English? Didn't the soldier realize he was standing on *German* soil? But, as if to answer this very question, a gust of wind caught the edge of an enormous flag situated high above a lamppost in the distance. The crimson stripes and white stars of America both dominated and defied his authority. Left with no choice, he softened his gray eyes at the invader, and politely responded, "*Ja, mir geht es gut,* (yes, I'm okay)," before abruptly walking away.

As he headed in the direction of the flag post, he was surprised by how much he was thrown. After all, he had mentally prepared for this day for quite some time. He rightfully imagined that the streets would be flooded with Americans and the belly laughs of their boisterous soldiers. That the crass sounds of the English language would grate upon his ears. He suspected that all the scarlet red flags and swastikas had been torn down long ago and replaced with those of the stars and stripes of the United States. But he supposed what he hadn't anticipated was how he'd feel about it all. How the loss of his culture, and values, and prominence would make him feel so... *how would one describe it? Humble? Yes, that's right.* He never could have imagined that he was going to feel this vulnerable and diminished.

As he stopped at a cross walk and waited for a bunch of jeeps to pass, a hostile set of green eyes met his, before the vehicle and its occupants turned into the entrance of the CIC building. The face of the man was unfamiliar to Parchmann, he determined, yet

159

he knew he was somehow recognized. Dressed in working clothing, with his silver hair cropped short, the former agent deemed himself unrecognizable from the impeccably dressed, haughty, domineering presence of his past. Yet in that moment, somehow, he knew his cover was blown. Once it was safe to pass the street, Parchmann followed behind those incoming soldiers, as it appeared they were headed to the same destination.

As he passed through the brick walled entrance, he attempted to again quiet those nagging fears. *Remember all that you heard: the courts have been reinstated by former members of the Nazi Party, along with all the prosecutors. The police are all run by the same members who served the Third Reich, and most importantly, the US has started to shift their focus from the Nazis to that of the spread of communism by the Russians.* As he walked up those steps, amongst the crowds of refugees, POWs, deserters, and displaced persons, he knew he would be fine.

Once he reported to the secretary at the front desk that he was there to surrender, he was immediately ushered to a room for questioning. He was surrounded only by military personnel until a lanky man in civilian clothing entered the room with the most suspicious of expressions—the very same man from the jeep. His antagonistic green eyes rested inquisitively upon Parchmann, while the former agent got ready to transcribe his official statement of surrender.

Soon after, an authoritative American briskly entered the room, and addressed Parchmann in unaccented German, "Hello, I am Special Agent Kurt David, and I am in charge of all captures and arrests of *Gestapo* and *SS* here at the CIC."

This announcement made the hairs go up on Parchmann's neck. He had heard tales of such men. Those German Jews who fled Nazi persecution only to then return as US soldiers to enact their revenge. They were commonly known as, "The Ritchie Boys."

"Guten tag." The man with the green eyes then suddenly spoke in German with a heavy Eastern European accent. "My name is Schmuel Berger, and I work as a translator here. However, because Agent David was born and raised in Germany, my services are not needed. I am just here to observe." With his intonation, overt hostility, and exceptionally lean frame, Parchmann's suspicions were raised. He wondered if this Schmuel was a former inmate of a concentration camp.

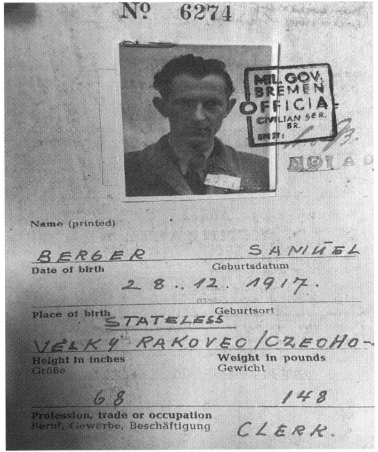

No. 6274

MIL. GOV. BREMEN OFFICIAL CIVILIAN SER. BR.

Name (printed)

BERGER   SAMUEL

Date of birth   Geburtsdatum

28.12.1917.

Place of birth   STATELESS   Geburtsort

VELKY RAKOVEC / CZECHO-

Height in inches   **Weight in pounds**
Größe   Gewicht

68   148

Profession, trade or occupation
Beruf, Gewerbe, Beschäftigung   CLERK.

Schmuel's ID Card for his work with the CIC.

"Ah yes, hello, gentlemen. I am here today to surrender for the crime of following *Gestapo* orders," Parchmann reported in a friendly fashion.

Agent David, dressed in particularly fine civilian clothing, pulled out a seat directly across from the *Gestapo* agent, and laced his fingers upon the table. He rested his steely gaze upon the criminal before him. Parchmann stammered in response to the confrontational posture taken.

"... I ... I myself am of no importance or power. Just an honorable, honest officer of the police," Parchmann continued, holding his hands to stop them from shaking. This was not how he was expecting this meeting to go.

161

The translator and sergeant then leaned in closely to one another to have a long exchange of words in hushed tones. Parchmann, unable to overhear, grew anxious. He began shifting nervously in his seat, and even ran his hands repeatedly through his silver hair. All the while, the men kept looking back at him. Now and then, the old Nazi offered what he hoped was a disarming grin in their direction. Without warning, the one who introduced himself as Schmuel Berger, unexpectedly dashed out from the room.

Parchmann remained seated after giving this testimony, and despite everything, was treated rather fairly by David and the Americans. *Maybe they believed my story, after all,* he hoped, growing a bit more optimistic when he was offered something to drink, and a bite to eat while he waited for—well, he wasn't quite sure why he remained there. As he settled back into his seat, as the hour neared four, a rush of activity just outside his doorway caught his attention. He heard a familiar voice give hurried greetings just beyond his line of vision.

No, not him. It can't be. He felt the panic grow in his heart, and straightened in his seat at the anticipation of facing the man now walking in.

Just beyond the doorway, standing before the agent, red in the face, and with none of the submission he usually possessed while in *Gestapo*'s presence, was the one man who could ruin Parchmann's chances of getting off. While he was a bit thinner than the Nazi remembered, his face more creased, and the lines around his blue eyes had certainly grown more prominent, Parchmann knew for certain it was him—the Jew, Carl Katz. The demoted Nazi looked upon this ghost from his past in horror—upon the one man he was certain hadn't survived. With panic settled in his chest, Parchmann instinctively shot to his feet, clicked his heels together, and gave a military salute to the *Schweinhund* (derogatory word for Jew) standing before him. The man who introduced himself as a translator standing beside Katz no longer looked angry. Instead, he appeared quite excited.

"This is him, the one I told you about," Schmuel Berger stated to Katz, enthusiastically. "I just returned back from Nazi hunting in the countryside, when this man surrendered to our office," he continued. His eyes suddenly clouded over, and dark shadows formed beneath them. His lips turned down in a hardened sneer, before he released a scornful accusation.

"After all these years, I can smell murderous Nazi scum from a mile away," the young man jeered while taking an aggressive step closer to the former agent. "I thought, *Herr* Katz, that you might help classify his true identity."

Parchmann looked nervously between the men in the room, while his body remained fixed in its military salute. It was now confirmed that the translator was not simply a man gifted in languages, but a Jew out for revenge. *What is happening?* he wondered as Schmuel looked as though he were going to murder him right then and there. *Will they all take their turns in bludgeoning me to my death?*

"Thank you, Schmuel. I do know this man. I know him well," Carl Katz responded, placing a firm hand on Schmuel's shoulder to hold him back. Parchmann exhaled in relief when it appeared his life would be spared.

Katz then took a moment to run his eyes up and down the man he had feared for all those years. At the one responsible for murdering so many of his friends and family, including Ruthie, Moritz, his wife's sister and brother, and little Rolf, along with the child's brother and mother. In that moment, Parchmann prayed that this Jew would remember his place. But when Katz approached him closely, and stared him down without the slightest bit of fear or hesitation, Parchmann knew his true identity would be revealed.

"*Du Aschloch* (You Asshole)," Katz muttered directly into his face.

While still standing only an inch from the murderous fiend, Katz stated for the record, "I know what he did. Everything. His name is Wilhelm Parchmann, he was head of the Jewish Department of the *Gestapo*. He led the action against Polish Jews in 1938, headed the atrocities of *Kristallnacht* upon the Jews of our city on November 9, 1938, he was a main participant in the expulsion of the majority of Jews from Bremen to the camps, and led the Minsk Transport, and should therefore be held responsible for all murders of Bremen's young families who died in those death camps, not to mention, the murders of countless others of our city's residents."

Parchmann was frozen in shock when the military police came from behind him and took his arms behind his back. "You are officially under arrest," Agent David recited, while ordering the other soldiers to clasp his wrists in metal cuffs before roughly shoving him from behind.

"You will be detained under the classification of '*Automatischer*' (serious offender)," he continued, as they then led the prisoner down the hallway and toward a row of dark holding cells.

The American agent shouted after him, "Transfer him to the Bremen internment camp!" before turning to face Katz and Berger with a nod and firm handshake. "Thank you, men, for your help in classifying him."

"Thank you for your service. For helping right the wrongs of Germany," Parchmann heard Carl Katz declare appreciatively.

"I do it for you as much as for myself. For my aunts and my other family members who weren't as lucky as I was in escaping those death camps."

Parchmann had to remain in the hallway for a moment while his arresting officers collected their paperwork. He was close enough to observe the discussion taking place between the Jewish men. He watched on as the sergeant looked off into the distance and tears formed in his abhorrent eyes. "I can still smell the burning flesh of the bodies in Dachau," David stated before meeting his gaze to Schmuel's. "I can't imagine what you had to see and experience in your time there." He then wiped a tear that had managed to escape before shaking Schmuel's hand again. He held onto it for a long while.

Piles of dead bodies the Americans witnessed while in Dachau. This photo was gifted to Carl by the US Armed Forces on the chance he'd encounter Holocaust deniers.

"I promise you, I want to get these guys," Kurt David vowed to both men before him. He then looked down the hallway and made direct eye contact with Parchmann. "I swear. It's the only thing I've got on my mind."

Chapter Twenty-Two
March, 1949
Never Enough

The Katz's new family home on Doandstrasse. *Carl's chocolate brown Wanderer parked out front.*

"Have a good day, I'll see you at dinner," Carl Katz stated as he landed a quick kiss on his wife's cheek and placed his hat upon his head.

"Are you dressed warmly enough? It's such a cold day to be at a construction site," she called out after him, as concern turned down the corners of her kind, blue-green eyes.

Carl hesitated momentarily before responding. "Don't worry, I have my scarf," he replied with a charming grin and wink before rushing out the door. He hoped she didn't detect the dishonesty in his voice. While it was true he was going to be at a construction site this morning, it would only be for a moment before his real commitment in the center of town.

He hopped into his car and drove the few minutes to his old neighborhood of *Neustadt*. As he pulled up to *Rudesheimerstrasse*, in front of the once bombed-out Cohen family home, he felt the usual lump of emotion rise in his throat.

He was grateful that Bremen was in the American enclave. It allowed him to acquire possession and responsibility of rebuilding the properties of all his murdered relatives. But this was no easy task. It wasn't the effort, nor the money, that was the issue. In fact, he was given a job of repurposing scrap metal, and there was certainly no shortage of that material in post-war Germany. He even got more than his fair share because of his good relationships with the American occupiers. Nearly all of them, at one point or another, had entered the Nazi death camps, and had seen firsthand the cruelty and devastation enacted upon the innocent. The Allies, therefore, were more than happy to give all business to a wronged Jew rather than to an Aryan businessman. Hence, these days, Carl had more income than he had opportunity to spend.

The rebuilt Cohen Family home in Neustadt.

Consequently, what haunted Carl, were the empty rooms—the vacant dining area where he had spent so many joyful dinners with his sister and brother-in-law, while the children would run upstairs to play. His eyes misted over as he approached the doorway of the unoccupied upstairs bedroom where Inge spent nearly every weekend of her childhood having sleepovers and pillow fights with her cousins Ruthie, Kurt, and Mary. He'd chuckle upon hearing from Inge at how they'd sneak out board games, like *Mensch*

166

argere Dich nicht, and played silently into the night after being reprimanded for staying up too late.

The burden of his heavy footsteps as they echoed through the now hollowed home was nothing short of heart-breaking. He really wanted Inge to help him with the process of rebuilding. He thought she might even find it healing to recreate the beloved home as a way to honor those she loved most in the world. But, surprisingly, his daughter stubbornly refused. Why, she even declined to walk down the streets of that neighborhood! It was probably the only time since her birth, that Inge outright refused her father any wish. What could he do then, but honor that appeal?

Outside the Cohen Family home lies their Stolperstein (literally "stumbling stone").
They are concrete cubes inscribed with the name and life dates of those exterminated by the Nazis.

"Yes, those look good," Carl said to the contractor already covered in dust. Paint was strewn all over his strong, worker's hands. The laborer held the tile sample of the kitchen flooring up to his employer for approval.

"These look exactly like they used to. Go ahead, and lay them in," he affirmed, before heading back out to his next commitment.

As Carl stepped out the paned front door and placed a hand upon the metal railing before the steps, a gray and black striped cat appeared from out of the shrubbery of the small front garden. Carl looked at the friendly stray inquisitively as she curled around the bottom of his pants legs.

"Hello there, friend," Carl spoke to his new acquaintance, when she turned her white face up to look at his.

Then, without warning, grief and fondness suddenly overtook him. Carl couldn't quite explain it, but in that moment, rather than leave to his next meeting—as he should have done—he paused. He even sat down upon the stone steps of that entrance. The cat, ever so lovingly, responded by jumping onto his lap. Carl then stroked the back and neck of the animal, as she curled in, and draped herself over his knees. While Katz never considered himself to be a religious, or even a spiritual man, for that matter, he pushed his practicality aside and recognized the divinity of this meeting. Even he had to acknowledge that this was no normal occurrence. With the last name of Katz, people often used this animal as a symbol of him and his family.

"I'm so sorry," he whispered into her black-tipped ear, while offering one last pat of his hand.

He took in a deep breath, and held it, while he cast his eyes upwards to the clouds. Images flooded his mind of what the Cohen family's last moments must have been like— of them all standing in the woods that night, hand in hand, awaiting their execution. Then he drifted to the vision of those empty chairs reserved for them at Inge and Schmuel's wedding only two years ago. Even though the Katzes felt truly blessed to celebrate that occasion, it was not an easy task to overcome the loss of their presence. As beautiful a bride as Inge appeared, behind that beaming smile, Carl knew there was a weight in her chest at not sharing the moment with Ruthie.

The despondency suddenly became too much to bear. *Enough!* Carl commanded himself. He needed to pull away from his horrific contemplations. It was not fair for him to remember the Cohens in those terms! Rather, Carl pretended for that moment, that he had just finished dinner. That his belly was full from Shabbat challah and roasted chicken and potatoes. That Inge, only a girl, was here now, upstairs in that large bedroom with her cousins whispering so as not to awaken her aunt and uncle.

He desperately tried to hold in the tears that wanted to escape, but it was an impossible feat. Without much of a choice in the matter, he allowed himself this moment to surrender to his grief. He permitted himself this time to mourn his profound loss.

****

Now running a bit late, Carl raced down the streets toward the center of town, afraid he'd miss the start of the hearing beginning promptly at 8:15 a.m. He blasted his horn at sleepy drivers, ordering them to get out of his way. They'd turn their faces at him in disgust at his obstinacy, but he paid them no mind. In fact, he rather enjoyed his rude and obtrusive behavior. For far too many years he had to shy his way around the city with his head lowered. He'd literally have to spend his days apologizing for his existence. But not anymore. Those days were long past. Many Jews remained meek—still afraid and cowering from the Aryans. But not Carl. No, he was not afraid to stand up. He was not afraid to hold them accountable for all they had done.

As he pulled into a good parking spot on *Am Wall*, and marched towards Nette's trial held at the Textilhaus building, he felt rather defiant and smug in his legitimacy. He bounded through the entrance of that stone slab, five-story building, and marched his way up the stairs to the first floor. As he approached the room where the trial was to be held, he suddenly stumbled in his steps at the crowd before the entrance. There they were—all three of the monsters who had made his life hell for all these years. Standing right there before him were none other than *Gestapo* Agents: Linnemann, Nette, and Parchmann. The faces of his past oppressors, wardens, persecutors, intimidators, and murderers of his friends and family were suddenly looking back at him now—right there where he stood. In a building so close to the old *Gestapo* headquarters, and right beside the *Polizeihaus* (police station).

It is 1949. The days of Nazi persecution have passed. You are free to once again live your life as a German and as a Jew, he reminded himself as sweat began to dampen his forehead at their presence. He pushed past the men after a curt nod of his head, and went inside to grab a good seat. As he turned the corner and away from their sight, he discreetly took out his handkerchief and wiped at his brow. Carl found a seat in what he found to be a surprisingly informal room. Another revelation was at how many Germans were occupying this unceremonious space. These trials, termed by the Allies as "denazification," was the process of bringing the National Socialist regime in Germany to justice and of purging all elements of Nazism from public life. While he assumed no Americans would be present, as they turned the courts (surprisingly, and as he considered, rather prematurely) back over to the Germans, he did hold out hope that they would be there to oversee that all business was conducted properly—and fairly.

The proceeding soon started, and after a few preliminary greetings, Carl Katz was called up to the witness stand by the presiding official, a German lawyer named, Udo Meineke. With conviction in his heart, Katz jumped to his feet when prompted. He sat in a chair facing the room. There weren't Americans in attendance by then, however. That fact made him nervous.

"Please state your name," the older German Prosecutor demanded. His silver hair a bit too long, and combed back off his bloated face.

"Carl Katz."

"Your age and residence?"

"I am forty-nine years old. I live on *Donandtstrasse* 18."

"In your opinion, why did Karl Bruck remain in Bremen?" he demanded, locking a steely gaze upon his witness. Katz was thrown. Why would he ask about his former friend and co-worker, Bruck, at a hearing for *Gestapo* Agent Bruno Nette's war crimes?

"Uh..." he stumbled for a moment. "He was married to an Aryan and therefore not under ordinance."

"Can you give me a reason why he stayed in Bremen until the end of the war?" the Prosecutor insisted.

"Cases, like Bruck, were only ordered to leave as of February of 1945, so it is beyond my knowledge, as I was deported from the city in 1942," Katz responded.

"And did you volunteer freely to go to the concentration camp, Theresienstadt?" the man stated aggressively, hands gripping at his lapel collars. There was not a trace of empathy to be detected—by anyone in that room for that matter.

"Was that even a possibility?" Katz responded incredulously. He was completely thrown at this line of questioning, and began to grow irate at the implication that Jews were willing participants in their demise.

"Is it even *conceivable* to you?" Carl challenged back, while pressing his hands firmly down upon the table before him, trying to keep himself composed and from jumping up and onto his feet.

"Of course I didn't volunteer of my own free will! None of us did!" he stated clearly while staring down the Prosecutor.

Once the lawyer turned his back, Carl took a moment to span the room. There were members of the press, and some citizens from the community, as well as the three *Gestapo* agents, the famed Nazi Prosecutor, Siegfried Hoeffler, along with his compliant Inspector from the police force, Charles Gerber. Carl felt the aforementioned had either well-known vendettas against the Jew they believed was responsible for their incarcerations, or worse yet, anger at his audacity to survive their murderous agenda. *Is this trial a farce? Am I here to relieve the Gestapo of their contributions of the murders of so many?* he now conjectured.

Katz couldn't believe the predicament he now found himself in—just sitting before them, uncharacteristically naive, on the witness stand, with not so much as a lawyer. His heart raced, and beads of sweat then soaked through his shirt. He had been tricked. While he was here to incriminate a Nazi, it was he, *der Jude* (The Jew), who was the one on trial.

"From those in your community in the Minsk Concentration Camp, did you ever hear from them?" the lawyer pressed on, with his back still turned.

Carl loosened the tie a bit from around his neck before replying. He needed to choose his words carefully.

"No, only five or six survived, and none of them were from Bremen. From Minsk, they were unable to correspond. We all thought we were going to an old age home according to all the paperwork and preparations we made before the move."

"And what kind of experiences did you have in Theresienstadt?"

"There wasn't much difference there as from my brief internment in Sachsenhausen after *Kristallnacht*. We were treated like cattle. The *SS* liked to push us to move. We slept on stone floors. The majority of us died there."

"Was it often you got together with Nette?" the lawyer queried, drastically altering the direction of the inquisition.

"Well, I lived in the *Judenhaus,* and my office was also there. Nette visited often."

"Were many bribes offered?" The Aryan stepped closer to Carl and now leaned down toward him. It was obvious he was attempting to intimidate his witness.

"I remember *Frau* Pieper gave Nette's wife a large diamond ring in exchange for her life and to avoid the transports. There were other small things, mostly, I don't remember everything. I gave him a suit from my brother-in-law, and would share drinks with him in my office. For me, these actions were merely a means to an end. For example, I wasn't in the mood to celebrate my leaving Bremen with him, but when you were in the grips of the *Gestapo*, you had to do what you had to do to survive," Katz explained confidently. While Carl was admittedly nervous, he made a promise to himself after he survived those horrors to never again live in fear of anyone.

"And at that time, was the transport to the Minsk Death Camp organized through you and the *Gestapo*?"

"No!" Katz responded loudly, his anger overtaking him. *How could he accuse me of having a part in that?* His suspicions of being on trial were confirmed with that last question.

171

"I spoke up against it. I suggested that the old and frail shouldn't go, but I had no power as I wasn't even the head of the Jewish community," Carl deliberately and slowly stated this obvious fact for the court's records. He had to play this smart.

"Hmmm," the Prosecutor replied, as he turned to glance back at the room of onlookers—suggesting that Katz's last statement was not to be trusted. "Did you have the impression that Nette knew what would ultimately happen to those people that were sent?" the lawyer proceeded, still facing the back of the room.

"It's hard to say," Katz replied, but then understood where the questioning was heading. "I truly thought we were going to an old folks' home when we left to Theresienstadt," he blurted out, defensively, to all in attendance. All the while, he cursed himself as to why he didn't have a lawyer at the ready.

"Could you imagine that former criminal agents wouldn't have been informed of the conditions there?" asked the attorney, now facing the "accused."

"By the *Gestapo*, they'd often change employment. That being said, my common sense tells me they must have discussed the truth of what was happening."

"Did Nette after the war try to get you to provide positive testimony on his behalf?"

"Yes, somebody came to my home—his son, Rudolf—but I threw him right out. I told him to, 'Get out of here.'"

"Thank you, *Herr* Katz, you may return to your seat now. We now call to the stand, Bruno Nette."

Carl, a bit shaky, rose to his feet. As he approached his original chair, Nette walked directly past him. Through his small, circular, wire rimmed glasses, the old *Gestapo* agent looked decidedly smug. From his confidence, it was easy for Katz to see that he was in for some sort of trouble. Once in his assigned place, Bruno Nette opened the jacket button of his neatly pressed, charcoal gray, pinstriped suit, before sitting. He appeared quite pleased to have this opportunity to state his side of the story for the record. After a brief introduction, Nette told his version of events.

"I lived in the best of friendships with Katz. He was the caseworker. I spoke to him about everything."

Chapter Twenty-Three
March 1949
History Revised

Building where Bremen's denazification trials were held. Source unknown.

"What? What is this nonsense?" a startled Carl demanded from his seat at Bruno Nette's claim of their friendship. Bruno looked around the room to witness the audience's reactions to his version of accounts. As planned, they all sat there, transfixed, while listening to *him*—a *Nazi*—declaring a Jew's collaboration. It was all too easy.

"I left all decisions to Katz. When I was assigned my position, I had to learn the ropes. I was never against Jews. I was never a hater of Jews, and if you state this, I am at a loss as to why. Katz," he called over to Carl, "am I not speaking the truth? Didn't we have conversations?"

173

All eyes then turned to the Jew in the room. Just as Nette had hoped, the unsuspecting witness was at a loss for words.

"Well…" Carl responded, finally finding his resolve after a moment, "I must take action against your words—'*Freundschaft*' (friendship) is far too heavy of a word. After all, Nette took his job very seriously, especially in Vegesack in dealing with Louis Neitzel and his family."

Nette felt his face turn red at the mention of his dark history in Vegesack—at Katz bringing to the light the shame and accountability the agent tried to hide all those years ago. Nette worked vigilantly to destroy all evidence of his unlawful wrongdoings to his late wife and children. He'd thought he had rid the city of the Jewish witnesses including Neitzel, and his brother, and Marie Huntemann with her suicide, before any had an opportunity to speak out. Katz just revealed that he was too late—as someone obviously met with the Jew before the transport to Theresienstadt. The agent was wrong to underestimate the cleverness of his adversary. He would be sure not to let that happen again.

With his hands held tightly in fists, Nette rose to Katz's challenge. "I celebrated the farewell of Neitzel and the rest of you, in that hotel lobby by the train station with champagne. Don't you remember?" Nette said as he leaned forward in his seat. The room of onlookers all gasped at the horrid declaration, as if to wonder how it was a Jew could do that to his own people? Encouraged by their reaction, Nette adjusted the jacket of the suit, the one the Jewish tailor, Gruenberger, had made for him in exchange for having his name removed from the transport list, before continuing his convincing tirade. "And I even accompanied you on your ride to Theresienstadt until Hannover. I sent the commander of Theresienstadt a letter of recommendation. You had it good there. That I know. You returned from the camps in good shape. You are today, again, a multimillionaire!"

Katz started to rise to his feet in objection, while the onlookers all turned their heads to look upon him with disapproval. Bruno, however, would not allow for any interruption of his attack. He had been preparing for this moment for years now. Every waking moment he resided upon the small, thin mattress, staring up at that leaking ceiling of his jail cell in Riespott, was for this day in court. He was just now getting started.

"You were my best assistant," Bruno stated, while offering a patronizing smile in his direction. "You were the one who chased *Frau* Huntemann into the Weser River!" Nette announced, finger pointed directly at his antagonist seated directly across the room.

The court room gasped again in response. They all gazed upon Katz in shock. Carl only looked back at the agent in confusion and horror. The former agent glanced to the back of the room where the journalists observed. With profound pleasure, he noticed the quick scribblings of their pens upon notebooks. *There. That ought to remind this Jew of whom he picked a fight with,* Nette scoffed.

"What did I have 'good' in the camps? Give me an example, please. Because all I ever experienced was starvation, torture, and the passing of friends and loved ones into mass graves. And who—for God's sakes—*who* is *Frau* Huntemann? She wasn't a registered member of the Jewish community. Therefore, I don't know her, much less ever went to her house. What are you talking about? How did I chase her into the water?" Carl stated quickly, obviously misunderstanding that the accusation made wasn't that he literally ran her into a river.

Of course, nothing the old *Gestapo* agent stated was truth, and indeed, it was made obvious that Katz had no idea who the woman was or that she had committed suicide. However, the courts chose not to recognize that, even less so, the court of public opinion. The room now frowned upon the wealthy businessman in response to his weak defense—just as Nette had hoped they would. The former agent looked back again at the journalists, and this time they were sitting still in observance. They had chosen their side. The old Nazi had easily won them over. This only encouraged his confidence further. He puffed his chest and raised the register of his voice to emphasize his next claim.

"I'm not surprised he'd say that," Nette addressed the room he now dominated. "This must all be so unpleasant for him today," the agent stated smugly before continuing his tirade. "In the case of the late Marie Huntemann, it is exactly as I stated. I couldn't have made this up, and I say this on my honor. Her family will attest to this!"

The agent intended to take full advantage of his foe's naiveté and lack of preparedness for the day's events. Why, the fool just sat there, dumbstruck. He obviously had no idea what to say or how to respond to the allegations. Bruno just had to keep the momentum going.

"In the case of Benno Schustermann, you told Agent Linnemann that his son, Lothar, went to a Jewish school," Bruno stated as he confidently reclined back into his chair. He lifted his chin while looking down the slope of his pug nose at the perplexed witness. "Therefore, you are also the one responsible for Benno's death, and the boy's imprisonment!"

Again, the room of onlookers huffed, and spoke excitedly to one another. A lightbulb briefly illuminated the room as it flashed a picture. *Now, let's see the fast-talking Jew try get out of this*, Nette taunted.

"But Benno never denied he was a Jew! His wife, Johanna, *she* was the one who divorced her husband, which absolved him from Aryan protection, and therefore *she* was the one responsible for getting him sent to the camps!"

175

Katz looked over to the mediator, Meineke, for assistance. It was obvious to Nette that Katz couldn't imagine that the lawyer would have allowed for such an onslaught of false claims and uninterrupted hearsay. After all, no legitimate court would tolerate an accused citizen to remain without suitable defense. But this was no legitimate court. The judicial system had again been reclaimed by the Germans. Nette could tell that the self-righteous Jew was finally learning exactly what that would mean for a man like him.

"How could you possibly know of their intimate affairs?" the lawyer intervened, but not at all in the way Katz could have hoped.

"Because the lawyer had been so upset at Johanna's request for divorce that he confided in me, and refused to work with Johanna. Ask Lothar! He is a good friend of my daughter's. He will tell the truth!"

"Lothar?" Nette interrupted. "Who do you think is the one making these claims? Who do you think offered this testimony of his own free will?"

"What?" At this, Carl, grew noticeably defeated, and slumped back into his chair. He appeared dejected and confused at this proclamation, just as Nette anticipated when unveiling the betrayal.

"That's impossible," Katz stated, barely audibly, about the boy he had looked out for all these years.

"You were my best person for info. You were raised as a Jew, Bruck was a Christian Jew. He didn't know anything. You were the only one who could help me."

"Why do you keep mentioning Karl Bruck? What does he have to do with any of this?"

"A lot, actually. He is a good friend of yours, isn't he?" Nette baited the witness.

"He was, yes, for many years," Carl answered. *Perfect,* Bruno thought, *he took the carrot right from my hand.*

"Would you say, then, that you had an open and honest relationship with him?"

"Of course," Carl said then paused a moment for impact, "before I knew that he was charged and served time as an informant and collaborator to the Nazis, that is." Katz stated this with a rise to his eyebrow, before going on. "We lived with Bruck and his family for a short while after liberation. Once I saw firsthand that he was on good terms and compliant with you—Nette, the criminally accused—even testifying on your behalf, that was when we had our falling out."

Nette wasn't all that surprised that the old Jew still had some fight in him, but it wouldn't be nearly enough to defend himself with what he was about to reveal.

"Exactly. That is what I thought," Nette responded. He was prepared for this response from the witness. He was well-known for his casting of webs, and Katz just landed himself in the center of it.

"What do you mean by that?" the Jew asked anxiously.

"Well, he didn't hesitate to offer you up. Being that you two were once on the same team, he had an opportunity to witness your involvement with the transports to and from the camps. He had quite a bit to say about how—or should I say, from *whom*—you acquired your wealth. For those of you in the room who don't know what I am referring to," Nette exclaimed, addressing the room of mesmerized attendants, "Karl Bruck testifies that Katz arrived home from the camps with many large suitcases full of riches!" Again, the courtroom collectively gasped at the thought of this Jew profiting from the deaths of his own people

"Nonsense! What? Wait—are you referring to the Jewish prayer books, ceremonial shawls, and burial cloths I brought back with me of those who were killed in the camps?"

Nette needed to gain control quickly. He knew he must not allow the witness any opportunity to present a logical defense or explanation. He raised his voice louder, so that he may drown out the reason from Katz's argument.

"Your friend, Karl Bruck, is the one willing to testify that you are the person who managed everything, while *I* was the one who just followed orders!" Katz's mouth gaped open in shock before springing to his feet.

"Impossible! These are lies! All of this!" Carl stated while on his feet. The engrossed journalists' cameras were being snapped away as the light from their bulbs flashed brightly, while the journalists enthusiastically documented the proceedings.

"I wanted to keep you out of Theresienstadt, but you told me in 1942 that you wanted to go. That you wanted to stay with the old people," Nette continued, undeterred from the outburst of his opponent.

"Why didn't you hold Katz back since he was your best informant?" Meineke then pressed Nette.

"I wasn't able to," the *Gestapo* agent stated simply.

"You didn't see yourself as a Jew hater?" the lawyer inquired. Katz, ignored by everyone, had no choice but to settle back into his seat—powerless of any recourse.

"No. I dealt with the Jew the same way I'd treat you. I never cursed out anyone or insulted anyone. Even though witnesses say I did. Maybe I did scold, but never insulted. Because of Katz I have been interrogated a hundred times by the Americans. Today I can see that I was correct. Because he is the head of the Jewish community, he acquired a great deal of testimony against me. Now he is a millionaire. He was in charge of everything regarding the Theresienstadt transport. He regulated everything, determined who would go and stay; I only supervised."

Nette, from the corner of his eye, caught sight of his comrade, Parchmann, suddenly scowl and shake his head ever so slightly in disapproval. Nette knew he had to move fast before anyone else took notice, or worse yet, his former associate decided to speak out against him.

With the courtroom now hanging onto his every word, *Gestapo* Agent Nette knew he had secured his acquittal with the court and public. He just now had to ensure his victory. "*Herr* Katz was the one who organized and headed everything! *Herr* Katz was a collaborator to the Nazis! I have people who will state for the court that they were more afraid of Carl Katz than they ever were of the *Gestapo*!"

With that damning closing statement, Nette quickly stood up from his seat, leaving no opportunity for rebuttal. As he walked off, he straightened his glasses over his pocked nose, and ran his hand slowly over his thin, graying hair. He was pleased with today's performance. After all, it wasn't enough for him to win the day. No, he understood that he had just succeeded in defiling this man's name and reputation for generations.

Ein unpolitischer Gestapobeamter?

Am Montag begann vor der Spruchkammer I die Verhandlung gegen den ehemaligen Leiter des Judendezernats der Bremer Gestapo, Kriminaloberssekretär Bruno N e t t e. Er ist angeklagt, drei große Transporte Bremer Juden für Minsk und Theresienstadt zusammengestellt und weitergeleitet zu haben. „Wenn er auch grundsätzlich nicht von der großen Linie der Befehle des Reichssicherheitshauptamtes abweichen konnte, so wäre es ihm doch möglich gewesen, in Einzelfälle mildern einzugreifen", heißt es in der Klageschrift. „Nicht so sehr seine Gesamttätigkeit, sondern das harte Durchgreifen in Einzelfällen wird dem Betroffenen von vielen Zeugen zur Last gelegt." Als Judengegner habe er darüber hinaus seine Stellung in der Gestapo ausgenutzt, um aus der Notlage der Verfolgten für sich und andere Vorteile zu gewinnen. In der Klageschrift wird Nette als Hauptschuldiger und als Belasteter bezeichnet.

Mit 95 geladenen Zeugen bildet dieser Prozeß einen Parallelfall zur Spruchkammerverhandlung gegen Herrlein, die in der vergangenen Woche zum Abschluß kam. Machte Herrlein den Eindruck eines biederen Beamten, so trifft dieses für Nette in noch höherem Maße zu. Es ist daher nicht verwunderlich, daß Herrlein gleich zu Beginn der Beweisaufnahme aussagte: „Ich habe mich immer gut mit Nette verstanden. Mir ist nicht bekannt, daß er wissentlich unmenschlich gehandelt hat. Er war ein guter Beamter, der pflichtgemäß seinen Dienst tat."

Wenn die Aussagen Nettes in eigener Sache zutreffen, so war er einer der unpolitischen Beamten. „Ich war immer bemüht, den Juden zu helfen. Was ich konnte, habe ich getan", sagte Nette von sich. Die Ausführung der Befehle des Reichssicherheitshauptamtes hielt ihn, wie er weiter aussagte, nicht ab, mit einigen Juden außerdienstliche Beziehungen zu pflegen. „Als der damalige Leiter der bremischen Bezirksstelle der ‚Reichsvereinigung der Juden‘, Katz, nach Theresienstadt verschickt wurde, habe ich sogar am Vorabend mit ihm Abschied gefeiert", klärte Nette die Kammer auf. Es klang glaubwürdig. (Wa.)

Newspaper article from the next morning stating, among other things, that Nette claimed, "I always tried to help the Jews. Whatever I was able to do I did. As the then head of the JCC, Katz was to go to Theresienstadt. I even celebrated with him the evening before his departure." The article remarked that they found Nette's testimony that day to be believable.

178

Chapter Twenty-Four
1949
A Painful Awareness

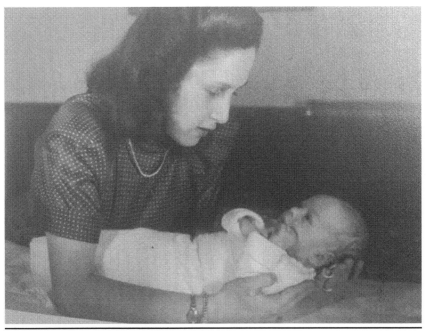

Inge, holding Carl and Marianne's first grandchild.

Carl pulled up to the front of his home. The hour was half past seven. After spending nearly ten hours at Nette's trial that day, he was physically and emotionally exhausted. He left the car running for a moment by the curbside, while he attempted to gather his strength. He was shocked at the day's proceedings. *What a fool I was!* he cursed at himself while slamming his palms on the top of the steering wheel. *How could I have ever believed it would be a fair trial? How could I not have foreseen that Nette would be up to his old tricks?* With the American occupation of his hometown these past four years, life had begun to feel so fair. The world felt right-side-up again. Why, in many ways, it resembled the Germany he had grown up in before Hitler came to power—the

Germany he loved—the Germany he fought for as a lad. For this reason, he had gained a false sense of security.

These last few dark years did too much damage. Perhaps the days of democratic governance, integration, loyalty, and a collective fondness of traditional customs, were now recessed too far in people's memories. *No*, he couldn't believe that. He couldn't possibly be back in the same predicament as he was in the 1930s.

The sudden barking of his cocker spaniel caught his attention. Ajax must have heard his master was home. By the sound of things, he was growing impatient at Carl's delay. *Times have changed,* Carl reminded himself, as he stepped out, and closed the door of his vehicle behind him. *First order of business will be to go about righting the wrongs of today.* Bright and early tomorrow morning, he would contact the Americans. They would never stand for the demonization of his character, nor for the *Gestapo* agent's futile declaration of innocence. It shouldn't be all that hard to clear his name of any damage Nette attempted to inflict. *After all, who could ever believe the words of such a discreditable witness?*

He walked past the block pillars of the front gate, and down the driveway towards the back entrance. Ajax's barking only grew more excited as Carl stepped into the kitchen.

"Hey, there, boy. How was your day?" he said warmly, while patting his black and white hound behind his ears—just as he liked it.

"You hungry? Yes? Did you get any *wurst* yet today?" The dog, understanding he was about to get his daily treat of pre-dinner sausage, started whining and hopping up and down excitedly.

"Shh! You're going to wake the baby!" Marianne scolded with a smile, before welcoming her husband home with a quick kiss on the cheek. Already prepared for his arrival, she placed a pre-cut slice of meat in Carl's palm for the dog.

"How is it going at my sister's?" she asked her husband with the quietest of voices. Even though it had been four years since Marianne learned of her and the rest of the Cohen family's death, she still couldn't speak about them without breaking out into tears.

"The house is looking really good. Almost just like it was before…" Carl trailed off, careful not to elaborate. He didn't tell his wife the real reason he was gone the whole day. He didn't want her or his daughter to have to deal with the former *Gestapo*—for any reason—ever again for the rest of their lives. He felt that they deserved that much for all that they had been through—for all they had lost at the hands of the agency. Carl allowed Ajax to lick at his palm in search of any last remnants, before standing back upright.

"I'll be back down in a moment. I'm just going to go upstairs to say hi to Inge," Carl remarked to his wife.

Ajax.

He left Ajax at his wife's ankles, where he liked to sit while Marianne stood over the stove preparing dinner for the family. Carl needed to be with his daughter a little while to recharge from the rough day he had, to help remind him why he fought so hard to survive, and for the strength to keep battling on, four years after the end of the war. Carl walked the flight of stairs to the second-floor apartment where Inge lived with her husband, Schmuel, and their new baby girl, Hanna. The child was named after Schmuel's mother. Tragically, the baby's paternal grandmother was one of the six million Jews that didn't survive the Holocaust. She was gassed to her death within minutes after the initial selection process of her arrival in Auschwitz.

"There she is!" Carl stated with elation in his heart.

He stretched out his arms so that he may cradle the newest member of his family. Inge promptly granted her father's request. As she lay the baby in the crook of Carl's arm, he couldn't help but wonder if it was a good idea to name a child after someone who met such a horrific end, but of course he respected their choice. Through a crop of dark hair, the infant's bright blue eyes met with his own. She looked upon him with the very same innocence and trust his daughter maintained to this day. Hanna reminded him so much of Inge in that moment. However, rather than give him the joy it should have, Carl felt fear and terror unexpectedly flood his chest.

"I can't—" Carl stumbled over his words, and hurriedly handed his granddaughter back to her mother.

"*Vati?* What is it?" Inge asked with concern. She briskly retrieved the child and instinctively rocked her against her chest. The only time she had ever seen fear like that wash over her father's face was during the war years. The child, feeling her mother's sudden unease, began to squirm in her arms.

Carl looked around the room so that he may center himself. But all there was in the chamber was a white crib, a small day bed, *Steiff* (stuffed) lions, and dolls adorned in lace dresses. The sweetness and innocence of it all overwhelmed the man. Rather than calm his nerves from the day's events, the nursery only exacerbated his anger at the injustice directed towards him and, ultimately, the family. Carl felt rage churn his belly that he was still being targeted—after all these years. He could not simply deny the incontestable truth that—one way or another—he would again have to fear for the lives of all those he loved most in the world.

"Shhh," Inge cooed gently into Hanna's ear. The baby, as though sensing the tension in the air, began to grow unsettled and whimpered. Inge began to pace the room to quiet the child, as her father looked upon them with the oddest of expressions.

In this very moment, in the safest of spaces, and with the most comforting of presences, Carl contemplated that danger, again, was just beyond his doorstep. Carl looked back at his daughter who briefly stopped her pacing to where she last stood; the baby settled down in her arms. With heaviness in his heart, he walked back over to where Inge remained. Carl put a gentle hand upon the baby, and kissed the top of her head softly. He then looked up, and met with the fearful eyes of his daughter. Almost choking upon his words, he said softly to her the statement that would haunt him for the rest of his life.

"You must go," he spoke, as a tear escaped the corner of his eye.

"*Vati?* What do you mean?"

"You have to go far from here," Carl said, breaking the vow he had made to his family all those years ago before his transport into the camp. The promise that they'd

182

never be separated—that the fate of one would be the fate of them all. That pledge was the only reason they endured Nazi rule with their lives.

But he now knew that what was safest for his family would be for his daughter to run as far from him as possible. That the Nazis would never be done targeting him. It was now painfully evident that he would be fighting them until the end of his days. He needed Inge to be no less than an ocean's distance away.

"You must take Schmuel and the baby and leave Germany at once," he stated solemnly.

Chapter Twenty-Five
March,1950
Undying Vengeance

Papers served to Carl Katz regarding the investigations and criminal proceeding against him from the Attorney General's office of Bremen. Courtesy of Staatsarchiv Bremen.

"They threw it out! I can't believe it! Who do those bastards think they are?" Arnold Schustermann exclaimed upon entering into Prosecutor Siegfried Hoeffler's office, with his sister-in-law Johanna, and nephew Lothar, in tow. Hoeffler remained seated and calm, even though he internally felt just as rotten at the news as the others in the room. Criminal Inspector Gerber stood beside where he sat.

"I was told you were the best. Or did I hear that incorrectly?" Johanna Schustermann ridiculed the lawyer upon charging into the room. She grabbed a seat, and settled back in her chair as it creaked loudly. She rested her arms over her thick waistline, and crossed her swollen legs at the ankles.

Hoeffler looked upon this reprehensible woman with disgust. *Someone ought to tell her that she is not young or pretty enough to have this ugly of a personality*, he couldn't help but think to himself as he ran his eyes over her unattractive form. However, as someone who always valued ambition over pride, Hoeffler hid his distaste of this offensive woman. She was a valuable witness, and therefore Hoeffler only politely replied.

"We will get him. I told you, I never lose a case," the attorney affirmed.

"Well, tell that to my late husband," Johanna said scornfully. "You couldn't seem to pin his murder on Katz, now could you?"

Gerber accidentally let out a small chuckle at Johanna's lack of decorum. But when she glanced up in his direction, he quickly averted his eyes and pretended to be clearing his throat.

"We will just have to push this further." Hoeffler exhaled loudly. "Please, Mr. Schustermann, Lothar, take a seat next to *Frau* Schustermann so that we may discuss the situation further. My associate, State Prosecutor Bollinger, will be here any moment."

Arnold Schustermann and his nephew did as they were told. Hoeffler then had his assistant serve his witnesses some tea. Arnold and Lothar accepted the offering with shy embarrassment from the pretty young girl. As Hoeffler anticipated, it didn't take much more than that to have the men's moods shift greatly.

"You know who's to blame here, don't you? It's those Americans! Those damn occupiers blow a whistle and everyone, like dogs, jump to their command!" Bollinger stated gruffly as the senior Prosecutor entered the office.

"If only the Americans were our biggest problem," Hoeffler responded to him with a sigh.

"What do you mean by that? What did the German courts state *exactly*?" Johanna inquired, dabbing at the tea that spilled down her chin with a napkin.

Hoeffler rustled through his papers to offer direct quotes, "Ah, right here it states to the charges concerning your son and husband: *according to the German Penal Code, a prosecution based on this angle would not do justice to the degree of wrongdoing in the action with which the accused is charged*."

"Preposterous!" Johanna exclaimed.

"Please, I am not finished," Hoeffler reprimanded before continuing. "*In various other cases, also incriminating the accused, a clarification, permitting any estimation pursuant to criminal law, could not be obtained.*"

"But what about the Americans? What excuse could they have possibly cited to absolve Carl Katz of his criminal participation in all those murders? In his collaboration with the *Gestapo*?" Lothar blustered, with his face a deep shade of red. He sat erect in his chair, and grabbed the armrests until his knuckles appeared white.

Both Gerber and Hoeffler looked upon this boy with interest. He was a handsome young lad, nicely dressed, with thick dark hair combed back stylishly from his face. Gerber, never one to leave a stone unturned, learned that up until recently, Lothar was a long-time friend of the Katz family. It was even well-known about town that he had pursued Katz's daughter with serious intentions in the years following the war. Why then the sudden change of heart? The obvious answer? *She didn't feel the same way back.*

"Chief Legal Counsel Johnson of the CIC tossed it. He said that there were no conclusive grounds for guilt, nor did he find any of the witnesses to be credible sources for an investigation," Hoeffler answered the jilted young man.

"*Excuse me?*" Johanna interjected.

"Listen, I've worked with the Americans on several occasions," Hoeffler responded to the hot-headed woman and her allies. "They are gullible. They are weak. They are war-weary and dream of returning home. I know them well, and know that they are lazy. They want their jobs done as easily as possible. They are tired of fighting. And that is precisely where we differ."

"How do you mean? What is your plan?" Bollinger inquired.

"We have all suffered. We have all been kicked around. We have all faced injustice. But unlike the soldiers, we are not tired." Hoeffler knew that his associate wanted a more pragmatic plan of action, but Hoeffler used this as an opportunity to inspire the room. He rose up from his seat, and raised his voice. "We are not afraid of a good fight. We are empowered by our obstacles! We will not stop. We will never stop until Carl Katz pays for what he has done to us! "

"Yes, yes, but what is your *plan*?" Bollinger insisted impatiently. He had heard enough of his pompous associate's emulation of Hitler's art of oratory persuasion.

"As I said before," a perturbed Hoeffler insisted, "I know many at the headquarters well. I've worked among them. I will fill out our case and deliver it to them personally. There has to be someone there with doubts, or else, can be persuaded to our side. Have faith, my friends. Even if it takes a lifetime, or that of our children's, or even our grandchildren's, we will get this man."

Chapter Twenty-Six
May,1950
Those Damn Nazis!

L-R: Carl, Marianne, and Inge, doting over baby Hanna.

Just as predicted, the next months of Carl's life were fraught with charges and accusations. Nette and his henchmen were relentless in their assault upon his character. Only a few short months after Nette's initial trial, he had his appeal, where the *Gestapo* agent's charges were reduced and classified as a Level Three Offender, a *Minderbelasteten*, namely, as someone who just followed orders. Around that same time, Katz was served his first set of papers.

Before he even read what was said, he knew exactly what the document was concerning. He unfolded the creases of the tri-folded letter, and took a deep breath before proceeding. It stated:

Under the direction of Chief Council Bollinger, and Assistant Council Sigfried Hoeffler Esq., Carl Katz is charged with the deportation of Marie Huntemann (section 2 of the statement of facts), the responsible party in Lothar Schurmann's deportation (section 1 of the statement of facts), all of which could be classified as of law section 239, subset II of the German Penal Code under "Deprivation of Liberty."

There are definitive testimonies of witnesses: English journalist Arnold Schustermann (brother of Benno and uncle to Lothar), former Gestapo Agent Bruno Nette, former Gestapo Agent Friedrich Linnemann, Lothar Schustermann, shopkeeper Johanna Schustermann (mother to Lothar and ex-wife to Benno), and Henriette (Huntemann) Lange (daughter of Marie who committed suicide to avoid her deportation).

The former members of the Nazi Party who now served the German Justice system were seeking approval from: *the American Occupying Authorities, pursuant to Art. III 1 d, to charge Carl Katz for* **crimes against humanity**.

Katz was dumbfounded at the paper he held in his now-shaking palms. While he had rightfully anticipated a counterattack for not testifying on the behalf of *Gestapo* Agent, Bruno Nette, at his denazification trial, he never could have, in his wildest dreams, anticipated this degree of vengeance. Instinctively, Carl crumpled up the notice, and tossed it as far as he could across his office. He slammed his hands down upon his desk, and jumped up from his chair.

"*Ihr verdammte Nazis* (You damn Nazis)!" he exclaimed aloud, and sent his chair crashing to the ground. This prompted his concerned secretary to run in.

"I'm fine! I'm fine. Get back to work!" he exclaimed gruffly while waving off the young woman poking her head through the crack at the door. Martha gingerly retreated from view and ever so quietly did as she was told.

Katz then raged over to his window, and threw it open. The early autumn winds blustered past the panes, billowed the curtains, and helped cool his hot forehead. He took in several long breaths before turning to look over at the document. He stormed over to the crumpled letter sitting upon the herringboned flooring, and brought it back to his desk. Without yet taking his seat, he smoothed out the wrinkles, before reading on.

Upon further observation, it appeared that they wanted to hold Carl responsible: *in accordance with Art. II 1 e, of Control Council Law No: 10, because the "accused," by his conduct, consciously furthered the performance of measures directed against the Jews. Also, that those who were deported and thus lost their lives in the camps, Carl Katz would be prosecuted for their* **murders** *or* **homicide**.

These papers on the investigation concerning criminal proceedings against the Chief Minister of the Jewish Congregation in Bremen, Carl Katz, merchant, of 18 Donandstrasse, Bremen, on charges that he did, in 1942, at Bremen, in his capacity was a liaison agent to the Gestapo, and is therefore guilty of committing a crime against humanity, in that he did, on several occasions, denounce Jews and Half-Jews who, in order to avoid deportations, had made false statements to the Gestapo.

Carl raised his chair from the ground, and sat upon it with heaviness in his heart. He was at a loss as to what to do. But he knew, as always, he'd find a way to fight back. He lifted the phone from its receiver, as he dialed the number of his contact at the CIC. As he rested his forehead upon his hand, he found a little peace at the revelation presented to him: these charges only confirmed his decision to have Inge flee the country as soon as was possible.

Chapter Twenty-Seven
1954
An Undying Love

Carl with his second granddaughter, Ruthie, 1954.

It was almost time to go. The trunks were packed and sat by the front door. All other furniture Carl provided for his family would be arriving shortly in New York by crate. He had prepared everything for an easy transition to their new lives. Even though he hadn't done so since she was a child, Carl remained beside Inge, holding her hand. But just then, little Ruthie was tugging on his pants leg. She, as always, wanted to be lifted up and into his arms. For only this reason, he let go of Inge and threw the nearly four-year-old gently into the air before hugging her close. She giggled, with that infectious smile of hers that never ceased to melt the old man's heart.

What would he do now without them all? he wondered, as the cab driver filled the car with all their belongings. But he urgently pushed those fears back down. *Everything will be just fine*, he told himself. *All that matters is that they are safe.*

"Let's go, *Opa* (grandpa)!" Ruthie beamed, her face only inches from his. Carl could already tell in this young child that she held the spirit of her namesake, his niece, Ruthie Cohen. Although still very young, her confident, spirited, adventurous, and kind nature was evident. He never told Inge the truth about her cousin's murder in all these years. As far as his daughter knew, Ruthie could find her way back at any time—even nine years after the war's end. Carl smiled warmly back at the child and pressed his nose against hers. She squealed out in laughter in response. He hoped his young granddaughters would help fill that hole the loss of his niece left in Inge's tender heart.

They all piled into the large Mercedes. And as the driver pulled the car past the house on its way to the Bremerhaven port, Inge sat next to her father. She stared out of the window longingly, saying goodbye to the only life she had known. While the vast majority of her thirty years were consumed with persecution, war, and loss, she was very much a product of her hometown of Bremen. All the good of the city had found its influence on Inge. She was sophisticated, intelligent, timeless, graceful, and maintained impeccable manners. Carl hoped all those attributes wouldn't clash too harshly in her new home city of New York.

"Hanna would have been the only Jewish child in her school," Inge stated softly to no one in particular. "Similar to how it was for me all those years ago."

Nothing much else was spoken in that somber forty-five minute car ride to the docks. Carl tried his best to maintain his positive and confident veneer. Marianne, on the other hand, didn't stop her sobbing the whole way there. Aside for those brief months Inge resided in Berlin before the outbreak of the war, the family had never once been separated. His wife just held Hanna tightly on her lap with one hand, while dabbing a pocket handkerchief to her eyes with the other. The only one of them who appeared excited about the move was Schmuel.

Carl's son-in-law was elated to leave Germany behind. As a Czech by birth, his only relationship with the Germans was that of the *SS* guards of the Theresienstadt, Auschwitz, and Dachau death and concentration camps. They were his torturers, as well as the murderers of his parents, grandparents, youngest brother, cousins, and countless friends. A few of Schmuel's siblings had also survived the camps, and they fled to America as refugees shortly after the war's end. They were now settled with their families in Brooklyn. While Schmuel agreed to remain in Bremen all these years as a

191

favor to Inge, he could barely stomach residing amongst those he viewed as the enemy. His only solace was his work for the CIC in bringing those perpetrators to justice. Needless to say, Inge's husband's eyes were bright and animated as he said his final goodbyes to the land and its people who stole his best years and his favorite people from him.

Hanna, Schmuel, Inge, Ruth pictured in ship window, 1955.

The Katz family pulled up to the dock. Standing before the ramp to the ship, the *SS Berlin's*, entrance, they each exchanged hugs and held each other close. While Marianne sobbed even louder, Carl was determined to remain stoic, confident, and encouraging.

"Don't fret," he stated to Inge as she dabbed at her eyes whilst in his strong grasp, "we'll visit you over the Christmas holidays!"

"But *Vati*." She then sniffled. "That is a whole six months away!" Inge cried out. It seemed with that statement, Carl had only made things worse.

"You will have a phone, won't you?" her father inquired.

"Yes, Dad," Inge replied impatiently. She knew where he was heading.

"And papers and pens?" Carl continued with a gentle smile.

"Of course, Dad, you know we will." His daughter couldn't help but crack a smile at being forced to respond to his silliness.

"Then there's nothing stopping us from communicating every day, is there?" Carl beamed down at her.

"No, I suppose not," she said as Carl gathered her into his arms and squeezed her even tighter.

Once he was confident Inge was doing a bit better, he stepped over to where Schmuel now stood, and shook his hand strongly. Looking into his eyes, he said, "I'm trusting you to take good care of my girls."

"Of course. I always do. I always will," the sharp, young man responded in an almost military fashion.

"I know, Schmuel. I know. You are a good man."

"Opa (grandpa)! I don't want to go!" young Ruthie interrupted the men, bouncing up and down in urgency to acquire her grandfather's attention.

"I know, my little *goldschatz* (treasure)," Carl said as he kneeled down right in front of her. He patted her upon her strawberry blond hair as they spoke.

"Can't I stay with you?" Ruthie then leaned close to whisper into his ear, "I can hide under your desk. I'll be so quiet!"

"Of course you can," her grandpa said with a kind-hearted chuckle, "just go with your mother now, and I'll be sure to ask her."

"Okay, *Opa.*"

"Ich liebe dich (I love you), Ruthie."

"Ich liebe dich, Opa."

With nothing much left to say, it was time for the Berger family to depart on their two week long journey across the Atlantic Ocean to America. But Carl realized that he had forgotten to mention one last thing. He called his daughter back for a quick word in hushed tones.

"I arranged it with the crew, and ordered a big marzipan cake to serve Ruthie for her birthday next week. Make sure they don't forget."

Inge just smiled back. Her dad always took care of everything. *What was she ever going to do without him?* She wanted to say thanks, but the words caught in her throat. Had she attempted to utter it, she would have surely broken down again. She didn't want her daughters to see just how distraught their mother was, and so she quickly turned back to ascend the ship.

Once aboard, the Berger family poked their heads through a small square window to wave down to Carl and Marianne. Before long, the ship's horn let out a giant bellow, and smoke puffed out from its enormous chimney. The crew urgently untied the massive ropes from the deck before jumping aboard. As the ship's engine began to separate the family from the pier, it had all suddenly become too real for Carl. He leaned over the railing, and began waving furiously at them. Sounds emitted from him that he had never before heard.

"INGE!" he screamed out, in an almost pained, animalistic tone. He did not recognize the sound as his own. Marianne grew fearful and immediately threw her arms around her husband's shoulders. With tears streaming down the old man's face, he became inconsolable. He screamed out for his daughter, again, and again, and again.

"INGE! INGE! INGE!" he cried out and remained in exactly this state until the ship disappeared over the horizon.

For the first time in his life, Carl was truly broken. Marianne, with the help of the chauffer, all but carried Carl back to the car. Leaning heavily on the driver's shoulders, the defeated man sat back into the nearly empty carriage. Where moments before it was filled with those he loved most, those who gave him an endless supply of happiness and cheer, it all now felt painfully barren. Looking out the car window upon the vast ocean, he was unsure of what else there was to live for.

By the time he returned home from the docks, he had regained enough strength to walk up the path to his front entrance. Ajax barked excitedly at his master's return. This helped alleviate the quiet of his now vacant home. Shattered, and with the tears on his cheeks not yet dry, he did the only thing he knew how to do. He sat behind his desk, while Ajax curled up atop his feet. As Carl rifled through his papers, ideas began to flood his mind about how best to go about rebuilding Germany to what it once was, and, of course, how to banish the lingering Nazi presence from his land with his last dying breath.

Epilogue

„Mein Großvater war kein netter Mensch"

Von **Frank Hethey** - 05.04.2017 - 0 Kommentare

**Bernhard Nette hat ein 344-seitiges Buch über
seinen Großvater Bruno Nette geschrieben:
einst Judenreferent bei der Bremer Gestapo.
An diesem Mittwoch liest er daraus in der
Zentralbibliothek vor.**

**Im Einsatz: Bruno Nette
(links) als Soldat im
Ersten Weltkrieg.**
(Bernhard Nette)

Als kleiner Knirps war
Bernhard Nette zu Besuch
bei seinen Großeltern in
Bremen. Ungefähr 1952
müsse das gewesen sein,
meint der gebürtige
Hamburger, damals sei er
sechs Jahre alt gewesen.
Noch ziemlich klar steht
ihm vor Augen, wie er
zum Milchholen geschickt
wurde. Anfangs habe
man ihn freundlich
behandelt. Allerdings nur,
bis er seinen Nachnamen
nannte. „Plötzlich
erstarrte der ganze
Laden", erinnert sich der
71-Jährige. Die eisige Reaktion: „Nettes werden hier
nicht bedient!" Der kleine Bernhard wunderte sich
zwar, dachte sich aber nichts dabei. Zumal auch der
Großvater gleichmütig auf die Zurückweisung
reagierte. „Es gibt auch woanders Milch", meinte
der achselzuckend.

Der gleichmütige Großvater starb im Sommer 1960,
sein Enkel studierte Geschichte und wurde Lehrer.
Mit einer Oberstufenklasse kehrte er 1987 nach
Bremen zurück, es ging in die Böttcherstraße. In
einer Buchhandlung blätterte er in dem damals
gerade erst publizierten Buch „Bremen im Dritten
Reich" von Inge Marßolek und René Ott. Und stieß
dabei unversehens wieder auf seinen Großvater:
diesmal als Judenreferent Bruno Nette, einen
Gestapo-Mann. „Davon hatte ich bis zu dem
Zeitpunkt keine Ahnung", sagt Bernhard Nette. In

195

man sich mal vorstellen", empört sich Bernhard Nette. „Noch im Februar 1945 schickte mein Großvater kleine Kinder unbegleitet nach Theresienstadt und schützte gleichzeitig Erwachsene." Das Kalkül dahinter: „Er stellte sich vor, die könnten sich später für ihn einsetzen." Was im Spruchkammerverfahren auch prompt geschah – es schlug die Geburtsstunde der Legende vom „Judenretter" Bruno Nette.

Das Ende einer Beamtenkarriere: Bruno Nette im April 1945 nach der Verhaftung durch britische Truppen. (Bernhard Nette)

Die Wahrheit sieht indessen ganz anders aus. Schon im Ersten Weltkrieg sei sein Großvater als Mitglied der Geheimen Feldpolizei mit stark antisemitischen Tendenzen in Berührung gekommen. Danach legte Bruno Nette eine eindrucksvolle Karriere als Kriminalbeamter hin. Bis der damalige Bremer Gestapo-Chef Erwin Schulz ihn 1939/40 engagierte. Das neue Aufgabengebiet nach dem Befehl zur „Endlösung": als Judenreferent die Todeslisten für den Abtransport in den Osten zu beschaffen.

Eine Aufgabe, die er nicht ohne die Hilfe von Carl Katz bewältigen konnte, dem Vorsitzenden der jüdischen Gemeinde. Auch dieses brisante Kapitel spielt eine Rolle in Bernhard Nettes Buch. Zwar betont der Autor, der wahre Verbrecher sei sein Großvater gewesen. Gleichwohl attestiert er auch Katz eine zwielichtige Rolle. Katz sei „religiös borniert" gewesen. Beim Zusammenstellen der Listen für die Deportation nach Minsk habe Katz alte Rechnungen beglichen, er habe es den vermeintlichen Verrätern am jüdischen Glauben heimzahlen wollen. Als Beispiel nennt er den Fall des schwer zuckerkranken Zahnarztes Ludwig Freudenthal. Den habe Katz ohne Not auf die schwarze Liste gesetzt. Der zynische Kommentar an Freudenthals Adresse: „Sie wollten bisher nichts von uns Juden wissen, jetzt werden Sie uns Juden kennenlernen."

Weil die Gestapo kompromittierendes Material verbrannt hat, schöpft der Buchautor sein Wissen aus Nachkriegsakten. In seinen Augen eine

2017. Book Review on a publication about Bruno Nette's life in Bremen's newspaper, The Weser Kurier. An excerpt reads as follows: Claims that while (former Gestapo Agent) Bruno Nette had to prepare the "death lists" to the East, this task couldn't have been accomplished without the help of Carl Katz (head of the JCC). Although the author acknowledges that the true criminal was Nette, he simultaneously attests to Katz having played a double role. Namely, during the compilation of the lists to Minsk, he declared Katz, as a religious fanatic, did so out of vengeance to those Jews who turned their backs on their religion. The author of this book is a well-known historian, teacher, and lecturer active today.

Carl and his wife, Marianne, remained in Bremen, Germany where he continued to run his scrap metal and textile business. In 1945, he used the goods brought back from Theresienstadt (the bags containing prayer books, challah covers, burial cloths, and prayer shawls) to re-establish the Jewish Community Center, where he was also elected as their president in 1945. Katz was simultaneously active in the governing board of the *"Zentral Komitee* Bergen Belsen" starting in 1945, and president of the Committee for Displaced Persons in the British zone while also head of the section for economic and welfare aid. Additionally, he was an active member of the *Zentral Rat der Juden* [Central

Jewish Committee] in Germany, proving instrumental in the re-establishment of Jewish life in Bremen as well as in greater Germany.

On January 12, 1960, Katz was awarded *The Order of Merit of the Federal Republic of Germany* in acknowledgment for his extraordinary service to the country and its people.

In 1961, in large part due to his efforts, and despite receiving numerous death threats and hate mail, Carl constructed the Bremen synagogue to replace the one destroyed during *Kristallnacht* in 1938. It is still standing today.

Katz's company was considered in April 29, 1961 in the *Bremer Buergerzeitung*, "[i]n the arena of recycled textiles to be the most important in the import and export field in West Germany. Katz was among the experts in this area." An aspect of his political and economic farsightedness and his entrepreneurial courage can be seen in his dealings between East and West Germany during the Cold War period. It was a perilous undertaking which met with much dissent. However, to repair and restore the Germany he loved, he persevered and became the president of the Trade Organization between East and West Germany in 1968 until his death in 1972.

Despite Katz's longstanding commitment to both the Jewish community as well as to the development of greater Germany, he has been pursued by the authorities and/or public, in their attempts to wrongly convict him of crimes against humanity and collaboration for decades. Regardless of that fact that the courts repeatedly threw out the cases due to discreditable witnesses, former *Gestapo* agent, Wilhelm Parchmann's, official testimony absolving Katz of any collaboration, and a lack of evidence to support any of the aforementioned claims, these charges pursued him until his dying day. In 2021, seventy-six years after the end of the war, and forty-nine years after his passing, various Holocaust historians and educators, descendants of the agents, as well as politicians who still adhere to Germany's "old ways," are still currently pursuing and perpetuating these false claims.

Never Enough is the first work released that exposes these abhorrent assertions to the larger public, all while allowing the accused an opportunity to state his side of the story. Nearly all accounts and occurrences written in this text were based on actual events obtained from the Bremen Archives and first person statements. While some of the dialogue had to be altered for purposes of clarification and storytelling, the vast majority of all wording in the book was pulled by the author directly from legal transcripts of court proceedings, investigations, and/or first person testimonies.

Acknowledgments

This book would not be what it is without the essential contributions of many others, especially the following whom I want to mention in particular.

Inge (Katz) Berger, my grandmother, who trusted me with her most precious recollections of what she endured during the war years as well as giving me the responsibility of gathering into this memoir many of her most intimate remembrances of those she loved and lost. It has been both an honor and a privilege. This is also to thank her for her faith in me that I would tell her story, and that of the others unable to do so, as they would have wanted those stories to be known. You have been an inspiration to me and all of our family. Now it is time to again let the world know just how truly special you are.

The late Sam Berger, my grandfather, whom I thank in spirit. His book, *The Face of Hell*, provided considerable information about his first-hand experiences in Theresienstadt. It was his intention in writing it to bring to the attention of future generations what horrors one nation was capable of inflicting on others in the hope that his readers will become better equipped to prevent such acts from ever recurring. I hope that my efforts further his objective.

My mother, Ruth Bahar. Ruth, who is not only my staunchest supporter, but the one responsible for this book having been written. Intent on clearing her beloved grandfather's name once and for all, she made the decision to tackle this extremely ambitious project. I thank her for entrusting me with the responsibility and honor of portraying her grandfather in both an accurate and affectionate light.

Menachem Z. Rosensaft, for his longtime friendship and support of the Katz/ Berger family. Ever since his parents first met Carl Katz at the Displaced Persons Camp of Bergen-Belsen, the families have continued to support each other for generations. Thank you for lending your voice to this project.

Frank Mecklenburg, for his longstanding support and encouragement of my projects. Without his assistance, I would not have accomplished such a degree of understanding and accuracy in my works.

Conrad Elmshaeuser and his staff at the Bremen Archives, this project couldn't have happened without all of your support and willingness to provide me with anything and everything required to make this story both legitimate and truthful. I am truly indebted to your diligence and sharing of information.

Birgitt Rambalski, you have been truly a gem throughout my writing career. So much could never have been accomplished without your dependable support and limitless enthusiasm. From the first day we met, you felt like family. I look forward to many more opportunities to collaborate.

Ina Navazelskis, thank you for breaking the rules to include this story in your Film, Oral History and Recorded Sound Collection interview. With newspersons of your calibre and conviction, I can rest easy that quality journalism is alive and well.

Thomas Hesslau, I will not soon forget that midnight drive through Bremen's Nazi history in your vintage Mercedes Benz. You have been instrumental in more ways than one, and I look forward to many more adventures in unearthing and righting the wrongs of the past together.

To all those family and friends I have mentioned in this book who have since passed. I pray that I have honored you, and your experiences, for all those still to come.

Notes

Chapter One

1. Information about Siegfried Höffler was obtained from Staatsarchiv Bremen, File Generalstaatsanwaltschaft Bremen Personalakten über Oberstadtsanwalt Dr Siegfried Höffler 4-10-AKZ-61-148 Pages 8–13.

2. Siegfried Höffler's ability to acquit Nazis was obtained from 2009-06-24 Schminck-Gustavus-Ermittl-Shoa-Bremen.pdf (864,1KB)

3. The lengths that Höffler would go to in trying to find incriminating evidence against Katz is obtained from Staatsarchiv Bremen, Karl Katz File 4,89/3–7, Informationsdienst Hansa page 143.

4. Siegfried Höffler's preparations in the case of Carl Katz is obtained from the Staatsarchiv Bremen Karl Katz File 4-89-3-007.

Chapter Two

1. Many of the events occurring during Krystallnacht were from interviews with Inge (Katz) Berger.

2. Events during Krystallnacht were also obtained from *Roses in a Forbidden Garden* by Elise Garibaldi published by Decalogue Books 2016 chapter two.

3. Carl Katz testified to events occurring during November 9,10,11, 1938, during the Spruchkammer of Wilhelm Parchmann obtained from the Staatsarchiv Bremen, Wilhelm Parchmann File Anlage 26 Vernehmung des 17 Zeugen Aktenzeichen 1177/47 pages 135–137.

4. Information on Krystallnacht in Bremen was also obtained from *Geschichte der Juden in Bremen und Umgegend* by Max Markreich Teil 15, 1938–1940 published by Temmen 2003.

Chapter Three

1. The chapter opens with Charles Gerber, but in reality, it was Chief Inspector Kurlensky from Police Station One that was conducting the interview of Arnold

Schustermann. Every subsequent interview was conducted by Gerber in Police Station five and for expediency, the persona of Kurlensky was exchanged with Gerber.

2. Information on Gerber was obtained from the Staatsarchiv Bremen File Gerber, Charles KL 89, Lebenslauf page 5.

3. The interview of Arnold Schustermann's accusations of Katz was obtained from the Staatsarchiv Bremen, Karl Katz File 4, 89/3–7 pages 5, 7–9.

4. Testimony of Katz regarding Johanna, Benno, and Lothar Schustermann was obtained from the Staatsarchiv Bremen, Karl Katz File 4, 89/3–7 pages 49–51.

5. Reasons stated for withholding reparations from Johanna Schustermann in July 15, 1949, due to the testimony of Carl Katz and Ilse Propper was obtained from the Staatsarchiv Bremen, Johanna Schustermann Reparations File page 50.

6. Arnold Schustermann writes to the Jewish Community Center August 6, 1949, to accept Johanna Schustermann into the community after his extensive research into her innocence, this information was obtained from the Staatsarchiv Bremen, Benno Schustermann's reparations file 2402 page 51.

7. Arnold Schustermann writes to the Senatspräsident Kaisen on August 8, 1949, that he doesn't make frivolous statements being an English journalist and an English citizen. This was obtained from Staatsarchiv Bremen, Johanna Schustermann reparations file 4-54-E-2402 part one page 54.

8. Johanna Schustermann converting to Judaism was obtained from Staatsarchiv Bremen, Johanna Schustermann reparations file E2402, Johanna and Lothar Schustermann Sache OH 2036/54 page 21.

9. Arnold Schustermann writes to the Landesamt für Wiedergutmachung that he wasn't in personal contact with the Schustermanns since they got married (1921). This was obtained from the Staatsarchiv Bremen File 4080/E10161/R page 123.

10. Former Gestapo agent Friedrich Linnemann stated on November 23, 1955, that Benno Schustermann was deported due to the divorce from his Aryan wife. This was obtained from the Staatsarchiv Bremen, File 4-54-E-24 Teli-3-von-3-2 page 47.

11. Gerber's hearing problems was obtained from Staatsarchiv Bremen, Gerber File KL89 pages 27–30.

12. Information on the apartment given to Gerber was obtained from the Staatsarchiv Bremen, Charles Gerber File KL 89 page 16.

Chapter Four

1. Information partially derived from Inge (Katz) Berger.

2. Katz testified of events on November 9, 10, 11, 1938 during the Spruchkammer of Wilhelm Parchmann in 1948. This was obtained from the Staatsarchiv Bremen, Wilhelm Parchmann File Aktenzeichen 1177/47 Anlage 26 pages 134–137.

3. Information was also obtained from *Geschichte der Juden und Umgebung* from Max Markreich, Teil 15 1938–1940, published by Temmen 2003.

Chapter Five

1. Information on the 303rd police battalion was obtained from *Polizei Gewalt:Bremens Polizei im Nationalsozialismus* published by Weser Kurier 2011 pages 124–128.

2. The Jewish tailor, Kurt Grünberger's relationship to Nette was obtained from the Staatsarchiv Bremen Bruno Nette File Two 4, 66-I-7840 Page 89.

3. Men being sent to personally invite Nette to testify against Katz was obtained from the Staatsarchiv Bremen, Karl Katz File 4-89-3-007 Page 19.

4. Personal information on Nette from his detention report was obtained from the Staatsarchiv Bremen, Bruno Nette File Three 4.66-1-7841 pages 21–22.

5. Nette's work experience in Riespott was obtained from Staatsarchiv Bremen, Bruno Nette File One 4, 66-1-7839 Page 33.

6. Nette's medical condition according to Dr. Rolf Ulrich was obtained from Staatsarchiv Bremen Bruno Nette File One 4.66-1-7839 page 27.

7. Official permission to vacation at home during Nette's internment from December 24, 1948 until January 5, 1949, was obtained from Staatsarchiv Bremen, Bruno Nette File One 4.66-1-7839 page 34.

8. Former Gestapo agent Heinrich Harms stated, while being interviewed by Arnold Schustermann, that Nette's son, Rudolf asked Katz for help in the case of his father. This

information was obtained from the Staatsarchiv Bremen, Karl Katz File 4-89-3-007 page 13.

9. The deposition of Nette against Katz where Nette at the end claims that he is not here out of revenge was obtained from Staatsarchiv Bremen, Karl Katz File 4-89-3-007 Page 20–22.

10. Katz states that he heavily accused the Gestapo agents, Nette, Linnemann, and Parchmann during their respective Spruchkammers and, "they therefore are now acting against me out of revenge." This information was obtained from the Staatsarchiv Bremen, Karl Katz File 4-89-3-007 page 156.

11. Bremen's justice and governing bodies were mostly staffed by former Nazis. Information obtained from, *Justiz in Bremen-vom Nationalsozialismus in der Nachkriegszeit*, von Ingo Kramer, Bremen NordÖr 5/2019 Pages 209–218.

12. Information on Bremen's justice system was obtained from *Bremen Im 3*. Reich by Inge Marssolek and Rene Ott pages 441–448.

Chapter Six

1. This chapter is almost entirely from interviews with Inge (Katz) Berger. Further information can be obtained from *Roses in a Forbidden Garden* by Elise Garibaldi, Decalogue Books 2016.

2. Katz's preparations for the Minsk Transport was obtained from the Staatsarchiv Bremen in the Festschrift zum 60 Geburtstag von Carl Katz *Zusammen Arbeit in Schwersten Zeit* by Dr Berthold Simonsohn, Frankfurt/Main pages 14–16.
3. Preparations for the Minsk Transport from testimony of Helmut Schmidt on March 2, 1966, in the Staatsarchiv Bremen, Max Plaut File 4.89-3-1119 Page 38–39.

Chapter Seven

1. Information on the post-traumatic stress disorder was obtained from the Staatsarchiv Bremen, Charles Gerber File KL89 page 33.

2. Mrs. Lange's statement was obtained from the Karl Katz File 4, 89/3–7 page 64.

3. Wilhelm Lange, (husband of Frau Lange), gave statements against Katz in the Staatsarchiv Bremen, Karl Katz File 4, 89/3–7 page 73.

4. Personal information on Charles Gerber was obtained from the Staatsarchiv Bremen, Charles Gerber File KL89.

Chapter Eight

1. Events surrounding the farewells at the Bahnhof during the Minsk Transport are from interviews with Inge (Katz) Berger and from *Roses in a Forbidden Garden* by Elise Garibaldi, Decalogue Books 2016.

2. Wilhelm Parchmann's reason that Katz was removed from the Minsk Transport was obtained from the Staatsarchiv Bremen, Karl Katz File 4,89-0-007 page 39.

3. Berthold Simonsohn gives account of Katz being removed from the Minsk Transport from the Staatsarchiv Bremen, 4.89-3-1118 Max Plaut-Schöffengericht Bremen page 64.

4. The interactions between Inge and Frau Katzenstein were obtained from interviews with Inge (Katz) Berger.

5. Carl Katz being removed from Yom Kippur services was obtained from Katz testimony at the Spruchkammer of Wihelm Parchmann from the Staatsarchiv Bremen, Wilhelm Parchmann File Anlage 28, Vernehmung of the 17th witness.

6. Louis Neitzel's feelings towards Nette can be seen in the testimony of Johanna Winter obtained from the Staatsarchiv Bremen, Bruno Nette File Four 4.66-1-7842 page 64.

7. Investigator M. Meyer said that Nette's Hobby was to go after "Geltungsjuden" obtained from the Staatsarchiv Bremen, 4.66-I Bruno Nette File 1887/12/22 Page 99.

8. Information on the home life of Nette and his wife's suicide was obtained from *Vergesst ja Nette nicht* by Bernard Nette published by VSA:Hamburg 2017 pages 32–38.

9. Reasons for Nette targeting the Jews of Vegesack was obtained from the Staatsarchiv Bremen, Bruno Nette File Four 4.6-1-7842 Page 137.

Chapter Nine

1. Information on Johanna Schustermann was obtained from Staatsarchiv Bremen, Wiedergutmachungsverfahren E2402/I/St page 120.

2. Johanna Schustermann blaming Katz for the death of Benno was obtained from the Staatsarchiv Bremen, Bruno Nette File Two 4.66-1-7840 Page 101.

3. Benno signing over power of attorney to Johanna Schustermann in December 1938 was obtained from the Staatsarchiv Bremen, Karl Katz File 4-89-3-007 page 61.

4. Insight into the relationship between Benno and Johanna Schustermann was obtained from the Staatsarchiv Bremen, OH2036/54 page 60.

5. Benno's notification of withdrawal to opposition of divorce was obtained from the Staatsarchiv Bremen, Karl Katz File 4-89-3-007 page 60.

6. Attorney Stutzer stated that he told Johanna not to divorce Benno since it would result in dire consequences for her husband was obtained from the Staatsarchiv Bremen, Karl Katz File 4-89-3-007 page 79–80.

7. Dr. Hergl writes that Johanna Schustermann threatened Max Cohen if he dared testify against her. Johanna said that Lothar would be returning shortly from the U.S. and would beat him up if he testified. This was obtained from the Staatsarchiv Bremen 4080/E2402 April 4, 1955, page 23, and page 100 red.

8. Letter that Johanna Schustermann writes to the Spruchkammer of Nette stating that she was emotionally unable to testify at his trial. She went on to accuse Katz of being responsible for the deaths of Fürstenthal and her husband and of the early incarceration of her son. She stated that she was more afraid of Katz than of Nette. This was obtained from the Staatsarchiv Bremen, Bruno Nette File Two 4.66-1-7840 pages 93–95.

9. Lothar Schustermann testified in the New York Consulate in 1955 that Gestapo agents had tried to get his mother to divorce his father. His parents also had spoken about separating. This was obtained from the Staatsarchiv Bremen, 4-54-E-2402 Page 11, and page 85 red.

10. Letter from Katz to Wiedergutmachung in June 1949 stating Johanna's deeds against Benno Schustermann was obtained from Staatsarchiv Bremen, Johanna Schustermann File 2402 page 42.

11. Carl Katz states that Johanna Schustermann must be behind the false statements of Emma Fernhomberg which was obtained from the Staatsarchiv Bremen, Karl Katz File 4-89-3-007 page 156.

12. Emma Fernhomberg states to Charles Gerber that Katz is responsible for the death of Ludwig Fürstenthal was obtained from Staatsarchiv Bremen, Karl Katz File 4-89-3-007 Page 156.

13. Emma's attempts at Fürstenthal's reparations and verdict that her claims were false was obtained from Staatsarchiv Bremen, E9569.

14. Emma bore witness in an unrelated case and served four months for perjury. This was obtained from the Staatsarchiv Bremen, Max Plaut File 4.89-3-1119 pages 67–85.

15. Claims made by Schmidt that Fürstenthal never intended to marry Emma Fernhomberg was obtained from the Staatsarchiv Bremen, E9569 4080/E 9569-1 page 26 red page 16&17.

16. Nette gave testimony in 1959 that Emma being engaged to Fürstenthal was entirely false. That Fürstenthal went to Minsk of his own free will in order to continue treating his patients. This was obtained from the Staatsarchiv Bremen, File E9596 page 40.

Chapter Ten

1. Interviews with Inge (Katz) Berger about their last days in Bremen.

2. Information on the coffins from Varel and Katz's final meeting with Nette before the Theresienstadt Transport was obtained from the Staatsarchiv Bremen Protokoll über die Sitzung des Direktoriums des Zentralrats page 68.

3. Statements of Benno Schustermann regarding his wife burning along with the house was obtained from the Staatsarchiv Bremen, E2402/R1 Aktenzeichen:04 2036/1954(E) Page 19.

Chapter Eleven

1. There were many meetings during the course of the Katz investigations and for expediency's sake they are combined in this chapter. Instances of one of these typical meetings was obtained from the Staatsarchiv Bremen, Karl Katz File 4-89-3-007 page 192.

2. Siegfried Höffler's fear that they lack credible witnesses. The former Gestapo agents have credibility issues, definitely in putting their blame for deportation on another.

Information was taken from the Staatsarchiv Bremen Staatsanwaltschaft Bremen Band Two Schöffengericht gegen Dr Max Plaut 4, 8913-1123 page 118.

Chapter Twelve

1. Information from interviews with Inge (Katz) Berger.

2. Further information may be obtained from *Roses in a Forbidden Garden* from Elise Garibaldi published by Decalogue Books 2016.

Chapter Thirteen

1. Information obtained from interviews with Inge (Katz) Berger.

Chapter Fourteen

1. Interviews obtained from Inge (Katz) Berger.

2. Information on the resistance was obtained from *The Face of Hell* by Sam Berger, Carlton Press, Inc. 1994. Page 68–69.

Chapter Fifteen

1. Information obtained from interviews with Inge (Katz) Berger.

2. Samuel Berger's experiences obtained from *The Face of Hell* by Sam Berger, Carlton Press, Inc. 1994.

3. The information on the Bialystok children was obtained from Theresienstadt 1941–1945, *The Face of a Coerced Community* by H.G. Adler published by Cambridge University Press 2017 pages 98–99.

Chapter Sixteen

1. Information obtained from Inge (Katz) Berger.

2. Further information may be obtained through *Roses in a Forbidden Garden* by Elise Garibaldi, Decalogue Books 2016.

Chapter Seventeen

1. Nette's children being mistreated was obtained from *Vergesst ja Nette nicht!* by Bernard Nette Publisher VSA:Hamburg 2017 pages 33–35 and 68–72.

2. Alfred finding his mother from *Vergesst ja Nette nicht!* by Bernard Nette, Publisher VSA: Hamburg page 36.

3. Information on Nette's wife's diamond ring was obtained from the Staatsarchiv Bremen, Bruno Nette File Band One 4.66-1-7839 Page 61.

4. Information on Alfred's return from the War was obtained *Vergesst ja Nette nicht!* by Bernard Nette Publisher VSA:Hamburg 2017 pages 234–235.

5. Ilse Propper testified to the cold blooded way in which Nette sent her seven-year-old boy to Theresienstadt in February 1945 which was obtained from the Staatsarchiv Bremen, Bruno Nette Band Two 4.66-1-7840 page 19 pencil page 16.

6 Lina Ramm stated that Nette sent her two children ages two and five to Theresienstadt in February 1945 as part of a work detail. This was obtained from Staatsarchiv Bremen, Bruno Nette File One 4, 66-1-7839 page 48.

Chapter Eighteen

1. Information obtained from interviews with Inge (Katz) Berger.

2. Information available in *Roses in a Forbidden Garden* by Elise Garibaldi published by Decalogue Books 2016.

Chapter Nineteen

1. This chapter combined the burning of the Gestapo files with the Gestapo fleeing Bremen though in reality this occurred several weeks apart. There is nothing stating that Nette was present but it is a probable assumption. This information of the files being burned in the inner courtyard of the Gestapo Headquarters was obtained from *Vergesst ja Nette nicht!* by Bernard Nette , Publisher VSA: Hamburg 2017 page 116.

2. Information on the Gestapo leaving Bremen from statements by Heinrich Herrlein was obtained from the Staatsarchiv Bremen, Bruno Nette File Two 4,66-1-7840 page 236.

3. Nette being arrested by the British was obtained from Staatsarchiv Bremen, Bruno Nette File One 4,66-I-7839 page 176.

4. Nette wearing the green police uniform while surrendering was obtained from *Vergesst ja Nette nicht!* by Bernard Nette, Publisher VSA:Hamburg 2017 page 43.

5. Information on Nette's background and Detention Report was obtained from the Staatsarchiv Bremen, Bruno Nette File Three 4.66-1-7841 pages 21–23.

6. Information on the destruction of Bremen was obtained from World War Two Today, The Royal Scots Fusiliers enter Bremen, ww2today.com.

7. Information on Nette's saving of seventy people towards end of war working in his favor was obtained from the Staatsarchiv Bremen, Bruno Nette File One 4.66-1-7839 page 73.

Chapter Twenty

1. Information on the liberation from Theresienstadt was obtained from interviews with Inge (Katz) Berger.

2. Further information on the liberation may be obtained from *Roses in a Forbidden Garden* by Elise Garibaldi published by Decalogue Books 2016.

3. Carl Katz's obligations after the war were obtained through personal correspondence of Carl Katz to Max Markreich, private family collection.

4. Information on Richard Frank's experiences in Minsk obtained from the Staatsarchiv Bremen in the File 4, 54-E 10521, E10520, and E 0523.

5. Richard Frank gives testimony in the Spruchkammer of Bruno Nette obtained from Staatsarchiv Bremen, Nette File Two 4.66-1-7840 page 132.

6. Interview with Hans Frank, "Die Menschen haben damals weggeschaut," Weser Kurier, November 18, 1991 page 15.

7. Benno Schustermann stating that his wife should burn along with the house was obtained from the Staatsarchiv Bremen, E2402/R1 Aktenzeichen:04 2036/1954(E) Page 19.

Chapter Twenty-One

1. Information on Wilhelm Parchmann's life was obtained from the Staatsarchiv Bremen, Wilhelm Parchmann File from his Lebenslauf of September 28, 1947.

2. The meeting between Katz and Parchmann was obtained from interviews with Inge (Katz) Berger.

3. The background and the capture of Parchmann's three pages signed by special CIC agent Kurt D. David was obtained from the Staatsarchiv Bremen, Wilhelm Parchmann File page 19.

4. Kurt David's personal feelings towards the Nazis were obtained from the Kurt David Collection, Veterans History Project.

Chapter Twenty-Two

1. The Spruchkammer testimony of Carl Katz was obtained from the Staatsarchiv Bremen, Bruno Nette File Two 4.66-1-7840 pages 121–124

2. Marianne Katz being shielded was a statement that she gave to the Weser Kurier in January 28, 1983 Nr. 23 Page 17.

Chapter Twenty-Three

1. Information from the Spruchkammer was obtained from Staatsarchiv Bremen, Bruno Nette File Two 4.66-1-7840 pages 121–124

2. The aftershocks of the accusations against Katz did last for generations. The Bremer historian, Dr. Guenther Rohdenburg, repeats the accusations of Nette (and therefore Hoeffler) again in the year 2006. In his book, *Die Beteiligung der Juden an den Deportation – das Problem der "Helfershelfer,"* published by Staatsarchiv Bremen, Rohdenburg tells of the first proceedings against Katz in 1949 when the "(P)ersecuted Jew Arnold Schustermann," states his accusations against Katz in great detail. There was at no time mention that Schustermann never met Katz, nor that he was not in Bremen those years. Rohdenburg tells in great detail of the many accusations of Nette against Katz as though they were truths. Rohdenburg states that in the opinion of *Gestapo* Agent Nette, "Katz was an Orthodox Jew who was the greatest hater of Christian/Jews, mixed marriages, and half-Jews, this category of Jews he would denounce while protecting the Orthodox Jews." The historian also tells of the accusations of Emma Fernhomberg (later

jailed for perjury) as truths. This defamation of Carl Katz goes on from pages 151–156. Rohdenburg states every possible discredited accusation against Katz from those declared disreputable sources as truths. Rohdenburg disregards every favorable piece of evidence in order to declare Carl Katz complicit with the Nazis.

Rohdenburg aimed to dishonor Katz's behavior in Theresienstadt despite reading many character references in the files stating his exemplary behavior in the camps. Rather, he preferred to quote statements against Katz from *Gestapo* agents, the discredited witness [later jailed for perjury], Emma Fernhomberg, as well as Lothar Schustermann's claims (proven false) that Katz sent his father to Aushwitz. Rohdenburg writes that while Katz, after the war, became head of the Jewish community and in charge of the economic and social help of the survivors, "for these survivors it was a dilemma, on the one hand to be sent by Katz to deportation since Katz's organization was supporting the deportation and finally after the War to return only to be dependent on Katz for support."

Rohdenburg also writes that, "for those people on the first transport to Theresienstadt in 1942, it appeared to them that their fellow Jews through the *Reichsvereinigung der Juden* were the ones that sent them to deportation, because all the organizational work was done through the Jewish organization. The orders were on the letterhead of the Jewish community and the signature was Katz and later Bruck."

This historian's book, *Die Beteiligung der Juden an den Deportation – das Problem der "Helfershelfer,"* as well as his claims, have been sourced and cited by many others in the historical, Remembrance, and educational societies internationally and within Germany. His researched "findings" inspired many others' works, and served to sway public opinion.

Chapter Twenty-Four

1. Information obtained from interviews with Inge (Katz) Berger.

Chapter Twenty-Five

1. Johanna Schustermann was not listed in the archives as having been in the meetings with Arnold and Lothar Schustermann and Höffler and Gerber, but she was a driving force behind the gathering of false witnesses and threats to those who opposed her. There were many additional false witnesses not mentioned in *Never Enough*, including, but not limited to, H. Singer, Haendler, and Lisiak.

2. Information that both Nette and Linnemann were witnesses for Johanna Schustermann in her reparations case was obtained from the Staatsarchiv Bremen 2402 page 92 red pencil 132.

3. There were meetings between Arnold and Lothar Schustermann with Höffler and Gerber to convict Katz through any means possible. Arnold Schustermann offered his services in contacting the Allies for incriminating evidence after Höffler explained the difficulties of the case. This information was obtained through the Staatsarchiv Bremen, Karl Katz File 4-89-3-007 Page 40–41 pencil 36.

4. Gerber states the urgency of the case against Katz and that these files should be hand delivered. Information obtained from the Staatsarchiv Bremen, Karl Katz File 4-89-3-007 Page 41.

5. Another attempt from the Attorney General to get the Americans involved in the Katz case occurred July 4, 1950. In closing, it was once again mentioned that Arnold Schustermann is a journalist and a British citizen and that Lothar Schustermann is stateless but residing in the U.S. Information obtained from the Staatsarchiv Bremen, Karl Katz File Pages 90–91.

Chapter Twenty-Six

1. Information on the formal charges against Carl Katz in English translation was obtained from the Staatsarchiv Bremen, Karl Katz File 4-89-3-007 Page 183–184.

Chapter Twenty-Seven

1. Information obtained from interviews with Inge (Katz) Berger.

2. Letter from the Attorney General on May 23, 1950, to the Senator for Justice and Constitution explaining that proceedings under German Law do not promise any hope for success, the only thing remaining is to give the case to the U.S. High Commissioner of Germany. Information obtained from the Staatsarchiv Bremen, Karl Katz File 4, 89/3-007 page 183–184.

3. Dr. Feine of the U.S. put a final stop on the proceedings against Katz on July 21, 1950, in a directive to the Justice Senator. Information obtained from the Staatsarchiv Bremen, Carl Katz File 4, 89/3-007 Page 93.

Bibliography

Books

Benz, Wolfgang: *Thereisenstadt*, 2012, Munich, C.H. Beck

Mueller-Tupath, Karla: *Verschollen in Deutschland*, 1994, Hamburg, Konkret Literatur

Marssolek, Inge—Ott, Rene: *Bremen Im 3. Reich*, 1986, Bremen, Carl Schuenemann

Rohdenburg, Guenther, Sommer, Karl-Ludwig: *Erinnerungsbuch,* 2006, Bremen, Staatsarchiv Bremen

Markreich, Max: *Geschichte der Juden in Bremen und Umgegend*, 2003, Bremen, Temmen

Adler, H.G.: *Theresienstadt 1941-1945*, 2017, Cambridge, Cambridge University Press

Garibaldi, Elise*: Roses in a Forbidden Garden*, 2016, New York, Decalogue Books

Berger, Sam: *The Face of Hell*, 1994, New York, Carlton Press

Nette, Bernhard: *Vergesst ja Nette nicht!,* 2017, Hamburg, VSA

Lindemann, Ingbert: *Die H. ist Juedin!,* 2009,Bremen, Donat

Luehrs, Marssolek, Mueller, Mueller-Tupath, Wrobel: *Reichskristallnacht in Bremen*, 1988, Bremen, Bremen Verlagsgesellschaft

Jakubowski, Jeanette: *Geschichte des Juedischen Friedhofs in Bremen*, 2002, Bremen, Donat

Archives

Karl Katz File, 4-89-3-007, Staatsarchiv Bremen, Germany

Generalstaatsanwaltschaft Bremen Personalakten ueber Oberstaatsanwalt Dr. Siegfried Hoeffler 4-10-AKZ-61-148 Staatsarchiv Bremen

Wilhelm Parchmann Aktenzeichen 1177/47 Staatsarchiv Bremen

Gerber, Charles KL89, Staatsarchiv Bremen

Johanna Schustermann Reparations File, Staatsarchiv Bremen

Benno Schustermann Reparations File 2402, Staatsarchiv Bremen

Nette, Bruno File One 4, 66-1-7839 Staatsarchiv Bremen

Nette, Bruno File Two 4, 66-1-7840 Staatsarchiv Bremen

Nette, Bruno File Three 4, 66-1-7841 Staatsarchiv Bremen

Plaut, Max File 4.89-3-1119 Staatsarchiv Bremen

Max Plaut-Schoeffengerict Bremen, 4.89-3-1118, Staatsarchiv Bremen

Schustermann, Johanna OH2036/54, Staatsarchive Bremen

Schustermann, Johanna 4080lE2402 Staatsarchiv Bremen

Schustermann, Johanna 4-54-E-2402 Staatsarchiv Bremen

Fernhomberg, Emma Reparations File E9569, Staatsarchiv Bremen

Fernhomberg, Emma Reparations File E9569 4080 Staatsarchiv Bremen

Protokoll ueber die Sitzung des Directoriums des Zentralrats, Staatsarchiv Bremen

Staatsanwaltschaft Bremen Band Zwei Schoeffengericht gegen Dr. Max Plaut 4, 8913-1123, Staatsarchiv Bremen

Pamphlet

Festschrift Zum 60. Geburtstag Von Carl Katz, September 14, 1959, Druck: Carl Schuenemann Bremen, Staatsarchiv Bremen

Newspaper

Interview with Hans Frank, "Die Menschen haben damals weggeschaut", Weser Kurier Bremen November 18, 1991

Schminck-Gustavus-Ermitti-Shoa-Bremen, 2009-06-24, pdf [864, 1KB]

Internet

The Royal Scots Fusilliers enter Bremen, WW2today.com

Kurt David Collection, Veterans History Project

Additional Photos And Documents

Carl (left) and Marianne Katz (right) with her brother, Hugo Gruenberg (center), 1923.

Marianne and Carl, 1923.

Marianne and Inge, age 14, 1938.

Inge (left) and Ruthie (right),in front of the Judenhaus 1941.

Touring Bremen in a Jeep. Inge was often driven around the American occupied zones of the city in one of the military vehicles. 1945.

Two weeks after returning home to Bremen from Theresienstadt. An apartment where Inge would often wait outside for her lost loved ones to return.

Carl and Inge on her wedding day, June 24th, 1947.

Hans Frank. Hanna, Inge, and Ajax in the garden of Donandtstrasse 18. Hans lived with the Katz family for several years after his father, Richard, couldn't handle his behavior due to the traumas endured during the war.

Family Portrait. Inge holding Ruthie, with Schmuel holding Hanna, 1951.

Arrival of furniture by crate to Inge and Schmuel's new home in Queens, New York, 1955.

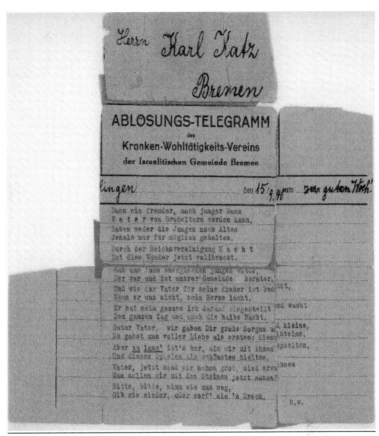

Des Kranken-Wohltatigkeits Verein (The Sick-Health Charity /Benevolence Organization) of the Israeli Community in Bremen, September 15, 1940. A grateful resident writes a poem to Carl Katz expressing his gratitude for the wonderful care provided.

That a stranger younger man can become the father of grandparents

Both young and old could not believe this

Through the *Reichsvereiniegung (Reich Association of Jews)*

Is this amazing thing possible

We got an energetic young father who is the advisor to our community

And as a father is always thinking of his children

When he sees us his heart laughs

He has focused intensely on us—during the day and during the night

Dear Father, we give you both little and big things to worry about

First you give us all your love

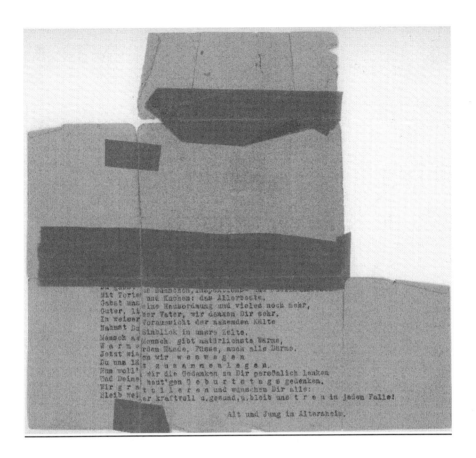

It was long ago that we played together with pebbles

Now we are gown up

What should we do with these stones

Please, please take them away

Give them away or throw them in the dirt

You gave us chickens and inspections and jubilee celebrations

With pies and cakes, all the best

223

You gave us direction and much more

Good father we thank you very much

Looking to the cold of the future

You look at our dwellings

Person to person provides warmth

Hands, feet and intestines are warmed

Now we understand why we are together

Now we want to thank you personally

We congratulate you and wish you

Remain strong and healthy and remain true to us

   -Old and Young in the Old Age Home

Written in June 1941 from the Judenhaus by Inge Katz. Marks of the Nazi censor in upper left hand corner.

Dear Frau Aronstein:

I hope that your trip went well and that you have landed happily with your family in America. I can't begin to explain it to you, how it was the first days after you had left, as though someone had died. On the return home from the train station, we hardly said a word. We also couldn't bring ourselves to enter into your room on that first day. It has become terribly quiet here. We miss our Adelheid so much.

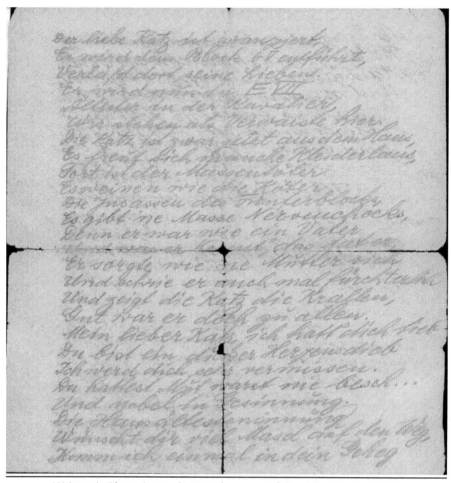

Written in Theresienstadt, 1943 by a grateful resident to Carl Katz.

The dear Katz has moved on he has been kidnapped from Block G V, leaving his loved ones behind. He now becomes the E VII Elder in Kavalier [Barracks], we stand here as orphans. As the cat is now out of the house, many a clothes louse rejoices, Gone is the mass slayer [of lice]. The inmates of Block 5 are crying like dogs. There's a mass of nervous shocks, for he was like a father and what he could do he did, He cared like a mother. And although sometimes he shouted terribly. And the cat showed its claws, He was good to everyone. My dear cat, I loved you, you were a big thief of hearts, and I will miss you very much. You had courage, you were never sh..[tty]And noble in spirit...

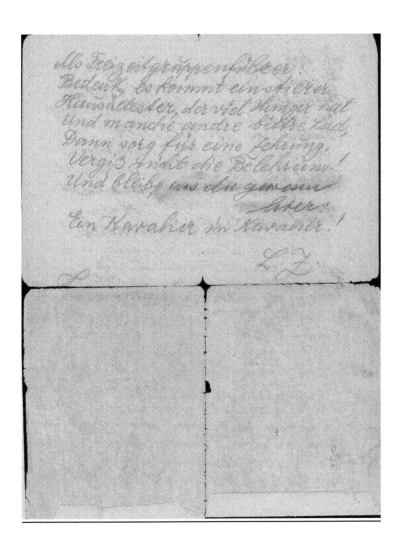

The House Elders Association wishes you much mazel on the way. If I ever come to your area as a free time group leader: Remember if there comes a stubborn House elder, with much hunger and some other bitter burden, then provide for a feeding. Do not forget these teachings! And stay what you have been here: A Kavalier [gentleman] in Kavalier [Gentlemen Barracks].

-L.F.

Bremen, den 8.11.
1945

Lieber Herr Markreich!

Die Copie Ihres Briefes- der Brief selbst ist
noch nicht angekommen, habe ich heute durch Fredi Keller
erhalten und daraus ersehen, dass es Ihnen und Ihrer
Familie gesundheitlich gut geht. Von meiner Familie und
mir, kann ich auch so weit schreiben, dass wir gesund
sind. Wir haben in der Georg Groeningstrasse 80 a eine
ganz nette 3 Zimmerwohnung und haben vorlaeufig keine
Not. Wie ich aus dem Brief an Fredi Keller ersehen habe,
fuerchten Sie, dass ich schon bald Bremen verlasse, aber
daran ist leider zur Zeit noch nicht zu denken. Einmal
besteht noch keine Moeglichkeit und zum anderen muss ich
erst meine Aufgaben hier beenden. Das Verhandeln mit den
Behoerden ist immer noch ziemlich schwierig und bedarf
es sehr viel Nachdruck, um alle die Projekte, die durch-
gefuehrt werden sollen, zum Gelingen zu bringen.
Dass wir uns am Osterdeich 17 vorlaeufig nie-
dergelassen haben, ist Ihnen ja bereits bekannt. Dieses
Haus ist von der Militaer- Regierung beschlagnahmt worden
und ist an und fuer sich gedacht fuer die juedischen
Soldaten. Die Synagoge haben wir gemeinsam und wir haben
in diesem Haus unser Gemeindebuero. Vielleicht kennen
Sie das Grundstueck. Es ist das Korffsche Erbe. Es
gehoert zur Zeit der Baumwollfirma Albrecht Mueller - Pearse
deren Verwaltungsgebaeude in der Langestrasse ausgebombt
ist. Es ist ein wunderbares Haus, herrlich gebaut und
gut erhalten. Ich beabsichtige evtl. dieses Grundstueck
zu kaufen, da zur Zeit noch keine Moeglichkeit besteht,
die Synagoge in der Gartenstrasse neu aufzubauen. Fuer
eine derartige Synagoge ist dort kein Platz. Ferner
duerfte die Bevoelkerung auch wenig Verstaendnis dafuer
haben, wenn in der heutigen Zeit, wo keine Wohnungen
vorhanden sind, Synagogen od r Kirchen aufgebaut werden.
Das Grundstueck ist fuer unsere Zwecke gut brauchbar.
Es wird wahrscheinlich RM 200.000.-- kosten.
stand angeDeRcFriedhof, den ich in einem furchtbaren Zu-

Letter from Katz to Mr. Markreich November 8, 1945, describing work in Bremen that needed to be done right after the war.

Dear Mr. Markreich

As I understand from your letter to Fredi Keller, you fear that I will soon be leaving Bremen, but alas that is not even a thought at this time. Firstly I don't have the possibility to leave and secondly I must first finish my tasks at hand. Dealings with the Authorities is still rather difficult and it takes a lot of prodding to bring all these projects to completion.

Den Friedhof, den ich in einem furchtbaren Zustand angetroffen habe, wird jetzt wieder hergerichtet. Nur ueber Truemmerhaufen war auf den Friedhof zu gelangen. Der Friedhof selbst ist mit Bombentrichtern uebersaeit. Ein grosser Teil der Steine ist umgeworfen und auch sonst verwuestet. Ein Teil Grabmaeler muss neu ersetzt werden, da dieselben nicht zu reparieren sind, u.a. der Grabstein unseres verewigten Rabbiner's Dr. Rosenak. Das Grabmal Ihrer sel. Mutter ist stehen geblieben und gut erhalten. Jedes einzelne Grab wird hergerichtet und im naechsten Fruehjahr sollen Anpflanzungen vorgenommen werden. Die Firma Roetsch habe ich wieder mit der Pflege des Friedhofs betraut.

Gerade heute sind grosse Zeitungsartikel ueber den 9. November 1938 in der hiesigen Bremer Zeitung (jetzt Weser-Kurier). Diesen Artikel wird Ihnen Fredi Keller einsenden und werden Sie daraus alles ersehen.

An Arbeit mangelt es nicht, im Gegenteil, ich habe keine Zeit, mich um eine Existenz zu kuemern.

Im frueheren Altersheim Groepelingerheestrasse 167 ist zur Zeit die Polizeiwache untergebracht und das Haus Buxtehuderstrasse 9 hatte die AG "Weser" gemietet fuer Arbeiterwohnungen. Das Haus Buxtehuderstrasse 9 ist bereits leer, aber stark bombenbeschaedigt und das Haus Groepelingerheerestrasse wird in aller Kuerze geraeumt und sollen beide Haeuser wieder als Heime eingerichtet werde,. das heisst, mit alten Leuten aus der Gemeinde, mit Fluechtlingen und evtl. mit juedischen Kindern aus den Ostgebieten Deutschlands. Sie ersehen aus diesem, dass ich es hier nicht ganz einfach habe, alle diese Projekte zur Verwirklichung zu bringen, besonders dadurch, dass ich eben von keiner Seite Unterstuetzung habe, dass ausser mir kaum einer aus der Gemeinde da ist, der diese Verhandlungen erledigen kann.

Die Moerder von Heinrich Rosenblum sind ermittelt worden und duerften in Kuerze verurteilt werden. Von Selma Zwinitzky hat man auch verdaechtige Personen verhaftet, aber sie noch nicht restlos der Taeterschaft ueberfuehren koennen. Leopold Baer ist 1942 eines natuerlichen Todes gestorben. Er war schwer lungenkrank. Ich habe noch an der Beerdigung teilgenommen.   b.- w.

Markreich November 1945 page 2

The cemetery which I found in horrible shape is now being repaired. The only way to enter the cemetery was over a pile of rubble. The cemetery was spared of the bombings. A large part of the headstones were overturned and generally all is in shambles. A number of headstones must be replaced as they are beyond repair, for example our honorable Rabbi Rosenak.

There is no lack of work, I have had no time to concern myself with my own livelihood.

Also, dass er eines unnatuerlichen Todes gestorben ist,
stimmt nicht.
Die Taeter von Erich Benz und Leo Freudenberg zu ermitteln,
ist bislang nicht moeglich gewesen.
Ob man Parchmann erwischt hat, ist unbekannt, da er in
den letzten Jahren in Jugoslavien Dienst gemacht hat.
Die Nachfolger des Parchmann sind selbstverstaendlich
in Haft.
Was Sie sonst an Fredi Keller resp. mir mitteilen, werde
ich nach und nach versuchen, zu erledigen, d.h. die Listen
anfertigen ueber alle diejenigen, die nach Minsk und Theresienstadt deportiert wurden. Ich bin bereits beimPolizei-
praesidenten vorstellig geworden, um diese Listen anfertigen
zu lassen. Durch die starke Zerstoerung Bremens sind saemtliche Unterlagen vernichtet. Es gibt weder eine Gemeinde-
kartei noch sind beim Polizeipraesidenten Listen vorhanden,
in die Einsicht genommen werden kann. Es ist nur noch die
gesamte Einwohnermeldekartei vorhanden und muss diese ganz
durchgesehen werden, nach dem Vermerk "evakuiert". Dieses
ist eine sehr schwierige Arbeit, aber ich hoffe, dass sie
bewerkstelligt werden kann.
Frau Henny Katz geb. Rosenberg und Schwester Frieda Rosenberg sind ebenfalls nach Minsk gekommen und haben dasselbe
Los gezogen.Schicksal erleiden muessen wie alle anderen.
Walter Goldberg koennen Sie ebenfalls bestellen, dass seine
Frau und Tochter auch nach Minsk gekommen sind und dasselbe
Los gezogen haben.
Sie fragten an, was die Bevoelkerung allgemein zu den Greueli
sagt. Heute selbstverstaendlich verwerfen sie diese Greuel
und erklaeren restlos alle, sie sind keine Nazis gewesen und
haben nicht gewusst, was in den KL geschehen ist.
Siegmund Koerbchen und Frau sind von Minsk seinerzeit nach
Sein bei Koblenz gegangen und haben als Pfleger bezw. Kranke
schwester in der juedischen Irrenanstalt gearbeitet. Von
dort sind sie mit den Patienten nach Polen ins Vernichtungs-
lager verschickt worden. Die Tochter ist von Berlin direkt
nach Polen gegangen und duerfte dasselbe Schicksal erlitten

Markreich page 3

You had asked what the population generally says to these horrors. Today they
naturally dismiss these horrors and all totally declare that they were not Nazis and
knew nothing of what was happening in the camps.

haben. Ihre Schwiegermutter, Jeanette Behrens, ist mit mir
im Juli 1942 nach Theresienstadt gegangen und Ende September 1942 dort an Entkräftung gestorben. Ich habe dieser
Tage, ich weiss nur nicht mehr von wem, einige Silber-
bestecke bekommen, die Frau Behrens dort vor ihrer Eva-
kuierung hinterlegt hatte, um sie Frau Goldschmidt aus
Oldenburg spaeter zurueckzugeben. Vielleicht gibt es
eine Moeglichkeit, Ihnen diese Bestecke als Andenken an
Ihre Schwiegermutter zu uebersenden.
Frau Scherbel ist auch nach Minsk geschickt worden mit
dem gleichen Resultat. Levy Weinberg ist am 27.5.44
in Theresienstadt verstorben, ebenfalls dort elendiglich
umgekommen. Die Ehefrau von Leopold Baer ist von Minsk
1944 nach Auschwitz gegangen.
Adolf und Frieda Hein waren ebenfalls unter denen, die
nach Minsk deportiert wurden.
Sobald ich also eine Liste derjenigen Juden habe, die
nach Minsk geschickt wurden, werde ich Ihnen dieselbe
zusenden.
Ueber diejenigen Personen, die 1942 nach Theresienstadt gin-
gen werde ich Fredi Keller eine Liste zur Weitersendung ueb-
bergeben, ebenfalls eine Liste derjenigen, von denen ich
ungefaehr die Todesdaten weiss, damit Sie die Angehoerigen
benachrichtigen koennen. Ich beabsichtige, spaeter hier
auf dem Friedhof einen grossen Gedenkstein mit saemtlichen
Namen zu errichten.
An das Baupolizeiamt wegen der bezahlten Mk. 5.500.--
fuer die Aufraeumungsarbeiten werde ich schreiben.
Saemtliche Gemeindegrundstuecke sowie Synagoge, und Ro-
senakhaus, Vohnenstrasse, Schnoor, hat Joseph Platzer, der
auch nach Minsk geschickt wurde, verkauft. Ich versuche
jetzt vor allen Dingen die Grundstuecke in der Gartenstr.
zurueck zu erwerben. Das Grundstueck von Heino Baumgarten in Wildeshausen, ist auch verkaufr worden und hat de-
den Verkaufsvertrag Heino Baumgarten noch selbst unter-
schrieben. Der Erloes ist an die Juedische Gemeinde in
Bremen ergangen und das Vermoegen auf Konto des Alters-
heims eingezahlt worden. Spaeter wurden alle Gelder auf
Weisung des Reichssicherheitshauptamtes in Berlin nach

Markreich page 4

Frau Scherbel also was sent to Minsk with the same result. Levy Weinberg died in Theresienstadt on May 27, 1944 also had a miserable death. The wife of Leopold Baer went from Minsk to Auschwitz in 1944. Adolf und Frieda Hein were also amongst those deported to Minsk. As soon as I compile a list of those that were sent to Minsk, I will send it to you.

For those people that were sent to Theresienstadt in 1942, I will give Fredi Keller the list to be forwarded, along with a list of approximate dates of their deaths so that you can notify their next of kin. I plan on erecting a large monument in the cemetery with all these names.

nach Berlin ueberwiesen.
Ihrem Brief habe ich ferner entnommen, dass beide Familien
Assenheimer wieder wohlbehalten in Antwerpen sind und dass
es Alfred Gruenberg nebst Frau und Kindern gut geht.
Lieber Max Markreich, ich wuerde es begruessen, wenn es
von dort moeglich waere, an die hier befindlichen Juden,
insgesamt ca. 100. Lebensmittel und auch Kleidung zu
denken. Es amtiert hier in Bremen ein amerikanischer
Chaplain Rabbi Poliakoff, dessen genaue Adresse ich Ihnen
nachfolgen aufgebe:

        Ch. M.M. Poliakoff, Bremen, Port Command.
        APO - 751 US ARMY.

Bestellen Sie bitte Alfred Gruenberg, dass das Grab seines
seligen Vaters in Ordnung und wuerdig hergerichtet ist.
Am Freitag Abend wird waehrend des Gottesdienstes eine
Gedenkfeier fuer die am 9. November 1938 und waehrend
der Verfolgungszeit umgekommenen Bremer Juden abgehalten
werden. Der Chaplain wird in englisch und ich werde
versuchen, in deutsch zu sprechen und fuer alle Maertyrer
gemeinsames Kaddish-Gebet verrichten.
Fuer heute, glaube ich, mein lieber Max Markreich, Ihnen
ausfuehrlich genug berichtet zu haben. Fragen Sie bitte
weiter an, was Sie wissen wollen und werde ich Sie auf
dem Laufenden halten.
Fuer heute verbleibe ich mit den herzlichsten Gruessen,
auch von meiner Frau und Inge, an Ihre werte Familie und
alle Freunde

                Ihr   (gez.) Carl Katz

Bitte Frau Adele Aronstein, mit der wir sehr befreundet sind
die Adresse kennt sicherlich Alfred Gruenberg - auch den
Brief zu zeigen. Wir haben von Frau Aronstein ueber Mr. Byrd
Byrd bereits ein Paket erhalten, sowie von Albert Seligmann
frueher Achim. Bestellen Sie bitte, dass die Pakete gut
angekommen sind und wir uns sehr gefreut haben.
Nochmals herzliche Gruesse.

Markreich page 5

At Friday night services there will be a memorial service for the Jews of Bremen that
perished in November 1938 and during the persecutions. The Chaplain will speak in
English and I will attempt to speak in German and to say the Mourner's Kaddish
[prayer for the departed] for all the martyrs.

```
                    283. WATFORD WAY,
                    HENDON, N.W.4.
                      HENDON 1759.

                            London, 24.6.48.


        Sehr verehrte Frau und lieber Herr Katz,

              die frohe Nachricht von der Geburt Ihrer
        Enkelin hat meine Gedanken vor allem zu Ihnen
        hingeführt. Lassen Sie mich Ihnen meine herz-
        lichsten Wünsche aussprechen. Nun liegt ein neuer
        Ausblick in die Zukunft vor Ihnen. Möge der Weg
        zu ihr Sie immer nur durch Gutes hindurch führen.
        Mögen stets nur glückliche Tage bei Ihnen
        einkehren.
              Ich denke oft an unser Zusammensein in den
        schweren Jahren zurück, und an wenige Menschen in
        diesem Kreise der Gefangenschaft denke ich so
        gern zurück wie an Sie.

              Mit herzlichen Grüssen und nochmaligen guten
        Wünschen

                            Ihr

                            L. Baeck
                            (Dr.Leo Baeck)
```

The letter from London on July 24, 1948 from Leo Baeck to Katz family. Rabbi, educator, intellectual, and community leader, Baeck was one of the most important figures of pre-war Germany. He decided to serve the Jewish community in Theresienstadt rather than flee Germany when given the chance. He and Katz remained close friends long after the war.

Dear honorable Mrs. And dear Mr. Katz

The wonderful news of the birth of your granddaughter brought my thoughts to you. Let me express my heartfelt wishes. Now something new is in your future. May the way always be good. May only good luck enter your life.

I think often think of our being together during those difficult times. Very few in this circle, during a time of imprisonment I only look fondly of you.

With sincerest regards and again good wishing,

Dr. Leo Beck

233

Zum Abschied.
-.-.-.-.-.-.-.-.-.-.-.-.-

Die Zeit ist nun herangekommen,
wo ich hab Abschied von Euch genommen.
Zum letzten Mal in Bremen hier
stand ich mit gemischten Gefühlen an Eurer Tür.
Es fällt mir wirklich schwer
Euch zu sehen vielleicht
garnicht mehr.
Ihr wisst allein,
wie oft ich hab bei Euch gesessen,
getrunken, geschlafen, gelacht, gesungen und gegessen,
dies alles weiss ich zu ermessen
und werde es auch nie vergessen.

Ihr wart, wie keiner wär zu mir gewesen,
4 Menschen so ganz auserlesen,
von Anfang an bis zum letzten Tag
ich wie Eure zweite Tochter behandelt wart.

Ich sag es heut und werd es immer sagen :
          "Bei K a t z, das sind für mich
                  unvergessliche Tage".
Drum nehmet dann von mir zum Schluss
noch einmal einen Abschieds-Kuss
und wünsche, dass in Eurem Heim
nur Masel und Shalom gehn ein und aus.

Ich weiss, ich allein kann Euch nicht genug dankbar sein,
drum möge dieser Euch belohnen,
der schwebt in höheren Regionen
und Euch von allem Golus verschonen.

            Dies schrieb Euch zum Andenken
                Eure immer Dankbare
                    Edith

A letter from Edith to the Katz family. She was a young girl from Frankfurt whose parents, brothers, and sisters were all murdered in Auschwitz. Although a stranger, the Katzes invited her to live with them in their home for as long as she needed.

A Farewell

The time has now arrived
When I have to say goodbye to you
For the last time in Bremen
I stand with mixed feelings in front of your door
It is difficult for me
Not to see you anymore
You know well
How often I sat with you
Drinking, sleeping, laughing, singing and eating
I know how to treasure all of this
And will never forget
You were to me like no others
4 people so special
From the first day to the last
I was treated as a second daughter
I say it today and always
"I will never forget these days at the Katz's"
At the end take from me
A farewell kiss
And wishes that in your home
Only good luck and peace enter
I know I cannot thank you enough
Therefore I wish that the one who reigns up high
Will reward you and save you from all harm
I wrote this as a remembrance
Yours in gratitude
Edith

235

Lieber Mr. Berger, meine liebe Inge, liebe süsse Hanna u. lieb Ruthchen, in einigen Tagen werdet Ihr uns verlassen u. sende ich Euch aus liebendem Herzen meine Abschiedsgrüsse. Ich hatte mir vorgenommen, Euch zum Dampfer bis zur Abfahrt zu begleiten, aber alte Leute gelten nichts mehr, das sehe ich bei mir. Ihr Lieben seid bevorzugt, werdet im fremden Lande von Euren l. Geschwistern empfangen, das tut wohl. Ihr habt mit Euren geliebten Eltern ein überaus gutes Familienleben geführt; ich kann es beurteilen, war ich doch viele Jahre zu allen Gelegenheiten u. an Festtagen bei Euch eingeladen, da denke ich mit Liebe noch gerne dran zurück. Sie lieber Mr. Berger haben sich sehr verdient gemacht, in unserer Gemeinde Bremen,

Written from the Jewish old age home in Bremen July 1955 to Inge and her young family. The Katz's cared for her while in Theresienstadt, and remained close friends long after the war ended.

Dear Mr. Berger, my dear Inge, sweet Hanna, and dear Ruthi

In a few days you will be leaving us and I am sending you a heartfelt farewell. I had planned to accompany you until your departure. However old people are useless, which I see in myself. You loved ones are privileged to go off into a strange land where you will be welcomed by your dear siblings which will feel good. I can attest to the fact that you have enjoyed an exceptionally good family life with your dear parents, since for many years I have been invited to all occasions and holidays to your home. I think back lovingly on those times. You dear Mr. Berger have been a very important part of our Jewish community....

It continues on the next page and is signed with wishes that she be remembered as the old loyal and good friend Rosa Wolff.

Manufactured by Amazon.ca
Bolton, ON

21340092R00133